AGING IN A CHANGING WORLD

GLOBAL PERSPECTIVES ON AGING

Series editor, Sarah Lamb

This series publishes books that will deepen and expand our understanding of age, aging, ageism, and late life in the United States and beyond. The series focuses on anthropology while being open to ethnographically vivid and theoretically rich scholarship in related fields, including sociology, religion, cultural studies, social medicine, medical humanities, gender and sexuality studies, human development, critical and cultural gerontology, and age studies. Books will be aimed at students, scholars, and occasionally the general public.

AGING IN A CHANGING WORLD

Older New Zealanders and Contemporary Multiculturalism

MOLLY GEORGE

RUTGERS UNIVERSITY PRESS

New Brunswick, Camden, and Newark, New Jersey, and London

Library of Congress Cataloging-in-Publication Data
Names: George, Molly, 1977– author.
Title: Aging in a changing world: older New Zealanders and contemporary
    multiculturalism / Molly George.
Description: New Brunswick: Rutgers University Press, [2022] | Series: Global
    perspectives on aging | Includes bibliographical references and index.
Identifiers: LCCN 2020057738 | ISBN 9781978809406 (paperback) |
    ISBN 9781978809413 (hardcover) | ISBN 9781978809420 (epub) |
    ISBN 9781978809437 (mobi) | ISBN 9781978809444 (pdf)
Subjects: LCSH: Older people—New Zealand—Attitudes |
    Multiculturalism—New Zealand—Public opinion.
Classification: LCC HQ1064.N45 G46 2022 | DDC 305.260993—dc23
LC record available at https://lccn.loc.gov/2020057738

A British Cataloging-in-Publication record for this book is available from the British
Library.

♾ The paper used in this publication meets the requirements of the American
National Standard for Information Sciences—Permanence of Paper for Printed
Library Materials, ANSI Z39.48-1992.

www.rutgersuniversitypress.org

Manufactured in the United States of America

For the three little souls that came into being
during this process

CONTENTS

ILLUSTRATIONS

FIGURES

TABLES

AGING IN A CHANGING WORLD

1 · AGING IN TIMES OF GREAT CHANGE

THE NARRATIVE OF THE RACIST OLD PERSON

The narrative of the old person as nostalgic, resistant to social change, and even racist, abounds. It's a friend's grandmother who always says cringe-worthy, politically incorrect things about people of different ethnicities, nationalities, or religions. It's the angry old man in the viral YouTube video shouting obscenities at minorities on the crowded city bus. It's the ready television or film trope of the "racist grandpa," like Clint Eastwood in *Gran Torino*, muttering and complaining about the immigrants moving in next door, ruining the neighborhood (Eastwood 2009). It's in popular stories about small town America, places like Albertville, Alabama, where older residents ostensibly "hated the changes" brought by large numbers of Latino immigrants (Glass and Meek 2017).

Everywhere in the media, the character of an "old bigot" persists, anxious and angry about increasing diversity and social change. In a recent article entitled "Will Racism End When Old Bigots Die?," the reporter writes that this title question is actually nothing new. In the United States, from Thomas Jefferson to Martin Luther King, Jr., to Oprah Winfrey the idea of race relations improving through our children has milled around the public psyche for generations. "The belief that our children's generation will be less racist gets repeated by teachers, parents, politicians and activists" (Donnella 2017). The inevitable flip side of this persistent narrative is that it is the old who keep racism alive, who resent diversity, who resist immigration, who shrug their shoulders at equality.

Various reports largely reinforce this narrative of intolerant older people. "It is old people everywhere" says one report, "who oppose immigration the most" (Winkler 2015a, 2015b). The author continues to say that older people across Europe disproportionately oppose immigration, regardless of income, education, or employment status, citing countries such as Hungary or Cyprus where "that figure is 80 percent" (Winkler 2015b). Other statistical survey reports from Europe show a positive correlation between age and prejudice (Pettigrew 2006;

Castillo et al. 2014; Heath and Richards 2018). A report out of the United Kingdom states, "it is now well-established that older people tend to be less favorable towards immigration" (Blinder and Richards 2020, 7), while another article states simply, "age increases prejudice" (Kunovich 2004, 33).

An article from the Centre for Global Development recently proposed that racism is "dying out" because, essentially, older people are dying. The author cites data that in France, young people are apparently significantly less likely than old people to say they did not want to live next to people of another race (Kenny 2017). The European Social Survey Findings found that younger people are more favorable to immigration than older people and put forth the following reasoning: "It is likely (although impossible to be certain) that generational differences lie behind the large age differences—generations who grew up in western countries before the years of mass migration are more negative than those who grew up more recently and for whom diversity has always been part of their experience" (Heath and Richards 2016, 11). Travel across the globe to Australia and a similar finding and explanation can be found. In a large racism survey, older Australians showed greater intolerance perhaps because "those aged 65+ were brought up in an era when Anglo-Celtic immigrants absolutely dominated immigrants . . . whereas those aged under 35 were a product of the post-White Australia" (Dunn et al. 2004, 415). In the United States, older people are the least likely to regard the country's growing population of immigrants as a change for the better while "millennials are well acquainted with the changing face of America and overwhelmingly think these changes are good for the country" (Pew Research Center 2011). Demographer William Frey suggested this is in part because baby boomers, mostly white themselves, came of age in a time of insulation, for example, in segregated suburbs with little exposure to immigrants (Frey 2015).

Dig deeper into analysis of generational differences in attitudes toward migrants and there are some gray areas of complexity discussed (Winkler 2015a, 2015b). But in public discourse, there has been a strengthening of rhetoric around older people's intolerance with two recent events. In 2016, the Brexit "Leave" vote and the U.S. election of Donald Trump perpetrated rhetoric of older people (and in many cases specifically older, white people) as not only nostalgic and anxious about change but also intolerant and blatantly racist. In the days and weeks after the Brexit "Leave" vote, prominent headlines included: "Stubborn old people . . . want to leave the EU" (Wilkinson 2016). As the media broke down the voting results by age bracket, old people emerged as having been much more likely to vote "Leave." Along with education, age was being called the "great fault line," with media outlets reporting that people younger than twenty-five were more than twice as likely to vote "Remain" (71%) than "Leave" (29%), whereas the picture among people older than sixty-five was nearly the "exact opposite" with 64 percent voting to leave and 36 percent to remain (Moore 2016). Older voters quickly became the targets of virulent anger by those who wanted Britain to remain in the European Union. In the hours and days after the vote, the old were blamed for having "screwed over the younger generations" (Dore 2016) and for "financially bankrupting the young" (Chu 2016). Young people took to social media with complaints of having their future "stolen" by older voters with Tweets such as, "We've lost our future because you wanted to re-live your romanticized past? (@dotttiejames)" (Kottasova 2016).

At the same time, on U.S. shores during Trump's presidential campaign, which has been readily labeled "vehemently anti-immigration" (Haltiwanger 2017), his rallies were described as "a sea of gray and white," "an abundance of the superannu-ated" as his supporters, "hobbled on walkers and canes" (Ball 2016). Trump's cam-paign was described as "a rebellion of the aged—a bygone generation's last furious grasp against modernity" (ibid.) and another journalist described the Republican National Convention as full of angry, old, white people (Whitlock 2016). A picture circulated of an older man raising his middle finger to the press at a Republican rally,[1] the epitome of the angry old person voting out of a desire to return to a *Leave It to Beaver* era—a white, 1950s suburban world (Staples 2016). In both the Brexit Leave vote and Trump's election, potent, juxtaposed images fueled, and continue to fuel, a delineated story of the young as tolerant and multicultural versus the old as bitter, nostalgic, resistant, and yes, racist.

Just weeks after the 2016 Brexit "Leave" vote, I attended the British Society for Gerontology (BSG) annual conference. Given the timing and the focus of the conference (aging), one of the keynote speakers deviated entirely from his intended topic and spoke about older people and the Brexit vote (Bell 2016). The tone in the room was tense as audience members, both academics and service providers for the elderly, were in the very early stages of investigating whether older voters had indeed voted "Leave" in such greater numbers, and if so, why and what the repercussions might be for the elderly themselves and others. In my observation, those in the room were overwhelmingly disheartened by and wor-ried about the "Leave" vote. For many in the room, a dire picture was emerging of an older generation that voted out of nostalgia as well as some understandable concerns, but who now may have inadvertently initiated the decline of the British economy. At the same time, an outspoken minority in the room vehemently rejected what they thought was an unfair scapegoating of the elderly. So soon after the vote, the topic was still emotive and at times certainly still is. Three years after this conference, the subtleties and complexities around who voted the way they did, and why, are still emerging, but a simplified narrative of the old, nostal-gic, racist "Leave" voter persists. For example, two years after the vote, Sir Vince Cable, Liberal Democrat leader in Parliament, said that older people who had voted "Leave" were driven by "nostalgia for a world where passports were blue, faces were white and the map was colored imperial pink" (BBC 2018).

Some cursory analysis of older voters has been included in some limited research drawing parallels between the "Leave" vote and the election of Trump.

Wilson (2017) wrote that the vote for Britain to leave the European Union and the U.S. election of Trump could arguably even be considered "a single phenomenon with shared causes"; a part of the "wave of populism that has swept across the developed democracies in the last ten years" (Wilson 2017, 543). Both the Trump presidential campaign and the Brexit Leave campaign purported to help make their respective countries great again, both invoked "xenophobia and racism" and "hostility to immigrants" (Wilson 2017, 546). And in both cases, older people disproportionately voted in support of the accompanying promises of renewed nationalism and reduced immigration.

As the results from the two votes rolled in—confirming Donald Trump's election and Britain's exit from the European Union—many younger people felt "betrayed by older voters" (Dorling 2016; Wilson 2017). Social media was full of angry, ageist exclamations; memes circulated such as an image of four older, white people laughing with the caption: "Votes for Brexit will die before being a victim of that decision!" (stevieco411 2016). In these contexts—the Brexit vote, Trump's election, and beyond—the story goes something like this: younger people have grown up with cheap flights, global media, more global migration and greater exposure to diversity; they are apparently more inclusive and tolerant. If simplified headlines are to be believed, "younger people are increasingly less racist" (Kenny 2017) than their older counterparts.

The research presented in this book offers a much-needed antidote to over-simplified depictions of the old as stagnant, oppositional members of increasingly diverse societies. Be it in the United States, the United Kingdom, or New Zealand—where the stories in this book unfold—many older people around the world have witnessed extreme social change related to the development of globalization and unprecedented global movement during their lifetimes. From London to Sydney, from Alabama to Auckland, older people who are aging in place are witnessing, reacting to, rejecting and/or embracing cultural shifts in their own neighborhoods that have accompanied global movement. Older people's lives uniquely span and encompass these recent decades of extraordinary social change; their experiences, perspectives, and reactions deserve far closer examination. Such an examination is offered in this book.

AGING IN PLACE WHEN THE WORLD COMES TO YOU

Migration is nothing new; it has been a constant throughout history and prehistory, not an aberration. However, it has never been as pervasive socially, economically, and politically as it is today. Migration since 1945 has involved more world regions until few corners of the world remain untouched by its impact. Processes of economic, political, and cultural change have transformed the relationships between rich and poor countries, creating the conditions for greater human mobility. This combined with improved transportation, communication,

TABLE 1   Population Composition by Age, Race

Ethnicities	White	Black	Hispanic	Asian
85+	85%	7%	5%	2%
65–74	79%	9%	7%	4%
18–35	56%	13%	20%	5%
Under 5	51%	14%	25%	4%

SOURCE: 2010 U.S. Census and Frey 2014, 2015.

and a rising transnational consciousness has all led to more human movement and greater diversity. Virtually all democratic states have growing foreign-born populations due to increasing and increasingly diverse, migration. International migration and the resulting rapid ethnic and cultural diversity have changed the face of societies, sometimes in just two decades.

Most developed nations have a youth cohort that is strikingly different from its older generations (Castles and Miller 2009). For example, as shown in Table 1, in the United States, the racial makeup of the nation's younger population is beginning to contrast sharply with that of baby boomers and seniors (Frey 2014). Specifically, "the oldest generation is markedly whiter than the youngest" (Ball 2016). Eighty percent of those over sixty-five are non-Hispanic whites, versus just 58 percent of eighteen- to thirty-five-year-olds. At the extremes of the age spectrum, the differences are even more pronounced: as of 2010, just 51 percent of children under five were white, whereas 85 percent of those over eighty-five were white (Frey 2014).

England and Wales present a similar phenomenon with over 95 percent of those over the age of sixty-five being white (with just 3% and 1% of those over sixty-five being Asian or black, respectively). Among young adults between eighteen and thirty-five, 81 percent are white, 11 percent are Asian, and 4 percent are black. Another way to look at this is that the median age of England and Wales' white population is forty-one, with Asian, black, and "other" ethnicities each having a younger median age of twenty-nine to thirty (Office for National Statistics 2018).

In many nations, such demographic shifts are bringing broader national identity into question. In this age of migration, immigrant-receiving nations are seemingly reeling and ungrounded while reexamining what it means to belong to their societies (Castles and Miller 2009). In countries such as Australia, Canada, the United States, and New Zealand, where massive and newly multicultural immigration has resulted in ever more ethnically diverse populations, complicated questions have arisen such as how to create a sense of shared belonging to a place that is not tied to race, ethnicity, culture, or religion (Dunn et al. 2004; Clark 2007). Contradictory sentiments can coexist, such as a belief that it is good for a society to be diverse paired with a belief that communities can only be strong in circumstances of cultural sameness (Dunn et al. 2004). In addition, the powerful *idea* of a particular place is increasingly more an imagined state of being or piece of nostalgia separate from the current *reality* of the place (Gupta and Ferguson 1992).

Many popular media and academic accounts present a division of older generations holding onto these nostalgic, imagined realities while the younger generations live contemporary realities in cities such as London or Auckland— pulsing embodiments of superdiversity (Vertovec 2010a, 2010b; Spoonley 2011). It is important to note that this feeds the narrative of a cultural generation gap where the older age cohorts are "voicing sharp resistance to . . . new racial change" (Frey 2015, 32). In the United States, demographer Dowell Myers (2007), argues that the older generation in the United States—the established white majority group—reflects the past, whereas younger generations made up of immigrants and diversity across race, culture, and religion represent the present and future. This "cultural generation gap" (Frey 2015) is spilling over into many social and political issues with older white Americans resonating differently than younger minorities. For example, on the topic of interracial marriage, 36 percent of baby boomers versus 60 percent of millennials found this to be a change for the better (Frey 2014). Demographer William Frey writes that in the United States, "more than half of white baby boomers and seniors said that the growing number of newcomers from other countries represents a threat to traditional U.S. values and customs" (Frey 2015, 32).

Some speak about what they see as an irony here: that "elderly people oppose immigration when they're the most likely to benefit" (Winkler 2015b). This discourse is often contextualized within "the problem" of population aging and, within the United States, with discussions of the sinking Social Security retirement system (Campbell 2018, 2019; Cassidy 2018; Antonio 2019). With less alarmist rhetoric, demographer Dowell Myers (2007) provided an interesting portrayal of how older people and younger migrants are economically bound in the United States. He directly proposed that it is immigrants who will buy the houses and fill the jobs of retiring baby boomers (not to mention help to care for them) and that it is in the boomers' best interest to invest in the education and integration of immigrants (Myers 2007).

With all of this discussion about population change and global movement, it is too easy to forget that migration is, in fact, the exception. Most people still live in the country of their birth (Castles and Miller 2009). Here, then, emerges one of the defining characteristics of this age of migration: even those who do not move themselves are profoundly impacted by those who do. This book takes a closer look at the majority in this age of global movement—those who have not recently (or ever) migrated themselves but who have been profoundly impacted by the movement of others. It specifically acknowledges older people as living at the center of contemporary multiculturalism rather than assuming they rest, out of touch, only at the periphery of such settings. During this unprecedented time of global movement, many older people may have indeed "stayed still" themselves, but the world has come to them. This book explores their current daily interactions with the diverse array of migrants now encountered while attending the same church they always have, while doing the shopping in familiar stores, while riding the habitual bus, or while chatting with the new neighbors in the old houses. The older people featured within this book serve to remind us that "aging in place" certainly does not mean avoiding change and novelty or new encounters with difference. In fact, without migrating themselves, many of today's older people live in a *very* different country than the one of their memories. This book prioritizes their voices.

WHY NEW ZEALAND?

Unprecedented/expedited demographic and sociocultural change has changed many nations dramatically; New Zealand is one of these. Perhaps more often under the radar in global discussions, Aotearoa New Zealand actually emerges as a fascinating backdrop for studying how older people are experiencing contemporary multiculturalism. Here, dramatic demographic change has exploded over just the last several decades, well within the memories of older people. During their lifetimes, New Zealand has shifted from a country characterized by Māori and British settlers and their descendants, to one now characterized as superdiverse. Māori, the Tangata Whenua or indigenous population, settled in New Zealand approximately eight hundred years before European arrival (Wilmshurst et al. 2008), while European settlers (primarily British) began settling in New Zealand approximately 190 years ago (Smith 2008). The process of establishing a political and social partnership between Māori and the British Crown began in 1840 with the signing of the Treaty of Waitangi and this process continues today (MacPherson 2005). Until the late 1960s, the structure of this bicultural framework and continued close ties with Britain acted to maintain a national population consisting of Māori and a nonindigenous population that was over 96 percent British settlers and their descendants. This high percentage of British settlers made New Zealand the most homogenous of the former British colonies (McMillan 2004; Ip 2003; Spoonley and Bedford 2012).

Some historians have referred to New Zealand's immigration policy through World War II as "whiter than white." Non-European immigrants, particularly those from Asia were actively discouraged (Ward and Lin 2005; Brooking and Rabel 1995). In the 1950s, when New Zealand looked (begrudgingly) beyond British settlers to increase its population, an agreement was made with the Netherlands to accept a large number of Dutch immigrants into New Zealand. The Dutch were considered ideal due to their whiteness and their high likelihood of assimilating, even being called "honorary Britishers" (Lochore 1951, 89; Roggeveen 1996, 4). Also, during the 1950s, Pacific Island immigrants were sought to fill New Zealand's booming postwar economic and labor needs. During this time and into the 1960s, however, overseas-born Pacific Islanders and Asians together still equaled less than 1 percent of the population, with foreign-born European residents not of British stock equaling less than 2 percent (Brooking and Rabel 1995).

Over the next several decades, there were other exceptions to New Zealand's "white New Zealand" immigration policy (such as accepting forty-six hundred Cambodian refugees from the Khmer Rouge between 1979 and 1992 [Beaglehole, 2013]), but New Zealand's ethnic diversity outside the Māori and British settler paradigm remained minimal. Careful preference was still enforced for immigrants from Australia, North America, Western Europe, and of course, first and foremost, the United Kingdom.

In 1986, however, immigration policies underwent dramatic restructuring in tandem with economic restructuring. This significant redesigning of the nation's immigration policy resulted in large numbers of various Asian and other non-European immigrants coming to New Zealand over the last thirty-five to forty years. The implementation of the 1987 Immigration Act and of a "point system" in 1991 effectively abolished traditional source country preferences and instead emphasized skills, language, qualifications, adaptability, and capacity to settle (Zodgekar 2005). It is important to note that it has been argued that this was done without Māori consultation and thus violates the Treaty of Waitangi (Hill 2010; Ip 2003). In just the ten years after these policy changes took place (1991–2001), Asian immigration increased 240 percent (Statistics New Zealand 2014; Ward and Masgoret 2008). Within twenty-five years of these alterations to immigration policy, overseas-born residents from "Asia" collectively overtook the United Kingdom and Ireland as the most common birthplace for overseas-born residents (totaling 31.6 percent of overseas born population in 2013) (Statistics New Zealand 2014). Asians and Pacific Islanders together now make up nearly 40 percent of New Zealand's overseas-born population (Zodgekar 2005).

Due largely (though not entirely) to changes in immigration, New Zealand now exemplifies most developed nations in having a youth cohort that is strikingly different from its older generations (see table 2) (Castles and Miller 2009). As in many nations, such demographic shifts are bringing broader national identity into question. New Zealand also uniquely grapples with having introduced multiculturalism while still striving for a meaningful, working biculturalism (Marotta 2000; Spoonley and Bedford 2012).

Immigration policies are typically driven by political and economic forces, often at the macro, global level. New Zealand offers a prime illustration of how these economic and political changes then filter down to have very real social ramifications for ordinary people. In New Zealand, older people's lives easily span and encompass significant sociocultural changes brought about by global

TABLE 2   Ethnicity by Age Cohort

Ethnicities	European	Māori	Asian	Pacific
Age 65+	91%	5%	4%	2%
Age 18–24	67%	18%	17%	9%

SOURCE: Ministry of Social Development 2010

movement and the nation emerges as a fascinating (and often overlooked) site for daily, individualized experiences of accelerated cultural change.

THE DETAILS: WHO, WHERE, AND HOW

I sought out older New Zealanders in two locales for their perspectives of the substantial changes that diverse migration has brought about during their lifetimes: Auckland and Dunedin. A city of 1.2 million people, Auckland fits the definition of a superdiverse city on par with London or Los Angeles (Vertovec 2010b; Spoonley 2011). It is home to one-third of New Zealand's population and two-thirds of all immigrants into the country (Friesen 2010). It is a high-density, diverse city with ethnic enclaves including a proposed "China Town" (NZPA 2011). Dunedin, on the other hand, is one of New Zealand's smaller provincial cities and acts as a hub for a sparsely populated, rural, and semirural province with a Pākehā (white/European) majority. A city of one hundred twenty thousand, Dunedin has a proportionally far smaller, more dispersed and less visible migrant population. Auckland and Dunedin demonstrate distinctive arenas for the enactment of multiculturalism in New Zealand (see table 3).

Because diversity, immigration, and multiculturalism are lived, dynamic, interactive experiences, "negotiated within or alongside everyday interactions, crosscutting ties between a number of groups" (Vertovec 2010a, 6), I also sought out and included immigrants who interacted with older New Zealanders in some way. Having both perspectives—older New Zealanders and the immigrants who interact with them—lends a rare balance to this research and adds a robustness to the story being told. Only with multiple lenses are we truly considering the multistoried, interactive dynamic of coexistence in multicultural settings.

Data from both Auckland and Dunedin were collected through the methods of participant observation (Emerson, Fretz, and Shaw 1995), thematic analysis of formal interviews (Garro and Mattingly 2000; Chase 2002), and some use of photographs and video (by both the ethnographer and research participants) (Pink 2006; Grimshaw and Ravertz 2005).[2] Data were simultaneously collected through the same methods with immigrants who interacted with older New Zealanders in some way.

TABLE 3   Auckland versus Dunedin: Overseas Born as Percentage
of Total Population

	Auckland	Dunedin
Total people	1,415,550	120,246
Total overseas born	517,164	20,661
Percentage overseas born	36.53%	17.18%
Birthplace of overseas born: Numbers and percentages of total city population		
Oceania and Antarctica (excluding New Zealand)	129270 (9%)	3186 (3%)
United Kingdom and Ireland	90432 (6%)	7377 (6%)
Northern and western Europe	13875 (1%)	1422 (1%)
Southern and eastern Europe	13629 (1%)	489 (0.4%)
North Africa and the Middle East	11502 (0.8%)	552 (0.5%)
Southeast Asia	46926 (3%)	1644 (1%)
Northeast Asia	101535 (7%)	2478 (2%)
Southern and central Asia	54813 (4%)	924 (0.7%)
The Americas	16383 (1%)	1503 (1%)
Sub-Saharan Africa	38799 (3%)	1086 (0.9%)

SOURCE: Table created by the author with data drawn from Statistics New Zealand. Dataset:
Birthplace (detailed), for the census usually resident population count, 2001, 2006, and 2013
(RC, TA). Data extracted on 25 February 2016 05:41 UTC (GMT) from NZ.Stat (data extraction
tool available at http://nzdotstat.stats.govt.nz/wbos/Index.aspx).

I spent six weeks immersed in the bustling city of Auckland and its inner suburbs. I had almost no firsthand knowledge of this city prior to stepping off the airplane to begin fieldwork. As I pounded the pavement among 1.4 million others, ethnographic fieldwork was characterized by fleeting encounters and observations in public arenas (such as on public transport and in supermarkets), punctuated with longer conversations, observations, and participation at service centers, *maraes*,[3] and community events. Some locations and events were purposefully targeted as those I suspected would be frequented by older New Zealanders, immigrants, or both. However, most locations, events, and encounters came about through serendipitous leads—one of the true strengths of entering an unfamiliar field with a willingness to engage with strangers and follow surprising paths.

The length of my ethnographic research in Dunedin is harder to pin down, as I normally reside in Dunedin; it spanned one to two years. Fieldwork in Dunedin had novel and unexpected components, too (as happens when you change your purpose and perspective, even in a familiar place). Unlike Auckland, however, fieldwork in Dunedin sometimes stemmed from existing connections. Furthermore, new connections were sometimes able to be sustained and resulted in longer-term relationships and involvement over a year or more. (See tables 4 and 5.)

TABLE 4   Fieldwork in Auckland

Auckland Fieldwork		
Duration—six weeks		
Older New Zealander interviewees	Immigrant interviewees	Participant observation
14	3	• "Pounding the pavement" and following countless serendipitous leads
		• Observation in various public "arenas of interaction"—supermarkets, pharmacies, public transit, *maraes*, service centers, and community events
		• Many "one-off" experiences and contacts
		Examples include (but are not limited to) the following, largely serendipitous events:
		• Zumba with senior citizens at a diverse community center
		• Several weekly public markets
		• Small music group performance at a social hall
		• New Zealand–China Friendship society meeting
		• Three days at an RSA (Returned Service Association) club
		• Line dancing and coffee at a kaumatua (seniors) morning at a *marae*
		• Opening reception of a photography exhibit on the "changing ethnic contours" of one of the city's main roads

The participant observation undertaken in these two urban locales is detailed in chapter 3 as a part of a timely discussion of urban fieldwork intricacies and recruiting urban strangers. This participant observation also then led to formal, recorded interviews with fourteen older New Zealanders and three immigrants who interacted regularly with older New Zealanders in Auckland. In Dunedin, nine interviews were conducted with older New Zealanders and another five with immigrants. Throughout this book, all names are pseudonyms with the exception of one older New Zealander who was a professional photographer and wished to be identified in relation to his photographs (two of which appear in this book). Interviews were between forty minutes and three hours in length. Most were conducted in the interviewees' homes, though eight were conducted in other places such as the public library, a *marae*, and a hostel where I stayed during fieldwork. Interviews consisted of open-ended questions and were conversational, typically unfolding as I sat across from my older interviewees on their living room sofas or at their kitchen tables with cups of tea and plates of "biscuits and slices." Preliminary emergent themes were verified by subsequent

TABLE 5   Fieldwork in Dunedin

Dunedin Fieldwork		
Duration: One year		
Older New Zealander interviewees	Immigrant interviewees	Participant observation
9	5	More consistent relationships and gradual networking. Long-term involvement with relevant groups and planned participation in pertinent events.
		Examples include but are not limited to:
		• Migrant women's group with weekly meetings—active member
		• ESOL group with weekly meetings—frequent conversation volunteer
		• Local Age Concern article about my research results in conversations and interviews
		• Met with the city "migrant support" coordinator; later attended her presentation about multiculturalism to a seniors group
		• Attended presentation on relating to immigrants at a seniors church group
		• Met with two in-home care coordinators
		Some "pounding the pavement" and serendipitous leads. *Examples include but are not limited to:*
		• Quick chats in an Asian supermarket
		• Observations at a pharmacy and corner shop; extended conversation with an immigrant in an antiques shop—all in a neighborhood with high concentrations of older people and immigrants

NOTE: ESOL = English for speakers of other languages.

participants, for example through questions such as: "Other people have told me that . . . Do you find this to be true as well or have you had a different experience?" Interviews were stopped when data saturation was achieved and when later interviews continuously confirmed earlier findings in this manner (Fitzgerald and Robertson 2006; Strauss and Corbin 1998).

Interview transcripts and the extensive fieldnotes from participant observation were entered into NVivo qualitative analysis software and mined for emergent themes. Along with the later interviewees themselves, my two PhD supervisors provided independent verification of emerging codes and the categorization of related codes into overarching themes. Thus, the resulting themes are derived from and "grounded in" the empirical data itself (Fitzgerald and Robertson 2006). (See Table 6.)

TABLE 6   NVivo Codes: Emergent Themes from Interview
and Fieldnote Analysis

Aging in New Zealand
- Economics
- Health care
- Social aspects

Older New Zealanders: Attitudes toward immigrants
- Acceptance of change
- Assumption that older New Zealanders will be racist
- Attitudes developing throughout life
- Fear of immigrants, bad outcomes
- Love–hate; contradictory thoughts on immigrants
  - Immigrants I know are good, overall it's bad
  - Struggling against oneself—knowing what one *should* feel
- Recollections of high-profile/media cases
- Older New Zealanders *more* accepting than younger
- Resentment
- Sympathy, respect for immigrants
- What "other" older New Zealanders think

Changes in New Zealand
- In general
- Immigration-related
  - Concerns
    - Competing resources
    - Fear of change or unwanted change
    - Looking forward, anticipated change
  - Positive changes
  - Then/now comparisons related to ethnicities/immigration
  - *Not* really a change for me

Contact
- Contact with immigrants impacts thoughts or experiences
- Cosmopolitan or multicultural interactions
- Diversity within one's own family
- Recalling first contact with immigrants
- Older people have not much contact with immigrants
  - Less contact now than previously
  - Mostly with my own kind, but not by design
- Seeking out multicultural contact
- Pākehā discussing contact with Māori as difference
- From immigrant point of view
  - Bad experiences with New Zealanders
  - Interactions with older people "back home"
  - Older New Zealanders help immigrants learn about New Zealand
  - Respect for older people
  - Social isolation and/or time on their hands
  - Sympathy for New Zealanders

(*continued*)

TABLE 6   *(continued)*

Context New Zealand
- Biculturalism
- Multicultural or not
- New Zealand and national identity
- New Zealand "norms"
  ◦ Immigrants and fitting in
  ◦ Immigrants breaking New Zealand norms
  ◦ Older New Zealanders "Mentors of 'Kiwiness'"

I also included a small, optional visual component in data collection by invit-ing interviewees to set out with a camera to capture some of the topics we had discussed in our interview (home, change, diversity, multiculturalism, and more). We would then meet again to discuss these topics further, guided by their images. This was reminiscent of "photovoice" (rather than a strict adherence to this methodology) in which participants are asked to use cameras and photographs to reflect on their communities and the photos then serve to elicit information as the participant and the researcher view the photographs together (Novek, Morris-Oswald, and Menec 2011; Pink 2006). Three older New Zealand partici-pants and one immigrant took up this task. In one case, over the course of a single interview with a professional photographer, he filtered through his digital and paper collections finding photographs that illustrated our discussion topics as they arose. Over decades, he had captured snapshots of community change and increasing diversity in his immediate surroundings.

As a former photography student, I also took photographs around both fieldsites as part of my process of observing, documenting, and interpreting what I saw. This process proved not only to be an enjoyable, creative outlet but also provided tangi-ble field recordings that proved useful in my data analysis. For example, photograph-ing what I saw around Auckland with my own eyes in 2012 (ten-lane highways, signage in countless languages, community events catering to a huge range of reli-gions, cultures, and more) drove home the sheer degree of change that had occurred when compared with older New Zealanders' recollections of the same areas in years gone by. (A short YouTube video in which the voices of two older participants recount how their area of Auckland "used to be" overlays images of the area as I saw it fifty years later: https://youtu.be/P2XewJPU1Lo.)

Categories and Positionality

How do you define older? Older people are often overlooked members of diverse, contemporary societies but they are the ones who can provide a time lapse of the past unfolding into the present. I settled on an age category of "65+" for two reasons. First, Statistics New Zealand keeps data on this segment of the population, allowing easy access to population statistics. Second, sixty-five is the current age at which New Zealanders are eligible for retirement and the public pension, making this a categorization with which people are familiar. A quick explanation that I was speaking to the "65+" group was met with nods of recognition and understanding.

The category "older New Zealanders" does not account for the diversity within this category—gender, ethnicity, nationality, a range of opinions, and so forth. Few New Zealanders over sixty-five would consider themselves to be, as such, members of a meaningful community, nor would they welcome generalizations about them based on being in that age bracket. What is more, as people are living longer life spans in New Zealand, the category is becoming even more arbitrary. (Here, it is important to recognize a measure of social inequality in New Zealand: the lower life expectancy of Māori compared with non-Māori [Pool 2015] [Pollock 2012]). Some participants were in their nineties, some had parents in their nineties; thus, "65+" encompasses two or more generations. There are significant differences between the life stories, memories, current life situations, health, mobility, and more for a sixty-five-year-old versus a ninety-five-year old.

Two participants in this research, Clare (Auckland, age seventy) and Charles (Auckland, age eighty) epitomize the significant differences in memories of those over sixty-five and how these memories might shape current views. Although only ten years older than Clare, Charles vividly remembers blackouts during World War II when his family had to cover the windows at night and a neighbor would inform them if any light was showing. He remembers the fear of being bombed, the suspicion of a Japanese submarine in the nearby harbor, the clear status of Japanese and Germans as the enemy. Today, he openly describes himself as a "racist bastard." Clare, on the other hand, says it is her parents who remember World War II, who remember when the Japanese and the Germans were the enemy: "Oh absolutely. And they would've influenced us a little bit as younger children because you get—'The Japs' would have been 'dangerous.' But we grew out of that." She said most New Zealanders who have firsthand memories of World War II have passed away now. She describes herself as being "reasonably tolerant" and is an English-language volunteer for elderly migrants and a homestay host for young foreign students.

But just when you think you might be seeing a trend that, for example, the "old-old" age group of "85+" might be less tolerant of diversity, then some individuals disrupt such generalizations—like Iris. Iris (Auckland, age ninety) spent several years volunteering in China in the 1940s, speaks fluent Mandarin, and loves surprising Chinese tourists and immigrants by speaking to them in their language. To summarize, this research uses a broad category of 65+ to respectfully refer to "older," with all the variety that this generalization inherently entails.

Who is meant by "New Zealanders?" In New Zealand's postcolonial, bicultural paradigm, this question is fraught with sociopolitical tension and requires careful consideration (see Callister 2004; Bartley and Spoonley 2005; Spoonley 2001). This question of "Who is a New Zealander?" hums along as a constant backdrop to conversations of national identity, biculturalism, and multiculturalism, occasionally coming to the forefront in popular media, such as when a popular television personality caused an uproar and was ultimately fired for stating that the current governor general, who was born in New Zealand and of Indian and Pacific ancestry, did not "look and sound like a New Zealander" (New Zealand Herald Staff 2010).

The debate around "New Zealander" has also manifested in census data. An increasing number of people are answering "New Zealander" in response to questions about ethnicity in official surveys—leading to the fundamental question of whether or not "New Zealander" can be considered an ethnicity. In the 1991, 1996, and 2001 censuses, those who wrote in "New Zealander" for ethnicity were subsequently regrouped by Statistics New Zealand as "New Zealand European" in spite of significant evidence that those answering "New Zealander" were also of Māori, Pacific Island, and other ethnic backgrounds (Callister 2004). In 2004, Statistics New Zealand recommended that this policy of regrouping be stopped (Callister 2004).

It is argued that a category of "New Zealander" allows those of, for example, European or Asian ancestry who hold no affinity with Europe or Asia to identify as a second "indigenous" group to New Zealand. Also, some people with complicated mixtures of cultural and ancestral backgrounds use the category of "New Zealander" as a new amalgamation (Callister 2004). The category of "New Zealander" as ethnicity is considered to be harmful to Māori, however. The reasons include that it creates problems for Māori/non-Māori comparisons, it does not sit well within a concept of the Treaty of Waitangi as being between two distinct peoples, and it is a step toward the creation of a second indigenous group, undermining Māori's status of indigeneity within New Zealand (Callister 2004; Statistics New Zealand 2004).

I realized that the complex category of "New Zealander" is also easily misunderstood internationally when I received feedback for a grant application from an overseas reviewer. The anonymous reviewer proposed that my research design was fatally flawed because s/he assumed that by "New Zealander" I was referring to a specific ethnic category of white/European background, and therefore was not including Māori (or, for that matter, any other ethnicity) in my research. After seeking advice from both Māori and Pākehā researchers, my intention had been, and still is, to use the term "New Zealander" as an inclusive nationality not indicative of ethnicity, though I certainly recognized the flaws and complications in doing so.

In my formal interviews, I carefully allowed the space and respect needed for each participant to explain their ethnic and/or national identity in their own words. To illustrate the variety of self-identifications that I heard and that typify New Zealand's population, and because it is particularly important to let participants speak for themselves when it comes to identity, here is a small selection of responses to my question, "How do you identify yourself?" in relation to the category "New Zealander." June (Auckland, age seventy-two) explained:

> I always acknowledge my iwi and my hapū and that I am a Māori. Even though I have Scottish ancestry. . . . And somewhere in between there's the stirring up of a Māori potpourri. [Laugh.] So I am Māori. And I'm a New Zealander. And uh, this is my heritage, it's my country.

Clare (Auckland, age seventy) explained that she could be placed in the Pākehā category, but that she would first describe herself as Kiwi. Another participant, Fran (Auckland, age seventy-five) told me before the interview began that she was "half Pākehā and half Cook Island Māori." When I asked directly at the end of our interview, she responded:

> A New Zealander. You know those forms you fill in when you come in off the plane? They haven't got anything in there that says New Zealander. They've got Pākehā, Māori, part-Māori, this that and the—. I just put down New Zealander.

Finally, Grant (Auckland, age sixty-eight) explained that while there are certain labels he is comfortable identifying with, he actually doesn't know his ethnic heritage:

> I'm happy to be called a New Zealander. . . . I mean first, "New Zealander," second, "Pākehā New Zealander." Although, because I was adopted, I actually don't know who my father was, so I mean I might be . . . part Māori, I don't know.

My interviewees also included four "older New Zealander" participants who were born overseas (in England, Scotland, and Australia, historically "traditional source countries" for immigrants in New Zealand before the 1987 Immigrant Act led to a far more diverse influx of immigrants [Bedford and Ho 2006]). All arrived as children or young adults and had been in New Zealand for at least forty-five years at the time of their interviews. Recruiting overseas born New Zealanders was not intended, however, these individuals approached me, or were referred to me, as "older New Zealanders" interested in participating in my research as such. Through my previous research on immigrants who have been in New Zealand for forty years or more, I know that long-term immigrants are often particularly insightful about their host country, viewing it simultaneously as a long-term local but with an outsider's eye (George and Fitzgerald 2012). Thus, their insights are particularly rich and still convey a knowledge of change over many decades within New Zealand. For example, Patty (Dunedin, age sixty-seven) was born in Scotland and migrated to New Zealand as a child. She described Dunedin as her home and like a comfortable old sweater while she spoke to changes in New Zealand experienced over decades. But her interview was also peppered with little insights from an immigrant's point of view.

Imposing clear-cut categories is tempting, appealing to an easy sense of order. But it is false. The older New Zealanders in this research remind us of what we in anthropology surely already know, that categories are inadequate simplifications of complex, fluid, contextualized identities. Contemporary ethics suggest people have a right to identify themselves in the manner that they wish to be identified (Callister 2004). Thus, I conclude this discussion of "New Zealander" by confirming that all twenty-three "older New Zealanders" in this research were comfortable identifying themselves and being identified as "New Zealanders" for the purposes of this research, although many would also identify as something else as well. Outside of formal interviews, in fleeting conversations in the urban field, I argue that it simply was not appropriate to ask the highly emotive and politically complex question about a person's identity. I detail this consideration in chapter 3.

Finally, what about the category of "immigrant?" My use of the term "immigrant" is intentionally ambiguous. By immigrant, I simply mean someone who was born in another country and has been in New Zealand for an extended period of time, years or more, and often settled here indefinitely. Most of the immigrants I interviewed would define themselves as such, although this did not preclude them from identifying as other things as well; occasionally, some now felt that they had become "New Zealanders," too! Two participants felt they did not fit their own image of a "true immigrant" because they did not have Permanent Resident status. The immigrants in this research stemmed from Iran, Indonesia, Germany, England, the Philippines, Korea, and China. All of them were comfortable being referred to as "immigrants" for the purposes of this research, including the two who would not have initially self-identified this way.

Outside of the interviews, I spoke with countless immigrants less formally. They represented a myriad of differing nationalities and circumstances. Some were refugees, most were not. Many were here permanently, some were here temporarily, many did not know. They spanned economic and educational ranges. They were from all over the world and were adults of all ages. Most were women, a point that will be briefly expanded on later.

My Own Shifting Role

During this research, my own identity demonstrated the permeability of categories. I switched frequently between "New Zealander" and "immigrant"—both as defined by myself and according to others. I first migrated to New Zealand in 2004 to undertake postgraduate study. After some years bouncing back and forth between New Zealand and my home country of the United States, I settled permanently in New Zealand in 2010. I am married to a New Zealander and have three children born in New Zealand. In New Zealand's bicultural context, my position, like that of many immigrants, is ambiguous. Clearly, I cannot be placed in the Māori or Tangata Whenua category of indigenous New Zealanders, who constitute one part of New Zealand's bicultural dynamic. By default, then, I fall into the Pākehā category, particularly with my white skin—the dominant marker of Pākehā-ness.

Positioning migrants such as myself into New Zealand society is tied up in complex, passionate, and long-standing arguments of New Zealand's national identity and the tensions between history, ideological visionings, and contemporary reality (Hill 2010; Ip 2003a; Bartley and Spoonley 2005). Is New Zealand multicultural? This label honors the diversity in the population and allows the approximately seven hundred thousand migrants a legitimate position but dangerously negates the position of indigeneity, the bicultural paradigm, and the founding document of the current nation-state, the Treaty of Waitangi (Hill 2010; Kukutai 2008; Walker 2004).

It proved surprisingly easy to develop a rapport with older New Zealanders that allowed them to reflect openly about immigration in New Zealand with me, an immigrant. I believe this is due to characteristics that allow me (or force me) to be placed into the Pākehā category—I am white, from a traditional source country, settled here long-term, married to a Kiwi, English is my first language, and I have only a "soft" foreign accent. There is a social and historical framework for immigrants "like me," at least in relation to the greater diversity of immigrants entering New Zealand since 1987. When conversation began to flow with the older New Zealanders I spoke with, it didn't take long before I typically heard something like "Oh well, you're practically one of us!"

I acknowledge that my immigrant status could have inhibited what older New Zealanders said on the topic of diversity and immigration, but I suggest that this inhibition around topics of race, ethnicity, diversity, and immigration can be present for many older New Zealanders regardless of whom they are talking to. There is a prescriptive discourse on topics related to race in New Zealand, which many people abide by to avoid being labelled "racist" (Tremewan 2005). The attributes of "openness" and "friendliness" are strongly presumed qualities of national character (Tourism New Zealand 2011). If I had heard only good things about immigrants, I would be concerned that my immigrant status and the general protocol for discussing (or avoiding) these sensitive topics might have combined to form a barrier to the expression of honest or complex feelings. It is precisely because I *did* hear a full range of opinions, including those that could be labeled "negative" or "racist" that I believe I largely overcame these obstacles.

I considered it a particular success when one participant complained to me about Americans!

When interacting with immigrants, I naturally felt "one of them." Conversation typically flowed through the topics that immigrants can share—how long we have been in New Zealand, what we miss about our homelands, what we like about New Zealand, and eventually, confessions about what we don't like about it. However, I was surprised to learn that some immigrants viewed me as "a New Zealander": those who were an ethnic and/or religious minority in New Zealand and who were learning a new language, sometimes assumed my transition to "New Zealander" was seamless.

In Dunedin, I attended an English-conversation group for Asian students and immigrants run by an eighty-year-old New Zealander, Alan. Alan would always introduce me as "a New Zealander" and in the context of this conversation group I would embody this persona. I could assist as a native English speaker and a long-term New Zealand resident. But when Alan would leave for a cigarette break, the other immigrants and I would often subtly shift to less formal interactions, empathetic conversations and camaraderie based on the broadly shared experience of migrating. Such contextual, flexible identities are typical for many today. Anthropologists such as myself are simply another embodiment of the transnational lives and the fluid, multifaceted identities that they study.

LIMITATIONS

My approach to fieldwork, like all fieldwork, had its limitations. My methods and approach did not allow a way to interact with older people who were *not* out and about to some degree, who perhaps have *not* engaged with the increasing diversity around them. Also, my interviews and extended conversations with older New Zealanders were with those willing to discuss the tenuous topic of diversity and multiculturalism in New Zealand. Those who were not interested or were unwilling to speak on this subject did not respond to my invitations to interact. My research, then, is more a reflection of the experiences of older New Zealanders with some degree of mobility, social interaction, and willingness to discuss the touchy subject of diversity.

My contact with immigrants was dominated by observing and interacting with female immigrants. In Dunedin, I utilized my existing network of a migrant women's group; however, my contact with female migrants might also reflect the social phenomenon that it is often female migrants who have contact with older New Zealanders. More and more immigrants are women (Castles and Miller 2009; Hochschild 2000, 34) (see also Vertovec 2010b). In New Zealand, carers for the elderly are being actively recruited from overseas, and these migrant caregivers are more often women (Badkar, Callister, and Didham 2009; Badkar et al. 2007). On the other hand, many women still do accompany a husband who is sponsored by a job offer and visa in New Zealand. Once here, the wife may have trouble finding paid work in her area of expertise, sometimes due to a language barrier, and may find work as an "unskilled" assistant in the rapidly growing industry of rest homes, or, alternatively, may begin to volunteer with agencies like Age Concern. I saw both of these things happen again and again in my own networks and fieldwork. So while I acknowledge that my interviews do not include any perspectives from male migrants who interact with older New Zealanders, they do reflect the reality that female migrants might be in contact with New Zealand elderly more often than male migrants.

Finally, my fieldwork methods lead to a sample of interview participants that is somewhat indicative of the variety of ethnic, social, and national identities that the category of "New Zealander" can include, but it is not a proportional sample. Māori are underrepresented and I did not conduct formal interviews with older Asian New Zealanders who together constitute approximately 3 percent of New Zealand's population that is older than sixty-five (New Zealand Ministry of Social Development 2010). In chapter 3, I delve further into my dynamic approach to the urban field and the process of recruiting urban strangers as interviewees. My hope is that the cosmopolitan approach that I describe—avoiding an unethical use of labels and categories in urban settings of diversity—will make a valuable contribution to discussions of contemporary urban ethnographic methods (George 2016).

CHAPTER BY CHAPTER SYNOPSIS

In the next chapter, chapter 2, I situate this new research within existing and developing research on global movement, multiculturalism, and aging. In chapter 3, I describe how during the course of conducting this research, I landed smack in the middle of several very current "hot topics" in contemporary social research that themselves became a central consideration in this research. Thus, chapter 3 focuses on my methods and particularly the complexities of carrying out ethnographic fieldwork in urban locales. I grappled with the common but troublesome question of "where to start" when treating "the city" as "the field" while also making conscious attempts to avoid the "pitfalls of anthropology by appointment" (Hannerz 2006, 77) that too often characterize current urban ethnography. I employed a somewhat risky and unconventional grassroots manner to find and speak with older adults going about their lives in contemporary settings of multiculturalism. Here, the New Zealand context facilitates an intriguing contribution to the timely discussion around urban fieldwork, in particular the problem of categorization. This chapter presents an evocative solution to the woes of categorization. I propose that labels and categories often utilized by anthropologists are not only difficult to employ but are unethical in urban fieldwork where fleeting interactions typify urban realities.

Chapter 4 locates older New Zealanders as aging actors within a dramatically changing world. When asked to reflect on current experiences, older New Zealanders traveled back in their minds, best able to describe their current reality in relation to "what used to be." In this chapter, their voices convey firsthand accounts of some of the many dramatic changes they have witnessed over their lifetimes, including increasing global migration, diversity, and the associated social and cultural ramifications. Their descriptions of a changing society emerge as rich autobiographic binaries of "then and now" that are at the heart of understanding what increasing diversity has looked like "on the ground." In the New Zealand context, these older people remember when they first noticed Chinese immigrants settling into Auckland suburbs and building a new style of housing; they remember their school class being all Pākehā and Māori in contrast to what they now see when they watch the kids flooding out of the school doors at the end of the day. They remember when garlic was an exotic spice and olive oil a rarity; this is in contrast to the current difficulty of finding a traditional New Zealand roast in the modern array of ethnic restaurants. They can even find evidence of population change in their own families—with sons- and daughters-in-law and grandchildren representing all regions of the world. Through sharing their memories, older New Zealanders bring banal, demographic statistics to life.

Given the amount of social and cultural change older New Zealanders have witnessed and experienced in their lifetimes, it is perhaps not surprising to find that their reflections include ample, significant concerns and complaints about these changes. Chapter 5 focuses on these concerns. Older New Zealanders relayed their concern about a perceived increase in crime, often expressed through some version of the phrase "these things just don't happen in New Zealand." Many worried about increasing job competition for their children and grandchildren as jobs are "snatched up" by immigrants. Many worried about the health-care system and told stories of friends being "wait-listed" for surgeries while the immigrants and refugees, who "come with these diseases," are tended to. They also expressed more intangible concerns, such as a loss of biculturalism, community, equality, and other self-described aspects of a fundamental "New Zealandness." In this chapter, all of these concerns were raised by the older participants themselves and were contextualized with various examples from the media and critical academic literature about the complexities of host–newcomer relationships.

Chapter 6 introduces the voices of immigrants. Their perspective moves this narrative in a surprising direction. First, chapter 6 begins by examining the existing assumption that older New Zealanders might be more racist, more resistant to difference, than their younger counterparts. We then turn to immigrants' reported experiences to the contrary. Rather than finding older New Zealanders to be intolerant of diversity, immigrants largely found them to be *more* approachable, *more* accepting, and less intimidating than younger New Zealanders. Immigrants described congenial interactions with older New Zealanders who were willing to have a chat in the botanical gardens or to repeat themselves if the immigrant had not understood something said. Immigrants described older New Zealand neighbors who took them to get a library card, who brought over a sample of New Zealand baking, or who warned of a mechanic to avoid. Several immigrants mentioned that interactions with older New Zealanders were comfortable because they could fall back on familiar social rules that govern interactions with older people in their home countries, things like politeness and deference. Immigrants also relayed having a feeling of "safety" around older New Zealanders; some had experienced discrimination and racist acts from younger New Zealanders. Some older people and immigrants both felt that older New Zealanders might have more free time and a slower pace of life (which I discuss as "cadence") that enables amicable interactions with migrant strangers.

Chapter 7 suggests that older New Zealanders can act as "mentors of 'Kiwiness'" with new immigrants. Many older New Zealanders freely and casually shared historical knowledge and narratives, little lessons that immigrants reported as unfolding exponentially, boosting their understanding of New Zealand and their sense of belonging in their host country. For example, an older New Zealand woman explained the historical and cultural significance of a local statue to her Fijian taxi driver as they drove past it; another explained to the migrant woman next door that making small talk about the weather would help her begin conversations with Kiwis. Be it deliberately or unknowingly, these older New Zealand mentors helped immigrants demystify the often ambiguous (but none-the-less very strong) parameters of an "ethos" of "Kiwiness." It is important to note that this chapter turns a common depiction of older people as the *recipients* of help on its head. In the common international scenario of pinched health-care systems, immigrants are sought to fill the gap of elder caregivers and thus relieve "the burden" of an aging population. However, this research reveals older people as the *givers* of assistance rather than receivers. Their micro acts of mentoring subtly but significantly aid the integration of diverse immigrants, a process that is an essential component of successful multicultural communities.

While this book began as a story about aging and the passage of time, chapter 8 clearly solidifies that it is also a story about difference; specifically, it is a story about how older people are living within and among difference that has developed around them. This chapter comes back to the idea of cosmopolitanism first introduced in chapter 3 as a method. Here, cosmopolitanism is introduced again as a framework for exploring the productive engagement with difference and the grounded expressions of hospitality to strangers that were revealed through this ethnography. Chapter 8 demonstrates the need for a view of cosmopolitanism that is plural and contextualized in the ambiguities of everyday life in diverse settings. It does this by highlighting the contradictions inherent in some older New Zealanders' reactions to immigrants: simultaneously openly complaining about immigrants while defending, helping, and befriending them. This chapter closes by proposing a new framework for the study of aging and diversity, that of older people having a "cosmopolitan cadence" or an ability to engage with difference in small, meaningful ways with individual migrants due to their slower pace of life. This chapter argues that older people's expressed macro concerns about the effects of immigration on society (the focus of chapter 5) do not deny or prevent their micro manifestations of cosmopolitanism; rather, the two seemingly contrary sentiments coexist.

Chapter 9, the conclusion, pulls the preceding chapters together in a cohesive discussion that engages with popular notions in contemporary understandings of aging in place and introduces a new paradigm for doing so in times and settings of great social change. The book concludes with a direct counternarrative to the old as resistant to change or as a collective liability in growing settings of multiculturalism, movement, and diversity.

2 · GLOBAL MOVEMENT, EVERYDAY MULTICULTURALISM, AND AGING

Nearly thirty years ago, cultural theorist Stuart Hall wrote that living with difference would be "the coming question of the 21st century" (Hall 1993, 361). Anthropologists have argued for decades that the discipline must move beyond "ethnic isolates" to consider instead how members of different groups within the same multicultural setting interact with and understand each other (Cohen 1978, 384). And yet enactments of multiculturalism, "negotiated within or alongside everyday interactions and cross-cutting ties between a number of groups" have remained "seriously understudied" (Vertovec 2010a, 6).

In current contexts shaped by global movement, people from numerous different backgrounds come into contact—be it occasionally or constant and routine—with difference. Living in contemporary settings of diversity has been referred to as "a being together of strangers" (Young 1990), "thrown togetherness" (Massey 2005), or "rubbing along" (Hudson, Phillips, and Ray 2009). The contexts hosting such contact with difference have been called "arenas of interaction" (Lamphere 1992; Vertovec 2015b), "transversal spaces" (Wise 2009), "zones of encounter" (Wood and Landry 2007), and "micropublics" (Amin 2002), to name a few. Louise Lamphere's (1992) edited collection, *Structuring Diversity: Ethnographic Perspectives on the New Immigration* is one early example of research that aimed explicitly to consider interactions in these settings by working to "uncover a more representative portrait of the full range of relationships between immigrants and established residents" (5). Concentrating on mundane, everyday interactions between migrants and established residents in "mediating institutions" and "arenas"—schools, factories, public spaces, churches, apartment complexes, Lamphere's research group purposely used the categories of "newcomers" and "established residents" to avoid thinking in terms of ethnic groups (Lamphere 1992).

Published years later, Baumann's 1996 ethnography, *Contesting Culture: Discourses of Identity in Multi-ethnic London*, similarly avoided focusing on one ethnic group and took the novel approach of considering the very diverse Southall, London, as one unit of analysis. Baumann wanted to see how the people of Southall defined their experiences of "community" and "culture." He painted a picture of lived multiculturalism where people shift their position and identity according to particular contexts. Some other works on everyday multiculturalism have looked at a variety of contexts, such as a "micro-geography" of a diversely populated residential street in Vancouver (Hiebert 2002) or a study of the dynamics between migrants and long-term residents in a small Eastern England city (Erel 2011). Others have considered difference as experienced in daily life settings such as coffee shops in Malaysia (Khoo 2009); shopping streets in Montreal (Radice 2011, 2000); and micro, mundane settings such as a body-building gym (Sherman 2009); a river (Goodall et al. 2009); a market (Watson 2009); and more.

Acknowledging that life in increasingly diverse cities is "marked by a coexistence . . . a plurality of ethnic affiliations, cultural preferences and life experiences linked with immigration," the large-scale Max Planck Institute Diversity and Contact (DivCon) project recently investigated the characteristics of social interactions between individuals (Diversity and Contact [DivCon] 2015; Schonwalder et al. 2016). Of all of the qualitative work associated with this project, I found the research that resonated the most with my own was undertaken by Susanne Wessendorf. In the super-diverse context of Hackney, London, with a notion of diversity as commonplace (a "normal part of social life and not something particularly special"), Wessendorf examined daily social relations and negotiations of difference among residents (Wessendorf 2013, 407; Wessendorf 2014b). She developed the idea of an "ethos of mixing"—a belief held by residents that people should mix in public spaces paralleled by the acceptance of more separate lives in private spheres (Wessendorf 2013, 407). She found that expectations of interactions can, and do, involve taking a deeper interest in other people's life worlds, and forming networks across "difference," but this is not necessary; the valued "ethos of mixing" could be maintained through public, associational spaces, even with a degree of indifference (Wessendorf 2013, 2014a). Her observations of Hackney fit an image of "unpanicked multiculturalism"— the manner in which difference is negotiated in everyday lives, away from state and media-driven anxieties (Noble 2009, 50)—or as one of Wessendorf's participants might put it, "just getting on with it" (Wessendorf 2013, 416).

All of these above works consider the "critical interplay between globality and particularity" (Lamb 2009, 11) and contribute to our understandings of everyday, lived multiculturalism. None of these specifically prioritize *older people's* experiences of increasing everyday diversity and multiculturalism, however, which is what this research with older New Zealanders aims to do. As older people age in place, only they can view global migration and multiculturalism longitudinally, through witnessing and participating in their own changing surroundings over time.

This research with older New Zealanders in increasingly diverse settings joins other anthropological works that recognize aging as interactive and socially embedded. In gerontology, a notion of aging as loss and decline dominated well into the 1970s, but anthropologists and some other social researchers have been producing an alternative focus and a strong counternarrative to aging-as-loss (Kaufman 1986, 1993). As with the research presented in this book, these studies have not dismissed or denied loss but have shown how loss is incorporated, adapted to, and negotiated within a variety of ways that confer meaning into life (Graham and Stephenson 2010a). These nuanced portrayals of aging include everything from older people who follow the sun in recreational vehicles (Counts and Counts 2001), to those who find love in late life (Barusch 2008). Studies of elderly people in Namaqualand in South Africa who have suffered under colonial oppression (Oakley 2010) to older Australian working class men who can no longer do hard labor (Russell 2010), to Puerto Rican women caring for their U.S.-based grandchildren (Rodriguez-Galan 2013), have all viewed aging in a web of intermingled life and contextual experiences that defy the simplified story of loss that is too often associated with aging, particularly in Western societies (Graham and Stephenson 2010a).

These sort of anthropological works are in opposition to much earlier theorizing of aging, such as disengagement theory (Cumming and Henry 1961), which posited that aging involves a "gradual but inevitable withdrawal or disengagement" between an aging individual and his or her social world (Victor 2005, 20). Instead, these studies reflect how loss in older age is far more multifaceted. Many social scientists have used the disengagement theory as a stimulant for rebuttals and countertheories, such as activity theory (Havighurst 1961) and continuity theory (Atchley 2000) (although these theories too have now largely been critiqued) (Victor 2005). However, anthropologists also readily critique one paradigm that appears to be the antithesis of equating age to loss: that of successful aging.

A single definition of successful aging is elusive. The term has been around since at least the 1960s and across the literature on successful aging, various themes have emerged, including individual agency and control; independence, activity, and productivity; and pursuing agelessness and permanent personhood (Lamb 2014). Although successful aging has emerged as a rebuttal to a "very powerful negative construction of old age as a time of inevitable disengagement and personal dissolution" (Andrews 2009, 74), it has many critics who warn against viewing successful aging as an "antidote" to aging itself (Andrews 1999, 303). Andrews proposes that the recent successful aging paradigm (depicted in images of tanned, fit, older couples playing tennis and cycling) presents aging essentially as an ailment that will be kept at bay by keeping active (Andrews

1999). A quick search through retirement community advertisements yields ample examples of the kind of imagery that Andrews criticizes as perpetuating the unspecified but preferred method of aging as not aging at all, or at least keeping its evidence to a minimum (Andrews 2009).

Among those advising caution around the successful aging paradigm is anthropologist Sarah Lamb. In her fieldwork in Bengal, India, she found that older people spoke openly about a readiness for death, an acceptance of decline, and an absence of a dedication to independence and physical and mental exercise. This threw "into relief" the assumptions and values built into North American models of successful aging with its emphasis on independence, activity, productivity, denial of decline and mortality, and the individual self as project (Lamb 2014, 42). Lamb argued that popular and scientific models of aging would be more productive, helpful, and even inspiring if they allowed for the realities of change, decline, and mortality. She spoke with older people who pointed out that a model of successful aging is actually contingent on things beyond one's control, like good health and economic resources, leaving some to be "doomed to 'fail'" (Lamb 2014, 49). Von Faber and van der Geest found that privileging notions of novelty, responsiveness, outgoingness, and even self-aggrandizement as "healthy" and normal leaves no room for personality differences or personal choice. Qualities and practices such as quiet listening, observation, reflection, and resistance are then understood to be the antithesis of successful aging (von Faber and van der Geest 2010). In their work, von Faber and van der Geest found that a group of older Dutch people, not one of whom would have met externally imposed criteria for successful aging, considered themselves to be aging well due to their "artful adjustment to changing circumstances" (Graham and Stephenson 2010, xi; von Faber and van der Geest 2010).

In recent years, anthropologists have joined other social scientists, notably sociologists, in utilizing a life course approach (also referred to as a theory, a theoretical orientation, a framework, a perspective, and a model). A life course approach can be broadly explained as the "contextual study of lives" (Elder, Johnson, and Crosnoe 2003, 7). This approach refrains from considering aging as a discrete life experience and from viewing the old as a delineated group. Terms such as "transitions," "trajectories," and "transformations" reflect that changes in states, experiences, or roles occur throughout life, conveying movement through time rather than disjuncture (Danely and Lynch 2013; Elder, Johnson, and Crosnoe 2003; Gardner 2009). A life course approach provides the scaffold for studying "phenomena at the nexus of social pathways, developmental trajectories, and social change" (Elder, Johnson, and Crosnoe 2003, 10) and "embodied journeys through time" (Gardner 2009, 229). For anthropologists, one of the central tenants of the life course approach is recognizing that physiological processes of aging may be largely universal, but are experienced, understood, and ascribed meaning according to cultural contexts (Gardner 2009). The life course approach informs my own research through its reminder to consider the processual, highly contextualized experiences of aging.

AGING IN PLACE IN A WORLD OF MOVEMENT

Aging in a Changing World sits precisely at the nexus of aging and the diversity associated with global movement. A small pool of literature sits here at this nexus, the vast majority looking at diversity *within* the aging population (such as policy-related research about working with diverse, aging populations (Torres-Gil and Moga 2002; Warnes et al. 2004). My own research with older New Zealanders sits with a smaller subset that considers diversity *as it impacts and is experienced by* older people. Rowles and Ravdal (2001) proposed that an older person's geo-graphical/environmental surroundings can change in two ways. The first type (most commonly written about) is change through the older person's own reloca-tion to a new area. So, for example, Ahmed (2015) considered British retirees who, ironically, moved to Spain in search of a feeling of community they felt had been lost by the transformative influx of migrants into Britain (perhaps like those who have since voted "Leave" in the Brexit vote). The second type of environmental change experienced by older people is when an older person stays still (or "ages in place"), but their surroundings change (Rowles and Ravdal 2001).

The genre of research on older people who move in some manner includes older people who migrate to join adult children overseas, who move into a rest home or retirement community, or who retire "in the sun" as a part of interna-tional retirement migration (IRM). A small number of studies consider those who migrated several decades ago and are subsequently "aging in place" in their adopted locale. These long-term migrants often have all the mixed and ambigu-ous experiences of "home" that more recent migrants have (George and Fitzger-ald 2012; Granga 2006; Izuhara and Shibata 2001; Leavey, Sembhi, and Livingston 2004). One such standout ethnography about migrants aging after migrating to an adopted country is Gardner's *Age, Narrative and Migration: The Life Course and Life Histories of Bengali Elders in London* (2002), which, like this book on older New Zealanders, sits at the intersection of globalization and aging in place over time. Gardner explored how Bengali elders were affected by global movement as they aged in the London borough of Tower Hamlets. As these older Bengali migrants aged, their home of London provided some of the best resources for aging bodies such as the national health-care system and network of other Benga-lis, including family, who now live in London, too. But for many, their heart still yearned for Sylhet, Bengal, as a sort of spiritual and emotional homeland.

Perhaps counterintuitively, these stories about older people who have moved or are on the move are actually some of the most powerful contributions to understanding aging in place. This is because they highlight the process of adapt-ing to changing contexts, which is increasingly recognized as a part of aging in place (Andrews et al. 2007). The theoretical roots of aging in place stem from environmental gerontology, which is concerned with the description, explanation, and modification of the relation between the elderly person and his or her environment (Sharlach and Moore 2016; Wahl and Lang 2003). The concept of aging in place has received substantial attention in recent years in academia, policy, health services, and in the media. Among policymakers and health service providers, discussions of aging in place focus on the physical home, functioning, safety, and support or care options at home (Andrews et al. 2007; Wiles et al. 2012). Among social scientists, the idea has broadened out to a focus on growing old within a familiar community, in a residence of one's choice, with some level of independence (Vanleerberghe et al. 2017; Wiles et al. 2012). The concept of aging in place is expanding further still to the dynamic relationship between person and environment. This broadening out is necessary once we recognize that aging is certainly not homogenous and place is not static (Sharlach and Moore 2016). This research with older New Zealanders contributes to an understanding of aging in place as a complex process whereby an older person is "continually reintegrating with places and renegotiating meanings and identity in the face of dynamic landscapes of social, political, cultural and personal change" (Wiles et al. 2012, 358). The passage of time is an often taken-for-granted but central aspect of aging in place because over time, both people and places change.

The smaller pool of research on older people who stay still and age in place while their environment changes around them considers environmental change in many forms, such as through the deterioration of a dwelling or the rerouting of a highway through the middle of an established neighborhood, or the movement of an unfamiliar ethnic group into the area. For example, one study in Amatango, Mexico, considered aging during the dramatic changes associated with "modernization" that came to the village over twenty years such as roading, modern schooling, electricity, wage-based urban jobs, and modern farm machinery (Sokolovsky and Sokolovsky 1982). By contrast, older people in a rural Appalachian town experienced great changes in the opposite direction as their town deteriorated and depopulated. While the town's elders had aged in place, the theatre of their lives had changed dramatically: they remembered a thriving town, though they now lived in a town of abandoned homes and boarded stores (Rowles 1983). (This latter and nearly forty-year-old-study is considered a foundational project in environmental gerontology [Andrews et al. 2007].)

More recently and across the Atlantic, another study of older people in economically declining areas in two urban centers in England and Belgium found that older people spoke about a "loss of togetherness" and declining sense of community due to the emigration of friends and family and the immigration of "new arrivals" of different ethnic backgrounds. The older people expressed sentiments such as "you feel as though you are being taken over" and "people don't have a chat anymore in the local shops because there are too many foreigners"

(Buffel, Phillipson, and Scharf 2013, 96–97). And finally, circling back to New Zealand where this book unfolds, a small study found that some Auckland neighborhoods had "significantly changed around older people." Some older residents found this difficult, even increasing their attachment to their private dwelling, while others found the changes brought new and positive connections (Wiles et al. 2009, 670).

Outside academic research, three recent films have also centered around the theme of older people encountering difference later in life. In *The Visitor*, an older college professor returns to his New York City apartment to find two illegal immigrants from Syria and Senegal living in his apartment (McCarthy 2008). In *Gran Torino*, a racist, retired autoworker and veteran is a longtime resident of a neighborhood that has changed around him and he is reluctantly drawn into the lives of his Hmong neighbors (Eastwood 2009). Finally, in the Australian documentary *Mary Meets Mohammad*, Mary, a Christian pensioner, is very opposed to a new refugee detention center opening in her area. Her beliefs are challenged as she forms a friendship with a young Muslim, Afghani male at the center (Kirkpatrick 2013). These films demonstrate that this "story" of older people experiencing a newly globalized world of movement is a meaningful depiction of how modernity filters down to touch individual lives.

This book rests with all of these artistic and academic depictions that specifically examine older people who are aging in place in times of great sociocultural change. This book joins those that acknowledge aging in place as a dynamic, continuous, interactive process rather than a static phenomenon or form of inertia (Rowles and Ravdal 2001; Lawton 1990; Erel 2011). Westerhof (2010), who studied how older people attribute meaning to cultural-historical changes in their lifetimes in relation to their own retirement, described growing old in a time of rapid change as "migrating in time." He found that

> Older people of today have eye-witnessed the vast and unforeseen historical events and cultural changes of the last century. As a result, the world they live in is drastically different from the world in which they grew up. (Westerhof 2010, 12)

Westerhof viewed older people's subsequent adaptation process, though they may have "stayed still" as a form of acculturation akin to that of migrants adapting to their new surroundings. Similarly, my research in this book counters assumptions of stasis by illustrating how, while aging in place, older people have actually adapted to profound change. It is a needed contribution to the underrepresented area of aging in place in cities, particularly cities being irrevocably altered by globalization (Phillipson and Scharf 2005).

Often the assumption may be that youth move forward while the old remain fixed in time and culture, old-fashioned and unchanging. Older people around the world who have adapted to significant social change debunk this common discourse; they are not victims of global change but are, in fact, crafting new forms of aging within it (Lamb 2014, 2009). Anthropologist Sarah Lamb found that many older Indian people were actively and dynamically reflecting on and adjusting to a globalized world they never could have imagined or anticipated. They had "complex and multivalent" reactions to the sociocultural changes associated with a globalizing world and, like the older New Zealanders in this book, they intertwined "celebration with denunciation" (Lamb 2009, 5). Perhaps most importantly, however, these older Indians were hardly devoid of agency, left only reacting to social change; rather, by creating new ways of aging, they were often agents of social change themselves (Lamb 2009).

In her 2009 book, Lamb called for further depictions of how the old are active, reflective, and capable agents of social change. With this book, I respond to that call. This book helps fill the gap in knowledge about "how older individuals deal with the impact of cultural change in their own lives" (Westerhof 2010, 12). It surfaces as a depiction of aging in place during a time of unprecedented global movement as a dynamic process amidst intense cultural change.

3 · CONSTRUCTING THE FIELD AND RECRUITING THE URBAN STRANGER

In anthropology, "the field" has traditionally been viewed as somewhere researchers "go to" and collect data by immersing themselves in a particular social context. How does one approach a city of more than one million people, such as Auckland, as "the field"? Or even a smaller city, such as Dunedin, of one hundred twenty thousand? Open and unplanned, I took a flying leap into Auckland and Dunedin—I wandered around, observed daily life, struck up conversations, followed unexpected hunches and opportunistic leads. I, perhaps ambitiously, aimed to first observe city inhabitants in their everyday surroundings, going about their daily lives, having conversations on-the-go, reflecting the reality of many urban encounters.

The best way to illustrate my approach to the field is with an example: I had heard from a colleague that the neighborhood of Papatoetoe, Auckland, had experienced rapid and substantial growth in population diversity in the last two decades. I found that there was an Age Concern office in this area and that became my destination for the day. In the morning, I took the train from central Auckland to Papatoetoe. Within a small stretch of a couple of blocks, there was the office for the Manukau Urban Māori Authority, a fruit and veggie shop seemingly catering to an Asian clientele, a large retail shop selling saris, a church with service times for people of various Pacific Island nations. I spoke with a few people in these offices and shops, and then easily found a café that seemed to have an older clientele. I sat for a while, watching interactions and having some informal conversations with those who could be classified as "older New Zealanders." Across the street, I noticed the RSA (Returned and Services Association, a club and organization for support of current and retired military) and wandered in. The bartender heard my story, took an information sheet, and made an unexpected announcement by way of introducing me and my research to the ten or so older people chatting over their cups of tea or pints of beer. She quietly told me that a lot of these people would appreciate some conversation and she welcomed me anytime. I spent the rest of the day at the Papatoe RSA, and then two more days, speaking casually with approximately ten older New Zealanders. This also led to three formal interviews subsequently arranged in their homes. This string of events was typical of my fieldwork in Auckland in particular, and to a degree in Dunedin as well.

I took copious fieldnotes, which were coded and analyzed alongside the formal interview transcripts. Although an article about my research was featured in a Dunedin Age Concern newsletter and led to several interviews, I never advertised for participants. Particularly in Auckland, I met them, organically, if you will, on the ground. This style meant that I first observed and found my participants in their surroundings, interacted with them there, and then met some of them again for a formal interview. In approaching the city this way, I was able to include some good, old-fashioned participant observation, open to the kind of serendipitous discovery that is the hallmark of so much fieldwork (Monaghan and Just 2000), such as when the Indian owner of the Auckland hostel where I was staying walked me across the street to a state pensioner flat to meet the elderly New Zealander who tutors her children, or when I met a Tongan man behind a Dunedin antique shop who talked at length about the dynamics between Tongan immigrant caregivers and the elderly (largely Pākehā) New Zealanders they care for. Ultimately, the key to ethnographic success, still, is being there, available to observe, available to follow up, available to take advantage of the chance event (Monaghan and Just 2000). It is "equal measures of serendipity and deliberate enterprise" (Amit 2000, 16).

I spent a significant amount of time in transit, an experience shared by other urban ethnographers. D'Alisera, for example, noted that the Sierra Leonians she was interviewing in Washington, DC, were dispersed across the city and its suburbs. To move between various members of the community she was studying, her fieldwork utilized "the subway, the automobile, the interstate highway" (D'Alisera 2004, 27). She knew her dissertation would include a map of the Washington, DC, metro system. Similarly, city bus timetables and a stack of detailed maps of Auckland were my constant companions (see figure 1). I had chosen to deliberately avoid renting a car in Auckland and instead considered the whole process of getting to and from certain areas or interviewees to be fieldwork. Locals bemoaned that the public transit doesn't facilitate getting anywhere quickly, but I would stretch the journey out on purpose: while waiting for a connecting bus, I would wander into a supermarket, library, or community center.

Such was the case one afternoon when I was headed to an interviewee's home. Helen was an immigrant living in a relatively quiet inner-suburb of Auckland. Bound by the bus schedule, I ended up in Helen's neighborhood forty minutes before our meeting time and so I began to wander around the neighborhood. From the business signs, it was obvious that this area had a significant Korean

FIGURE 1. A fieldwork map: Auckland bus map with a blue, movable arrow that marked my destination, typically to an interviewee's home. (Photo by the author, 2012)

and Chinese population. I began to pay attention to the few people driving slowly along the residential streets. Many *appeared* to be older Pākehā New Zealanders and many also *appeared* to be people of Asian ethnicities. Happening upon the Community Centre, I wandered in. What seemed to be a young Korean mother's group was just leaving the building. I looked at the content of the information on the notice boards: English Language Partners, wearable emergency alarms, a driving service for the elderly, a companionship program for the elderly, and settlement services for new migrants. I knocked on the door of the office and two women greeted me. One, an older woman, was suspicious but reluctantly talked with me about my research topic. I asked if I was correct in my observations that this neighborhood seemed to have a lot of older New Zealanders and Asian immigrants. She perked up at my specific but accurate observation and confirmed that the area consists mainly of both these categories. She told me that she belonged to a choir group and an orchestra group, and now that she thought of it, both were made up precisely of older New Zealanders and Asian immigrants. With her own interest now piqued, she elaborated: the average age of the groups was rising as few young New Zealanders were joining the choir or orchestra, but then the neighborhood began to fill with Asian immigrants, who, she felt, commonly value music and often became keen new members of both groups. In her words, if I were to come to a gathering or a show, I would see "an audience of gray-haired New Zealanders and young Asians." In her opinion, the boost and revival that the Asian immigrants offered to these musical groups was appreciated and represented a positive realm of interaction among the local, older New Zealanders and new immigrants.

As I wandered Auckland and Dunedin, this sort of spontaneous but pertinent string of events, observations, and interactions happened again and again. Furthermore, one person's insight would guide me to other relevant locations, gatherings, or events. In the case of the older woman I spoke with at the community center, her insight about "Asians" and "older New Zealanders" in her choir and orchestra inspired me to keep an eye on small, regional music groups as another area where older New Zealanders and immigrants might interact. Attuned to this "arena of interaction," a few days later I noticed an advertisement for a small community music group gathering and I went along. Over the cups of tea and biscuits that followed the small performance, I chatted with a few of the older people present and this led to scheduling a formal interview in one woman's home.

Contemporary anthropologists face many pressures—tighter PhD schedules, the "audit culture" in research institutions, and "output-based" assessments in academia (Drozdzewski and Robinson 2015, 274). They also face the temptation to utilize ubiquitous online information about nearly everything everywhere. Maintaining openness to whatever comes your way is actually a challenge in and of itself. Furthermore, in urban settings, "anthropology by appointment" might seem the necessary approach as cars zoom by and anonymity and suspicion characterize fleeting encounters of lives comingling for a second and then parting ways (Hannerz 2006, 77). However, overly firm fieldwork plans can come at the cost of undermining the strengths of ethnography: a willingness to adapt and seize unforeseen opportunities when they arise (Amit 2000; Hannerz 2006). In hindsight, it feels like my approach was quite a gamble. But in the end, rich unplanned moments made up much of my fieldwork. Against the constant hum and movement of the city, I wandered through it—successfully stumbling, following, watching, learning, and occasionally plucking a person here and a person there out of their daily life and asking to chat.

DEFINING/CONSTRUCTING THE FIELD

In reading other anthropologist's musings on their fieldwork experiences, I related to D'Alisera (2004) who questioned whether her fieldwork—urban and close to home—was "authentic" enough. Gmelch and Gmelch (2009) found that students doing fieldwork in the Australian city of Hobart similarly questioned if they were doing "real ethnography" in comparison to the Malinowski experience they had been taught in the classroom. D'Alisera, who had to suddenly abandon fieldwork in Sierra Leone and shift instead to research with Sierra Leonians in Washington, DC, found it rather disconcerting when her husband drove her to "the field" in their own car. Her new fieldsite was not only close to home, it was a city and it was familiar. Did this familiarity mean that Washington, DC, was not "away enough" to be the field? Furthermore, was it a valid fieldsite even though it was a city? "This isn't even rural. This isn't really fieldwork" she thought to herself (D'Alisera 2004, 20). Forty years before D'Alisera was doing fieldwork in Washington, DC, Hannerz undertook fieldwork in the same city. The underlying assumption, he wrote, was that fieldwork in *any* urban, Western setting was not quite "away" (Hannerz 2006, 77). Through my own fieldwork—urban and contestably "at home"—I deeply engaged with both of these contemporary discussions about the reality of fieldwork experiences in relation to iconic, traditional fieldwork imagery.

In anthropology, "the field" has traditionally been viewed as somewhere a researcher "goes to," for an extended time, and then "returns from." The vision of the anthropological project was solidified by this paradigm of "home" versus "away" (D'Alisera 2004)—a distinct, fundamental separation. The field is "away" and is the "site where data are collected" by a geographically displaced anthropologist immersed in extended face-to-face encounters with "exotic others." Being alone, on a solitary endeavor, has also been an assumed criteria of being "away"—a romanticized, stoic mission (Frohlick 2002). The duration in the field has also been a defining characteristic of valid fieldwork—traditionally, fieldwork must be long-term, thorough immersion whereby the anthropologist's intellectual, physical, emotional, political, and intuitive resources are engaged (Amit 2000; Okely 1992). Furthermore, a fieldsite has traditionally been viewed as a container of a particular set of social interactions that the ethnographer could enter to study; that container of interactions could then be compared to the contents of other containers elsewhere (Falzon 2009b).

This rendering of ethnography is familiar and yet, Amit argues, it no longer suffices "even as a serviceable fiction" for many contemporary ethnographers (Amit 2000, 2). Some anthropologists stay put in the field for many months, others visit the field (or multiple field sites) in shorter, repeated visits, while still others visit only virtual fieldsites, never meeting participants in person. Rather than fieldwork always being conducted by a lone, fully immersed ethnographer, many (especially female) ethnographers are both accompanied by family and in frequent professional communications with those "back home" due to the simultaneous pressures of family commitments and the need to "maintain an uphill trajectory" in the "unrelenting pace of the neoliberal university sector" (Drozdzewski and Robinson 2015, 374). The "farce" of comprehensive immersion constituting authentic fieldwork "flies in the face of actual practices of many anthropologists" (Amit 2000, 5).

Furthermore, a view of a fieldsite as an independent, bounded site is now faulted as a colonial fiction and completely inaccurate in a world of "manifest global relationships" (Olwig and Hastrup 1997, 2; Tsing 2005). Culture as geographically grounded and centered within boundaries has been replaced with a notion of contingent relationships among collective identity, places, and social networks (Amit 2000). In a world of infinite interconnections, the ethnographic field does not just exist; the ethnographer is increasingly central in the active construction of the field (Enguix 2014). Sometimes the ethnographer creates a social category and is the only person in touch with all of the members of a so-called community who do not actually know each other (Amit 2000). Such was the case in this research with "older New Zealanders" and "immigrants," although some of my participants did know each other and, in one instance, two older New Zealand participants met each other completely by chance at an Auckland Tai Chi class, realizing their shared status as interviewees in my research through casual conversation.

In spite of prolific discussions about the reality of contemporary fieldwork in contemporary settings, anthropologists are still presumed to be "sojourners"— going to a bounded "there" and returning to a separate "home" (Stoller 2012). My position within my field exemplified the true ambiguity around what constitutes "home" and "away" when living in and conducting fieldwork within a modern world of movement. Undertaking fieldwork in Auckland and Dunedin, was I an Irish American looking at urban centers in a small, remote island country? Or was I a New Zealander "hanging out" in my own back yard? My two fieldwork sites each had elements of the "familiar" and the "unfamiliar." For example, I arrived in Auckland with a suitcase full of digital recorders, printed consent forms, and an array of maps, with no key contacts, no schedule, and no knowledge of how to even get from the airport into town. Unsure where to start, constantly double-checking maps, exhausted after missing busses, and ending up at closed businesses, having doors closed in my face and facing other (literal and metaphorical) dead ends, I certainly had more than a taste of being the bumbling apprentice conducting fieldwork in a novel land (Van Maanen 1988). On the other hand, Starbucks and familiar department stores dotted the streets and I seemed to have an instinctive knowledge of navigating the public transport. My husband came and stayed with me for a weekend and I visited a friend who lived an hour outside the city. In contrast, in Dunedin, where I had resided for a number of years, I utilized some of my existing connections and networks, such as a migrant women's group, with older Kiwi women as informal hosts and mentors. Attending the weekly group for over a year, I shifted between an ordinary group member to an anthropologist scribbling notes; the separation between my private and research worlds blurred. Historically, the "nearby" has been assumed not to hold the alchemy, the essential tension of a site that is culturally and spatially distant but is then rendered familiar by the ethnographer (Amit 2000). However, Rapport (2005) argues that anthropologists have traditionally used outward signs of travel as validation of what is actually, more crucially, an experiential and cognitive movement. Fieldwork is a set of practices *and* a mindset.

Once I had made the cognitive shift to researcher in Dunedin, my eyes were attuned to where older New Zealanders might encounter new diversity. One day, I noticed an Asian supermarket right in the middle of an area dense with pensioner flats. Excitedly, sure that this must be a relatively new establishment, I went in to ask how long the shop had been there. The owner nonchalantly replied he had been right there for twenty-six years; I'd simply never noticed. When conducting fieldwork in Dunedin, it became a place I had never seen before.

My experiences conducting fieldwork in Auckland and Dunedin stimulated constant reflection on the experiences, merits, liabilities, and implications of fieldwork "at home" versus "away." Furthermore, my fieldwork became an intense journey into reimagining ethnographic fieldwork methods for urban centers shaped by global diversity. In the next section, I hope to make a contribution to this complex but fundamentally important task.

URBAN FIELDWORK AND RECRUITING URBAN STRANGERS

The need for and legitimacy of urban ethnographies is obvious as most of the world's population now resides in cities and urbanization will continue to grow (Prato 2012). However, some lingering uncertainty about urban ethnography lies in the difficulty of approaching the modern city as the field. Traditional methods do not always apply but contemporary, urban ethnographic methods are rarely taught (Pardo and Prato 2012). In simply wondering how to approach Auckland as the field, I was not alone (Foster and Kemper 2010). Alma Gottlieb, for example, wrote that after several months in her field of Lisbon, she was not even sure "if or when I'd actually started fieldwork" (Gottlieb 2012, 93).

To make the city more approachable through traditional ethnographic methods, anthropologists largely study city life through the lens of one neighborhood or one subculture within the broader city (Foster and Kemper 2010; Radice 2011). But Radice (2011), who conducted fieldwork in Montreal, wrote that the problem with this approach is its implication and assumption of the city as an urban village, a collective of parts, rather than examining "the city at the ontological level at which it exists" (Radice 2000, 17; Huyssen 2008). Radice questioned, "How can we capture the city as a city, at the level where its urban qualities— density, heterogeneity and mobility of population—really matter?" (Radice 2011, 13). In breaking the city down into its parts, much of what is truly urban can still be missed. Some anthropologists have focused instead on specific public places, like a market or plaza—grasping some of the interactive, relational nature between diverse people.

Finding participants can be a challenge of urban fieldwork (Foster and Kemper 2010). D'Alisera expressed this conundrum in her early weeks and months of fieldwork in Washington, DC: "I constantly wondered where and how to begin. I was not even sure where 'the field' was." And about her potential informants, she questioned, "But where would I find them, and how?" (D'Alisera 2004, 25). Anthropologists' traditional strategy of living amongst their subjects of study cannot apply when members of a group being studied may be dispersed across a city (Caldwell 2010; Foster and Kemper 2010). Anthropologists George and Sharon Gmelch (2009) have run a field school for their social anthropology students for over thirty years and recently the location was changed from various villages in Barbados to the Australian city of Hobart. Their fieldwork students in Barbados villages would leave their homestays in the morning and encounter potential informants. Nearly all residents were aware of the student's presence. In contrast, when the Hobart-based students left their suburban homestays, they seldom encountered anyone and struggled to approach strangers. After two weeks in Hobart, a student wrote in her fieldnotes, "'I'm still not sure how to find informants.' No student in Barbados ever reported that problem" (Gmelch and Gmelch 2009, 297).

For the students in Hobart, informants were often found through contacts and connections, and eventually through prearranged internships with a certain group, club, or service. Oftentimes, interviews were set up by phone or e-mail with a person that the student ethnographer had never seen before and would never see again. Gmelch and Gmelch (2009) found that student fieldwork in an urban setting showed a heavier reliance on formal interviews and less opportunity to see their participants in their natural surroundings, which also meant fewer fieldnotes. This sort of urban fieldwork emphasis on interviews with less time spent in classic participant observation is what Hannerz refers to as "anthropology by appointment" as opposed to "anthropology by immersion" (Hannerz 2006, 34). One criticism of this heavy focus on scheduled interviews is the gap between knowing what participants say and knowing if that is really how things play out in unobserved life (Gmelch and Gmelch 2009).

I was very aware of the "pitfalls of anthropology by appointment" (Hannerz 2006, 34) where research interviews exist suspended in space, decontextualized from the person's daily life and habits. From the get-go, I was determined to minimize this reliance on preplanned, structured interviews. From the many fieldwork accounts I have read, I feel most affinity with Wessendorf (2014b) as she described her very similar approach to the field of Hackney, London. To view interethnic interactions in the area, Wessendorf attended knitting groups, an IT class, a youth club on a housing estate, a parents' morning coffee, and dropped into a center for migrants. She carried out participant observation in public spaces such as shops, parks, and a market where she "hung out by one of its curry stalls, observing traders' and customers' interactions" and in playgrounds where she chatted with parents (Wessendorf 2014b, 16). She writes that her fieldwork drew on a "myriad of encounters, conversations, interviews and observations" and included meeting "anyone and everyone" she could without simplifying and isolating categorical units (Wessendorf 2014b:18).

In an approach to the urban field, such as Wessendorf's and my own, "categories" and "labels" still pose a challenge. As already discussed in chapter 1, the category of "New Zealander," like many categories, is one that is fraught with political, historical, and emotional complexities. In the early days of my fieldwork, I began to doubt my original intention of using "New Zealander" as a national category, reflective of citizenship and not ethnicity. After all, in spite of anthropology's ample talk of decolonizing methodology (Smith 1999) and recognizing the falseness of categories and the inappropriateness of reification (Falzon 2009a; Gupta and Ferguson 1992), unease and doubt still abound about research that does *not* focus on a particular ethnic group (Vertovec 2010a). I felt the weight of this lingering pressure to specify the ethnicity of my research group. I considered narrowing my focus down to an attempted category of older Pākehā New Zealanders. This would have certain benefits including avoiding confusion and controversy over who was being included or excluded as well as allowing me to refute any possible accusations of "studying down" (Hannerz 2006, 59) as I myself can (contestably) be considered Pākehā. Thus, I almost succumbed to what Tolich (2002) has called "Pākehā Paralysis." According to Tolich (2002), many Pākehā researchers, aware of the historical exploitation and resulting resistance to research "on" Māori recognize the issue as a "political minefield" and go so far as to exclude, and coach their students to exclude, Māori participants from their research (Tolich 2002, 167).

Speaking as an indigenous New Zealand researcher, Linda Tuhiwai Smith (1999) wrote that anthropologists in the past have approached indigenous New Zealanders with "innate superiority," stealing knowledge that benefits only the researchers: "They Came, They Saw, They Named, They Claimed" (Smith 1999, 56, 80). This complicated history in New Zealand must be recognized and thus research about Māori by non-Māori is complex and conceals unequal power dynamics harmful to Māori (Smith 1999). However, Tolich (2002) argues that when research is on or about the general population of New Zealand, the exclusion of Māori participants violates the ethical obligation to avoid doing harm. When Pākehā researchers avoid Māori participants, it presents a violation of the Treaty of Waitangi as this act then also excludes Māori from any *benefits* of the research, research that is largely state funded (Tolich 2002).

To keep a broad, inclusive category of "New Zealander," I then briefly toyed with the idea of a purposive sampling of older New Zealanders that mimicked the ethnic breakdown of the 65+ population. Statistically, the ethnic breakdown of New Zealanders older than sixty-five looks like this: 91 percent European, 5 percent Māori, 4 percent Pacific Island, and 2 percent Asian (New Zealand Ministry of Social Development 2010). Roughly mimicking these statistics in my own sample seemed to offer an enticingly "neat and tidy" response to questions and doubt around the ambiguity of "New Zealander."

During the brief time that I had a proportional sample in mind, however, fieldwork was a stressful disaster. Moving through the amorphous urban fields that I have described, trying to single out those who fit particular ethnic categories, I felt not only desperate and vulnerable, but worse, I felt voyeuristic and exploitative. Sensitively inquiring about a person's ethnic identity during a one-hour (or longer) interview is one thing, but in the large portion of my fieldwork characterized by serendipitous interactions, I did not know the ethnic identity of the people I encountered. I had to try to judge based on appearances, I had to ask too soon and abruptly, and therefore disrespectfully, a person's ethnic identity—as if this was for my taking and allowing me to mentally tick a box. Although my foray into proportional sampling was an attempt to fairly represent the different ethnic identities under the umbrella of "New Zealander," I was instead perpetuating the violence of singling people out according to their ethnic identities and ascribing labels. It felt like a regression back to the ossification and essentialization of fluid and complex categories of social identity, the kind of behavior that Smith writes has led many indigenous writers to "nominate anthropology as representative of all that is truly bad about research" (Smith 1999,11). I quickly gave it up.

Instead, I believe my methods have been in line with a cosmopolitan approach characterized by consideration of the human "over and above proximal categorizations and identifications such as nation, ethnicity, class, religion, gender and locale" (Rapport and Stade 2007, 223–224). Cosmopolitanism does not negate the importance of difference, but it institutes a social space beyond membership of groups. It celebrates the freedom of individuality and the value of each life. Cosmopolitanism delegitimizes categorical thinking so that individuality is never confounded by classificatory, collective identifications or stereotypes (Rapport 2012).

Rapport presents an interactional ethos—"cosmopolitan politesse"—which he describes as a set of manners, a politeness, that assures that *Anyone* might be everywhere recognized as themselves, an individual, and admitted into interaction simply on that basis (Rapport 2012, 72). Politesse is a superficial polite engagement with another, a polite style of public exchange and an ethic of individual dignity and freedom. Central to the idea of Rapport's cosmopolitan anthropology is the idea that public identities are *voluntary*. Allegiances and affiliations are not *ascribed* nor do they equate to or subsume the identity of the individual (Rapport 2012). Politesse anticipates that *Anyone* passes from one kind of life to another, from one stage to another; it recognizes and respects that people have unknown futures. Rapport's politesse is perhaps akin to discussions of the often overlooked "productive potential" of a degree of "detachment" (Candea et al. 2015, 1) or Wessendorf's (2014b) "ethos of mixing" whereby intimate knowledge of the other is not needed for successful coexistence. For Rapport, it is "good manners" to retain *Anyone's* right to take part in routine social exchange with anyone else while occupying space in his or her own way.

My urban fieldwork had unexpectedly led me into this careful consideration of the ethics of encounter. This led me to the writings of Emily Beausoliel (2014), who argues that ambiguity must be accepted in all encounters. To avoid the violence and benevolent imperialism inherent in a unidirectional gaze of the Other, a dispositional ethics refrains from prescribing encounters in advance and means maintaining an openness to that which we do not yet know or understand instead of resorting to familiar strategies of self-preservation by labeling the foreign (Beausoleil 2014). Ronald Stade points out that anthropologists will still want to make sense of how human beings use and experience collective and categorical terms, but a cosmopolitan anthropology suggests it is unethical to turn the Other into an object of knowledge through categorical designations. A cosmopolitan anthropology, then, desists from claiming intimacy with another (Rapport and Stade 2007).

Speaking as a Māori New Zealander, Smith writes, "It galls us that Western researchers and intellectuals can assume to know all that it is possible to know of us, on the basis of their brief encounters with some of us" (Smith 1999, 1). A central component of politesse is interacting with *Anyone* at a respectful distance without presuming to know or encompass the other. These good manners safeguard a public space for *Anyone* to occupy regardless of the private significance given to their behavior. Politesse entails a balancing act—maintaining public respect for the individual while acknowledging ignorance of that person's private self (Rapport and Stade 2007). I suggest that maintaining the respectful distance inherent in the notion of cosmopolitan politesse, of *not* claiming intimacy and *not* assigning labels, is to attempt to avoid what Smith describes as treating people as "specimens" and "stealing" knowledge from them (Smith 2008, 56).

I propose that a respectful distance, of not claiming intimacy and familiarity, is particularly important in urban fieldwork since urban encounters are often fleeting and anonymous. Episodic, occasional, partial, and ephemeral social links pose particular challenges for ethnographic fieldwork (Amit 2000), but such moments are at the heart of ethnography. One evening in Auckland, I attended a small community music group performance. During the intermission, I spoke with an older gentleman about the performance and about my research. After the show, when he heard I was catching the bus back to my hotel, he stated, in abrupt hospitality, "You'll come with us," meaning he and his wife would drive me there. In the car, casual and polite conversation easily revealed they were well over sixty-five and they had lived their whole lives in Auckland. As we zoomed along Auckland's motorway at speed and then slowed in its clogged inner streets, they told me about the huge amount of change they have seen in their neighborhood and their city. Janice told me a story about being on a full bus nowadays and occasionally thinking: "If the driver suddenly said something like, 'Ok, everyone who is not born in New Zealand disappear,' then that would leave me and that fellow up there on the bus!" Jim mentioned that he needed to learn to read Chinese, so he knows what's inside the various shops. They contrasted this to their memory of the wave of Dutch migrants that came to New Zealand in the

1950s who were expected to strictly adhere to "Kiwi norms." "Nowadays," Janice lamented somewhat wistfully, "you'd struggle to even define what 'normal' is."

As we neared my hotel, Jim and Janice found their way by recalling their student days when they used to navigate this particular part of town, pointing out different buildings that had changed purposes or telling me what "used to be" on each block. They dropped me at my hotel and I thanked them for the lift and the interesting conversation. They wished me good luck. I never saw them again. I do not know how Janice and Jim would identify themselves in terms of ethnicity or ancestral background. It would have been completely inappropriate to ask or to attempt to place them into certain "categories" to merely appease any unfortunate anthropological tendency to still, in spite of so much discussion to the contrary, label people too readily. In a New Zealand context, this means that I cannot specify the proportion of my interactions that were with Pākehā, Māori, or other ethnicities.

"It is the circumstance which defines the method rather than the method which defines the circumstance" (Amit 2000, 11). In my approach to the urban field, I employed a cosmopolitan politesse in the field, refraining from labeling, categorizing, claiming intimacy, or saying that I "know" something about a person based on his or her possible grouping. And so I suggest that a cosmopolitan anthropology might be an ethical approach to urban ethnography—since we cannot, and should not, claim intimate knowledge through fleeting encounters and because labels are somewhat unknown and even arbitrary when the city and its diverse inhabitants are "the field."

4 · "THEN AND NOW"
Narratives of Change

As I sat with and listened to the older people in this research, they spoke easily and readily about the many profound changes they had witnessed around them over the decades of their lives. I realized early on that what I was interested in—population change and an increase in immigration and diversity— was just one of countless, significant changes they could recount in detail. And so, I begin here by mimicking the experience of speaking with these older participants—hearing first about so many memories and changes, before zeroing in on the issues at the heart of this research. Allowing older people, such as these older New Zealanders, the space to recount a wide variety of memories, positions them as aging actors within a dramatically changing world.

For example, in a Returned and Services Association (RSA) club in South Auckland, I sat listening to a group of older men recalling fishing "at the bottom of Queen Street." In their memories, it was certainly an urban area, but fishing there was a relatively quiet experience. I cast their shared recollections of Queen Street against my own experience of it earlier that day: a bustling, noisy center for a city of over one million people, filled with skyscrapers, commuter ferries, a major bus and train terminal, construction around every corner, restaurants and retail packed side by side with tourists, business men and women, students and shoppers moving in every direction.

In another example from a different fieldwork outing, Beth (Auckland, age seventy-two) drove me around the West Auckland area where she grew up. Again, the juxtaposition of her memories against my own observations formed a dramatic contrast. As I rode in her car, I looked out at traffic, brake lights flashing in front of me, crowded, rainy intersections, and strip mall after fuel station after supermarket. She, however, waived her arm across the scene around us and spoke of a rural, agricultural landscape. She spoke only of what "used to be" and described a landscape of endless orchards, one of which was formerly her own family's apple orchard. As we drove, Beth moved simultaneously through two spaces—one, sitting next to me and controlling the car's movement through the congested, urban roads on a rainy day; the other, walking on the warm grass, under the quiet shade of fruit trees.

The older New Zealanders in this study spoke easily and readily about the population growth they had witnessed over decades and of the accompanying increase in infrastructure and traffic. As another example, Leonard (Auckland, age eighty-one), painted a vivid picture of the area he grew up in—a ten-acre block with a hawthorn hedge along the road. Every day his father's cows waited for him at the gate and, as there were no cars coming along the road, Leonard would open the gate and take the cows across to another field. He remembers others moving "big mobs of cattle" and "sheep by the thousands" along that road where there were "just a few houses and a few farms." His wife, Anne, spoke of the "adventure" of riding her bike to the next township to get an ice cream from the one-and-only shop. "We'd maybe be passed by about five cars," she said. After our interview, I left the cozy confines of their home and set out on foot to have a look around the area they had described. Sixty years after Leonard and Anne were moving cows across the road and biking to the ice cream shop, my newcomer's eyes saw only cafés, restaurants, countless cars and shops that reflected the contemporary diversity of the area: Chinese, Indian, Pacific Island, Māori; Hindu, Buddhist, Christian, Muslim.[1] In the background, was the constant hum of speeding traffic on the nearby ten-lane highway!

While the increase in traffic and pedestrians and the erection of buildings and roads was most notably changed in Auckland, "Dunedin-ites" had stories too. David (Dunedin, age seventy-three) told me his fondest memories of sleeping in a tent, or even just in a sleeping bag on a warm night, laid out on the sandy lakefronts in the "sleepy little towns" of Queenstown and Wanaka. These two areas are now thoroughly developed, ever-growing resort towns with an international airport, hotels, and lakefront properties featured on the cover of architecture magazines. The "freedom camping" of David's memories is now strictly prohibited.

On and on older New Zealanders went, recounting the significant changes they had seen during their lifetimes, of which transportation seemed to be one of the most dizzying. Patty (Dunedin, age sixty-seven) remembered when the Dunedin railway station, now more of a museum and tourist attraction, was "a working railway station . . . a busy transport hub." Nowadays, "everybody [owns a car] whether they can afford it or not!" crooned Paul (Dunedin, age eighty-five). Ellen (Dunedin, age sixty-five) explained how the reliance on buses used to mean that people gathered in their own neighborhood instead of socializing all over town the way they do now. A twenty-five minute bus ride into Dunedin, she said, used to mean a twenty-five-minute conversation with someone. Now "people get into their cars and zoom around. I do too," she lamented. For an island nation in the South Pacific, the revolution in international transport has been equally salient. Kay (Dunedin, age eighty-three) joked, "I don't go back as far as the horse and coach but, you know, I did see the airplanes start." Paul

(Dunedin, age eighty-five) whose grandparents migrated to New Zealand from the United Kingdom by boat, agreed: "My grandparents wouldn't have ever dreamt of [taking] a boat trip back to the U.K. Wasn't so much the cost but how do you give up work for six months? Whereas now you can be in the U.K. on Monday morning if you like."

Everyday technology also featured large in these older New Zealanders' accounts of what has changed in their lifetimes. Paul spoke of his father getting a gramophone in the 1930s before later getting a radio. But he told me, since the 1980s, his has been "a house of computers." During our interview, he showed me pictures of his family on his iPad and complained of being up all night downloading a new operating system for his desktop. Ninety-six-year-old Eve (Dunedin) received several texts during our interview, stopping midsentence to chuckle at the content of each message. Kay (Dunedin, age eighty-three) described technology's prevalence more disparagingly: "I don't understand people having funny things that they talk to each other on. Twitters and tweeters and whatever they all are. I just don't understand it. . . . I always muck those things up, having just blown up my microwave yesterday."

An increase in consumerism was another popular rendition of "what's changed." Two interviewees in Auckland remembered the Grand Opening of the "first supermarket" along with the raging public disapproval of it. Patty (Dunedin, age sixty-seven) remembered when a single apple, wrapped in tissue paper, would be carefully distributed at school, and an orange was a Christmas gift. Kate (Auckland, age seventy-four) remembered not only the more limited stock of items but also the limited opening hours: "Things would be all shut up and closed, that's how New Zealand was. Now things are open late at night and at weekends." Dee and Beth (Auckland, ages seventy-one and seventy-two) spoke of repairing old or broken goods instead of buying new ones. In midconversation with each other, they stopped to ask me if I understood what they were talking about; I didn't. They then described to me the process of mending their stockings on a darning mushroom.

Several female interviewees described changes in gender roles—from the scandal of a woman working well into pregnancy to the limited job range for women: "nursing, teaching and offices," but any woman who worked in an office, added June (Auckland, age seventy-two), simply "made the tea." Eve (Dunedin, age ninety-six) told me how early in her married life she was offered some temporary work but received "an anonymous letter" accusing her "of holding down a job that should go to a single woman." She had to resign; it was the only time in her life she earned money. Fran (Auckland, age seventy-five) illustrated the confines women were expected to stay within:

If I wanted to be, I could be a mechanic now. . . . In my day, a mechanic? Don't talk such rubbish! . . . In my day, we learned, besides the ABC's and then the 123's, you learned to knit, you learned to sew. You learned to cook.... Ladies played tennis or netball and everybody was "a lady."

Clare (Auckland, age seventy) commented on how women are out and about so much more now, particularly with their own cars: "they are not stuck at home waiting for their husband to be kind enough to take them out. Or not."

The older New Zealanders I spoke with were also quick to point out that, indeed, things certainly were not always better back then: "Things were very narrow.... You never had anything—people forget!" According to Dee (Auckland, age seventy-one), nobody had any money and top price was paid for everything; wages barely covered expenses. Nowadays, in contrast, there's "such a range of products and such a lot of sales." Kay (Dunedin, age eighty-three) spoke specifically of today's ease compared to the hardship of the Depression: "That was THE Depression, not what people call a Depression these days. I mean we didn't have socks for our shoes, we were hungry. We lost our house" Iris (Auckland, age ninety) remembered that her dad was lucky in never losing his job, but other men came over to do a task, like chopping wood, in exchange for a meal. "That was a sad time. It really was." However, many older interviewees complained with worry about the increase in social inequalities over the decades of their lives. Patty (Dunedin, age sixty-seven) remembered a time when, as she described it, nobody had much but everybody generally had enough and far fewer people experienced true deprivation then as compared to now. Iris said, "We are a much more striated community" and Ellen (Dunedin, age sixty-five) spoke extensively about how the "people at the top are earning a lot more than they used to and people at the bottom are earning a lot less."

"When you think of what you've seen, you've seen an awful lot," Leonard (Auckland, age eighty-one) told me—his eyes wide with the wonder of it, but with a sigh at the overwhelming magnitude of it, full of pros and cons. While some say that in old age, there is a tendency to become more nostalgic, these are not simple, unreflexive memories—they are conscious and structured proof of time's passage and evidence of a changing society. Though "fundamental and inescapable," neither time nor aging can be apprehended directly; it is only through effects on the mind, body, and social relations—as well as through memories such as these—that time becomes evident (Hockney and James 2003, 41).

It is within this context of salient, emotive recollections of many great changes that the older New Zealand participants then went on to speak extensively about just one change—increasing ethnic and cultural diversity through immigration. Conversations around that topic formed the bulk of this research and inform the rest of this book. With their unique ability to relay change over decades, older people's narratives illustrate the very personal ramifications of economic, political, and technological shifts that have led to more and more people from more and more countries moving around the world.

COMPARING "THEN" AND "NOW"

When I asked older New Zealanders to reflect on current experiences, they quickly traveled to the past. It was as if the only way to describe their current reality was in comparison to what "used to be." Particularly for Aucklanders, contemporary descriptions of their city were almost always relational: they could not explain their current surroundings to me without seamlessly transitioning into a memory of a different kind of place. For example, when I asked her to describe her current social environment, Dee (Auckland, age seventy-five) immediately leapt into a description of what her West Auckland neighborhood used to be like: "Everybody would have been just like us. They would all have been white New Zealanders." Similarly, June (Auckland, age seventy-two) explained her current social environment by explaining a time gone by, when it felt like all Māori in her area knew each other and Māori and Pākehā were nearly the only ethnicities around. In Dunedin, David (age seventy-three) explained his current view of the increasing diversity in Dunedin in relation to the "almost mono-cultural" environment of fifty years ago. The reverse was also true: when I asked older New Zealanders to reflect on "what used to be," they typically and readily did so in relation to what was true for them now. In other words, flowing between descriptions of "now" compared to "then" and "then" compared to "now" seemed to be the best way, perhaps the only way, to relay the magnitude of the population change they have seen. Thus, a sort of before-and-after juxtaposition easily emerged.

The older New Zealanders in this research typically described a far less ethnically and culturally diverse country in years gone by. Speaking of the local high school, Leonard (Auckland, age eighty-one) told me that if I went to watch the students arriving at the nearby bus and train stops, "you'd be lucky if you saw one or two white people. That's what it's like now." He immediately contrasts this to his time at the same high school: "we had one Chinese guy in the room with us and we had a class of, it was around about forty-eight I think . . . And there was a Māori boy, lovely guy, great big bloke. And all the rest were little whities." Katherine (Auckland, age seventy) described a similar memory in terms of her children's school in the 1970s: she recalled that the teachers were all New Zealanders and the student body consisted of Pākehā, Māori, and some Pacific Island children. At the time of our interview, Katherine volunteered at the primary school that her children had attended forty years ago. She had recently asked a class of fifty children to tell her about their families. Most children were either from the Pacific Islands or India, or their parents came from these countries, in which case she noted it was interesting to see that as they grew up here, "you are getting Indian children with no accent." She also pointed to the current school staff as a reflection of change by telling me that the principal was named "Mohammad" and most of the teachers were "Middle Eastern, but they don't wear the garb. And there's Indian and Island teachers. There's a few Western-faced ones, they are usually the older ones. It's a massive change."

Through these "before and after" juxtapositions, many older New Zealanders can recount what the development of contemporary multiculturalism has "looked like" in a variety of everyday contexts. Beth (Auckland, age seventy-two), for example, described what she had noticed about corner dairies[2] in her lifetime. She remembered the dairies being run by husband and wife New Zealanders: "they'd put in long hours for several years, then retire." She added, "then the Indians came and now you won't find a white person in any of the dairies around Auckland." She felt the same thing had happened with the service stations and cafés, adding, "sometimes it's now the Asians, you know the Chinese, say, who own and operate many cafés."

For Katherine (Auckland, age seventy), the most salient example of her experience of increasing diversity was through the ethnic makeup of the church she had attended for forty years:

> When I first went there—mostly Western people. There was the odd Island person. But over the last ten or fifteen years as the cultures have come in . . . it's really totally altered. . . . In 1974, it was almost totally Western people. But they have, my age, have got older, they've moved to other areas . . . and of course their places have been filled by families that want to use the schools. So it's understandable that if your church is going to remain growing that they've got to reach out to the mixed cultures. . . . I think our Chinese church has been going about twenty years, they have their own congregation, about two hundred of them, they have somebody speaking in Mandarin, interpreting our minister. . . . At the same time, that same minister would be ministering to the Middle Eastern people but there's someone, perhaps up in a box with the headphones and everything, and they all carry headphones, and they get the interpretation in Farsi. See? They get the interpretation in Farsi for the Iranian people.

While Katherine illustrated population change over time through her church congregation, June (Auckland, seventy-two) explained it through the weekend markets she frequented in South Auckland. She remembered when the markets first started, they "used to be all Māori and Polynesian and that was it." Now, she said, the market stalls and shoppers also include large numbers of Asian people.

Kate (Auckland, age seventy-four) noticed the change all around her, on the bus, at the bank and on her street, which she said is "a pepper-pot of different people." She said her neighborhood center used to be

> like a village community with its own butcher shop, insurance company, hardware shop, dairy, all the regular shops, you could go and do your shopping. Well that's now all, just about all of it, Chinese with all the Chinese characters up

on the signs and a lot of take-aways and restaurants. It's changed the character of it. They were recently discussing in the news that perhaps that should be a China Town.

Kate also noticed the change in the ethnicities, languages, and nationalities represented at the hospital. Many older interviewees described the diversity they now encounter in the health-care sector, but Kate worked as a nurse and recalled: "We were all Pākehā nurses. I had to go to hospital this year and the only Pākehā was the doctor who was doing the procedure on me. All the rest, including the technician in the operating room and the registrar and all the nurses were Asian or Indian." Just as Ahmed's (2015) British retirees in Spain explained how the Britain they remembered had been fundamentally changed by immigration, older New Zealanders in this study demonstrated that in many realms of life population change through increasing migration and diversity was self-evident and undeniable. As another older New Zealander summed up: "It's been a complete and total change, whether you are at the shops, whether you are at the supermarket, whether you are in church or you are walking down the street. It's very, very different."

Early Memories of "New" Diversity

Several of the older people in this project readily recalled their first or earliest contact with an immigrant. Elaine and Irene (Auckland, ages sixty-nine and seventy) are two friends who have both hosted a variety of foreign newcomers in their homes over the last several decades. Irene began doing this in 1981: "Actually the tourist bureau asked me if I would take somebody because they were short of accommodation in Auckland and we had a very nice house then." Irene explained that the long-term foreign student was a Frenchman and he stayed with her family for a year. She was then asked to take in an "Asian," and was "a wee bit reluctant . . . because I thought their cultures were so different, I wouldn't be able to handle it." She went forward with it, however, and has since hosted a wide variety of nationalities. On the other hand, the circumstances under which Elaine first became a host were financially motivated. As a single mother of two, she was looking for a source of income when she began taking in homestay students—her first was a Japanese boy and she has since hosted people from around the world, several of whom have become permanent residents of New Zealand. At the time of our interview, at nearly seventy years old, she was hosting two young Iranian sisters in the process of permanently settling in Auckland.

Alan (Dunedin, age eighty) remembers that his first encounter with immigrants was experienced with hesitance and caution. He and his wife were asked by their church to entertain a new migrant family for dinner. This was several decades ago and Alan's initial reaction was "No." He worried that he and his wife were "too old" and they would have nothing to talk about with these migrants.

Alan eventually had this family for dinner, however, and the experience led him to more and more interactions with migrant families.

June's (Auckland, age seventy-two) earliest memories of contact with immigrants is less characterized by one-to-one encounters and more about being struck by the apparent wealth and number of Asians settling in some Auckland areas in the early to mid-1990s. Her husband was a landscaper and June recalled a day she accompanied him to work in one of the areas increasingly populated by Asian migrants.

> They had these huge big mansion homes with the pillars in the front and they had all the white pebble stones in the front and out the back. . . . All these flash Chinese people coming into New Zealand with these flash cars and these flash houses. . . . I looked at the carpet, pale, pale pink or the colors, white or cream, and I, "God, father, wouldn't want my *mokos* [grandchildren] live in this house, they'd have the carpets black within an hour!" And the gardens—they have their dragons and all this, their beliefs, absolutely beautiful. . . . That was when I first realized there was a lot of Asians, when he went to work for landscaping gardens. . . . We never noticed so much the Indians, was just the Asians because they came out in a rush, eh . . . we recognized [an] influx of Asians.

When I asked June if she remembered what she felt at that time, her response was simple: "curiosity."

Kay's (Dunedin, age eighty-three) first memories of immigration and population change were also ones of scale. She recalled a day, years earlier, when she saw the number of "Asian students" emerging from a local high school at the end of the school day:

> I used to walk down into town . . . and I used to go past [the high school]. And then, the Asian people from [the high school] just came out in a flood as you went past at about half past three. And that's when you really knew how many people lived here. . . . And I hadn't really realized how many—. I say "Asian" because I never saw one from the other, I couldn't sort, you know. But I thought, "my goodness." . . . It was just seeing them like a little flood, coming out the gate and running down Stuart Street.

Many of these Asian high school students were likely to have been foreign students, immigrants, or the children of immigrants. In any case, Kay's assumption that they were first- or second-generation migrants contrasted to her own memories of attending high school, during which her school "didn't have one foreign person."

Recounting the Different Waves of Immigrants

Older New Zealanders' personal observations of the population diversification around them over the last forty-plus years richly illustrated historical immigration patterns. For example, several participants readily recalled the wave of Dutch immigrants that came in the 1950s. Beth (Auckland, age seventy-two) remembers the impact of many new Dutch immigrants who took up employment at the same biscuit factory where her mother worked at the time. Her mother felt "out of it" when they spoke their own language. But Beth remembered her mother saying, "they were jolly hard workers." Dee also recalled the Dutch immigrants being hard workers: "they'd work every hour and relish every opportunity because they'd come from hard times." Dee remembered her father employing a young Dutch immigrant as an apprentice and how frugal his family was while attempting their new start in New Zealand. These and other memories reflected the "assisted passage scheme," a government policy for bringing immigrants to New Zealand. Originally the scheme sought out British immigrants to come to New Zealand just after World War II. The overseas passage cost ten pounds—giving these British migrants the nickname of "Ten Pound Poms" (Hutching 1999). In the following years, however, due to labor shortages, this scheme was extended to small numbers of other Western Europeans and in 1950 the scheme was extended to the Netherlands. As mentioned in chapter 1, the Dutch were considered most desirable after the British, because they were commonly perceived as the most likely to assimilate into New Zealand society (Lochore 1951; Roggeveen 1996). Ellen (Dunedin, age sixty-five) offered autobiographical, narrative "proof" that the Dutch did largely end up assimilating to a high degree when she relayed her memories of meeting Dutch people who had been in New Zealand only a matter of months and were speaking English, "I was quite amazed how quickly they picked it up." By 1971, Dutch were by far the largest non-British migrant group in New Zealand, with over twenty thousand Dutch people scattered throughout the country (Phillips 2013).

After describing the Dutch wave of immigration in the 1950s, the older New Zealanders chronologically moved on to then describe the Pacific Island immigrants coming in large numbers through the 1950s, 1960s, and 1970s. Elaine (Auckland, age sixty-nine) remembered primarily having contact with British New Zealanders and Māori only until about 1965 when her work as a school dental nurse put her in contact with Pacific Island children. Around the same time, Clare (Auckland, age seventy) remembered "a great influx of Islanders" at her church. These sorts of memories are personalized illustrations of the growing Pacific Island population from the 1950s through to the early 1970s. In the context of a growing postwar economy, with manufacturing on the rise, the New Zealand government looked to its close Pacific neighbors as an inexpensive and convenient source of unskilled labor (McMillan 2004). The number of Pacific migrants grew exponentially during this period (Friesen 2009). Between 1945 and 1966, the number of Pacific Islanders resident in New Zealand rose tenfold from 2,159 to 26,271 (Spoonley and Gendall 2010).

Ellen (Dunedin, age sixty-five), who lived in state housing for several decades, was able to recount the distinct waves of immigrants that came through her housing complex: first the Dutch came while she was in high school in the 1950s; then, the Samoans, Tongans, and Cook Islanders in the 1950s, 1960s, and 1970s. She continued, "In the seventies and eighties, that'd be Cambodians and Vietnamese." These two nationalities represent some of the various small-numbered groups that have come into New Zealand as refugees since World War II. Between 1979 and 1992, about forty-six hundred Cambodians fleeing the Khmer Rouge were given asylum to enter New Zealand, as well as several hundred Vietnamese refugees (Beaglehole 2013).

Similarly, Grant (Auckland, age sixty-eight), having taught in an art school for four decades, easily recounted some of the country's "pattern of immigration" as evidenced in the student body. Grant referred first to the "Dalmatians" who, historians have noted, had quite an impact on West Auckland during the first half of the 1900s, particularly in their domination of the wine and fruit industries of the area (Walrond 2016). Grant then described the students as manifestations of the increasing numbers of Chinese, Korean, and Indian migrants, and then "just occasionally black people," too. Into the 2000s, Grant described the student body as comprised of students from nearly everywhere. Thus, he said, the nation's immigration trends have been "reflected through the school's enrolment. Possibly even proportionally, funnily enough."

The collective implications of all these earlier "waves" of migration and the subsequent growing diversification of immigrants entering New Zealand after the 1987 Immigration Act is summed up in older Aucklanders' descriptions of their neighborhoods. Grant, who described the diversification of the art school where he taught for decades, was one of several older participants who described the diversification of their own neighborhoods as immigrants brought the world to their local streets. Grant told me his area west of Auckland was all Pākehā and Māori through the 1950s. He remembered recently meeting a Pacific Island man who had been in the area since the 1960s. This experience was both surprising and noteworthy to Grant as he felt this man must have been one of the earliest Pacific Island residents of an area that is now heavily populated by Pacific Islanders. Grant went on to describe the Indians and Indian Fijians in his area before saying the following:

We've got even a few black people, you know, Africans and I think one woman I met, lives around the corner here somewhere, she's Ethiopian. So it's become much more mixed. We have a Christmas Parade every year and everyone gets out there and you see quite an ethnic diversity.

Leonard and Ann (Auckland, ages eighty-one and seventy-eight) described their neighbors in a similar vein—these ones are from here, those ones are from there. They remembered just one other man, a New Zealander, who had been in the neighborhood even longer than themselves and who still kept a traditional lovely, tidy garden.

Iris (Auckland, age ninety) says her neighborhood used to be all Pākehā New Zealanders and "one or two" Māori families. Her vastly different description of her neighborhood at the time of our interview was a common one among the older New Zealanders I spoke to in Auckland:

> It's changed a lot in the last twenty or so years. I mean I was just thinking how next door that way, we've got a Filipino family . . . And, um, then across the road, well the front family is Indian . . . And there's a New Zealand Chinese family live at the back, and we've had a lot to do with them . . . And then, another family who've just sold their house and some Koreans have come to live there. . . . So, we've got all sorts round about.

Dee (Auckland, age seventy-one) told a similar story about how her level of exposure to different ethnicities and nationalities had drastically changed right within her own neighborhood. She began by telling me about her walk home from primary school as a child:

> I used to go past this boy's house. . . . His mother was a rather large—. And she had an accent and [was] rather swarthy. Look, she might have been Yugoslav, something like that, I don't know. But that would be . . . 1947–48, I think it was. And his name I think was Slavin. And I would love to have asked how come he had a name like that. . . . There was always that question mark. Everybody that we knew in our streets, were all just very basic names. . . . I would hear mum, mum especially, you know when they talk to the neighbors, "Who's that? Where would they have come from?" "They're not like us." It was very much that "not like us." . . . Maybe my circle was very narrow.

When I asked Dee to describe her neighborhood now, she told me this:

> Oh I have Indian people [next door]. And I did have Chinese in the big house down at the back, but they have now sold to the Indian family who have the dairy up the road. But I don't know them. And there's something like Iranians, or something, in Ruth's old house, after she died they sold that house. They wear the sort of pantaloons-style things in white. . . . I would say Middle Eastern, I really couldn't say. But they put the big fence up.

Dee's narrative, and those of many other older New Zealanders in this study, exemplify how the political and economic policies that have brought more and more immigrants from a greater variety of countries into New Zealand have had personal and social implications.

In Dunedin, interviewees' descriptions of their neighborhoods reflect the more dispersed immigrant presence largely characteristic of this smaller city with its lack of ethnic or immigrant enclaves and a lower ratio of immigrants to New Zealand–born inhabitants. Most interviewees in Dunedin said their neighborhoods were relatively unchanged with the exception of a few immigrant families peppered here and there. Ellen (Dunedin, age sixty-five) explained that from her point of view, the impact of immigration and population diversity is less obvious in Dunedin simply because it is a smaller, less populated area overall. However, older New Zealanders in Dunedin still recounted noticeable change, like Patty (Dunedin, age sixty-seven), who cited the subtle but noteworthy presence of a mosque as an indication of immigration and accompanying religious and ethnic diversity. All of the nine older interviewees in Dunedin cited the array of restaurants owned and operated by immigrants from Cambodia, Turkey, India, Korea, Mexico, and more, as a symbol of population diversification. Several mentioned that they noticed the diversity apparent in the people "near the university" or "at hospital." As opposed to Auckland, where the recounting of immigration and diversity was often about scale and obvious change everywhere one looks, in Dunedin, population change over time was about personal, individual stories, such as one-on-one encounters with a migrant caregiver or a newly settled foreigner in the folk dancing club.

In both locales, individual encounters with diverse immigrants sometimes took the form of immigrants entering one's own family. Perhaps no one exemplifies this phenomenon more than Paul (Dunedin, age eighty-five). After our first interview, I asked Paul if he would take or share any photos with me that illustrated the presence of immigration and population change in his life. He e-mailed me a photo of his family with the caption: "My extended family, once entirely British, is now genetically and culturally quite varied." Upon meeting again in person, he explained further that his family history is "very much Anglo-Saxon," but that "the next generation has taken partners from all over." Looking at the photograph of his family with me, he explained that he has Russian and Australian daughters-in-law, an Indian son-in-law, a half-Japanese granddaughter, a Japanese grand-daughter-in-law, a half-Japanese great-granddaughter, and a half-Egyptian grandson. Tales of sons- and daughters-in-law, and grandsons and granddaughters-in-law from around the world were relatively common. June (Auckland, age seventy-two), who described her ancestry as Māori and Scottish, said she had a Malaysian Chinese daughter-in-law and two grandchildren who are part-Samoan and part-Niuean. Jolene (Auckland, age unknown but over sixty-five) told me all three of her children have foreign spouses and she now has "an international family."

Diversity Manifested in Food

Another common theme when retelling the impact of immigration and multi-culturalism in New Zealand was the resulting array of international foods and products. Christine (Dunedin, age sixty-seven) explained:

> We grew up in an era of roast and three veg. And my mother ... grew up on a farm where the shearers expected their roast and three veg. ... But even in [outer Dunedin suburb], I can buy Indian food, I can buy Indian take-away, I can buy Turkish take-away, I can buy Chinese take-away and there'd be a few satay dishes as well. ... The willingness of New Zealanders to try foods they were not familiar with at their mother's table! ... I think the move has been enormous with food!

In a previous research project, in which I spoke with older immigrants who had migrated to New Zealand in the 1950s and 1960s, the limited palette and food product availability were strong features of their memories of their first decades in New Zealand. Iso, who migrated to New Zealand from Spain in 1955 recalled having to buy olive oil for her Spanish cooking from the pharmacist. Her Kiwi work colleagues turned their noses up at the mere mention of garlic, an ingredient which was commonplace in her traditional Spanish kitchen (George and Fitzgerald 2012). Several of the interviewees for this research remembered the novelty of garlic several decades ago. Dee (Auckland, age seventy-one) told me about an Italian she knew through her office and the very noteworthy fact—at that time—that he ate garlic! When I was hanging out in an Auckland super-market between interviews, I had these stories about the rarity of olive oil and garlic in mind and could not help noticing the now commonplace assortment of international foods and the variety of products, including a bulk spice section (see figure 2).

This was not a specialty shop, but a mainstream supermarket. I paused to reflect on how not so long ago this would have been unheard of for the residents of the retirement village next door to the supermarket.

Fran (Auckland, age seventy-five) used to work as a chef and has found the influx of flavors available in New Zealand to be fantastic; Moroccan seasonings, lemongrass, and Turkish breads are among her favorite additions. Fran was not alone in her enthusiasm for the extreme increase in food variety in New Zealand; this was commonly referred to as a positive result of immigration, perhaps even the only positive result of immigration according to a few who were not so sure if there were any other positive results. But one older New Zealand man's contrary opinion stands out. He wanted to take his wife out for an anniversary dinner of traditional Kiwi roast. As he told me this story, we were walking together where

FIGURE 2. Bulk spice section in an Auckland supermarket. (Photo by the author, 2012)

they had walked—along the main street in their area of Auckland—one filled with countless ethnic restaurants. Ed (Auckland, age seventy-three) and his wife were much begrudged that they simply could not find a restaurant that served traditional Kiwi fare! They ended up getting the closest thing they could find— roast chicken from a Pacific Island eatery. Though still dismayed that they could not find a roast, he admitted, they liked the chicken.

On the other hand, John (Auckland, age sixty-eight) spoke at length and with more enthusiasm about the change in food in New Zealand in his life:

> I grew up with parents who made the Sunday roast, which is always the same, potato, maybe *kumara* and maybe an onion and uh maybe some pumpkin and roast beef or roast lamb or something like that. Very sort of, in those days, well we didn't have chicken. That was something that became cheap and more available later. But things like garlic, my parents looked down their nose at garlic, they didn't like the smell they said, coming from, I guess, British stock. And so things like garlic weren't part of our diet.

John, who is a photographer, searched his archives to find a photo that would illustrate the degree to which his experience of food had changed over time. After giving up on his digital archives, he eventually found the old print he had in mind amidst his boxes of prints. It was a photo of his parents' kitchen

FIGURE 3. Turner Family Series—Kitchen Safe. (Photo by John B. Turner, 1968)

safe in the early 1960s—they did not have a refrigerator but rather a vented cupboard.

He explained the contents of the kitchen safe (see figure 3).

> And this is typical ... see here's the family roast, which would be lamb or beef. Then mint sauce goes with it. . . . That looks like butter, here's where they have the gravy, you know the gravy thing. Some tongue or something up here. Eggs ..., golden syrup. . . . But anyway, that's an indication of the Sunday roast, a typical meal that you had.

When I asked what a typical meal would be for him now, he said he can hardly describe some of it—delicious, full of noodles, vegetables, and meat. His partner is from China. He told me that just the other night, his partner, for the first time and just for fun, made what she called "a Western meal." It was a roast with potatoes, the very thing Ed and his wife complained that they could no longer find.

I remembered John's photo and his description of his parents' 1960s kitchen safe when some weeks later I saw an elderly New Zealand man in the supermarket in Dunedin. I imagined that this man's parents' cupboard, as he grew up, might have been much the same. Symbolic of the diversification of food, in his shopping basket now was just a small selection of ready-made meals, perfect for one person and easy to heat—packaged *chana masala, dahl mahkni,* and *palak paneer*—no doubt adapted for the Kiwi palette but imported in bright little boxes from India.

CHANGING EXPECTATIONS OF ASSIMILATION

In the text above, older New Zealanders have described a changing environment subsequent to the increase in numbers of immigrants and the diversification of the countries they come from. In addition, older New Zealanders also recounted how more recent immigrants assimilate into New Zealand society to a lesser degree than immigrants of the past. Older New Zealanders remembered a time when immigrants were quickly absorbed into the mainstream. Historically, New Zealand has adopted a variety of methods to pursue a goal of culturally assimilating immigrants as expeditiously as possible. During and after World War II, for example, New Zealand considered whether or not to accept refugees from Poland. In the end, mainly orphaned Polish children were actively sought and accepted because children were considered to present the least difficulties in terms of full assimilation (Beaglehole 2013).

New Zealand of course also kept to its unofficial "White New Zealand" immigration policy by selecting only immigrants of European ethnicity with the presumed high likelihood of assimilating into Pākehā New Zealand (Ward and Lin 2005; McMillan 2004). As previously mentioned, qualities that made the Dutch a sought-after secondary group to British migrants after World War II was their high likelihood of assimilating fully, their willingness to integrate, and their membership in the desired "race" of central and northern Europe (Bönisch-Brednich 2002a). Races, nationalities, or ethnicities perceived to be less likely or able to assimilate to this ideal were largely not granted entry into New Zealand. According to Beaglehole, for example, although New Zealand was well aware of the atrocities occurring against Jews in Europe before and during World War II, the government maintained a restrictive postwar Jewish immigration policy; not even relatives of Jews already in New Zealand were allowed to enter (Beaglehole 2013). Another group seen as unlikely or unable to assimilate, the Chinese, was subjected to "a series of legislative measures, endorsed by popular sentiments and everyday discrimination, from the 1880s [that] did not dissipate until the 1950s" (Spoonley and Bedford 2012).

Furthermore, the immigrants that did eventually arrive in New Zealand during the years of World War II and after were largely prevented from settling in the same area as others of the same nationality or ethnicity. Instead, immigrants including the Dutch, Hungarian refugees after the 1956 Uprising, the "Old Believers" (Russian Christians from China) and more—well into the 1980s—were dispersed around New Zealand in a process known as "pepper-potting" (Beaglehole 2013, 15). This process was carried out to ensure that immigrants and refugees were resettled in places where their labor was required and also to explicitly prevent unwanted "alien enclaves" (Beaglehole 2013, 111). Only after 1980 was new arrivals' need to be close to each other, to offer support, recognized (Beaglehole 2013).

New Zealand society, as these snippets of life stories and interviews have suggested, leading up to and well through World War II, was one that valued and urged conformity. New Zealand was "a society in which there was widespread agreement about what was right and what was wrong, about what constituted appropriate and inappropriate behavior" (King 2003, 375). In the years following World War II, New Zealand was slowly becoming "more pluralistic" but New Zealanders still highly valued conformity and predictability (Robbins 1998, 369), and the older interviewees quoted in this chapter frequently remarked with a sense of wonder at the openness of current lifestyles and options. In earlier times, there was little variation in recreation, creativity, or food. After World War II, there was a "desire of the nation as a whole to enjoy the good times and not rock the boat" (King 2003, 434). New Zealand historian Belich wrote that "social retrospects on the 1950s and 1960s range from 'our country's golden age' to the most boring time and place on earth" (Belich 2001, 307). Bönisch-Brednich (2002a), who has written about German immigration into New Zealand from the 1930s through to the 2000s, wrote that the socially admirable goal of equality has often been interpreted as conformism, so that being different was seen as a fault. One German immigrant told Bönisch-Brednich that New Zealand in the 1930s and 1940s was "generally speaking a working class and middle-class New Zealand where everybody was expected to operate at that level and if you didn't then something was terribly, terribly wrong" (Bönisch-Brednich 2002a, 37). Immigrants through these decades and well beyond did not speak their language in public; many did not speak their language with their New Zealand–born children (Bönisch-Brednich 2002a; George and Fitzgerald 2012).

From the colonial period through to the 1970s, New Zealand's immigration policies have been based on the assumption that selecting immigrants based on race and ethnicity meant that the incoming migrants would be culturally similar to those already resident in New Zealand and would create few problems "fitting in." The cultural diversity of those arriving since the 1960s, and particularly since the 1980s, has raised very different issues and questions about migrant settlement, social cohesion, and integration (Spoonley and Gendall 2010). Older New Zealanders in this research remembered this national background of immigrants who nearly disappeared into mainstream society. For example, one older New Zealand woman told me she remembers that the most controversial thing done by immigrants was the Dutch allowing their children to play in the street. Some of the older New Zealanders in this research recalled the small number of Chinese that have been present in New Zealand for as long as the older New Zealanders can remember. But the Chinese who feature in older New Zealanders' memories "kept to themselves." As Patty (Dunedin, age sixty-seven) said, "they didn't advertise their Chineseness, if you like, they didn't put Chinese signs up on their shops and things like that." This degree of quiet assimilation presents a strong contrast to the current reality of diversity that can, at times, pervade all senses: one where older people now hear multiple languages on the street, see signage in a myriad of unidentifiable languages, drive or walk past mosques and Hindu temples, smell or taste a huge range of foods; one where diversity is "celebrated" through cultural festivals such as Chinese New Year, Diwali, or Pasifika Festival.

DIVERSITY IS NOT ENTIRELY NEW

It is important to point out that many older New Zealanders recall that some degree of diversity of ethnicities and nationalities was always present in their areas or broader networks. Together, Indian and Chinese people made up just 0.39 percent of the population in 1945, 0.74 percent in 1966, and 1.66 percent in 1986 (Spoonley and Gendall 2010). However, older New Zealanders' most frequently cited early memory of immigrants (and later their New Zealand–born descendants) was of Chinese and/or Indian fruiterers. Though small in number, the Chinese in particular had a strong community presence as market gardeners. Both Paul (Dunedin, age eighty-five) and Ray (Dunedin, age eighty-four) mentioned the presence of a small Chinese community in Otago that dates back to the late 1860s gold rush. Most Chinese men left, but some stayed on when the rush was over, many turning to market gardening. Clare (Auckland, age seventy) said, "ever since the year dot," the green grocers were often run by Indian people. Christine (Dunedin, age sixty-seven) explains that even sixty years ago, "you were quite likely to find in small towns that the fruiterer, the guy who sold the fruit and groceries, was not a New Zealander . . . I don't see it as a recent phenomenon."

As previously mentioned by Grant (Auckland, age sixty-eight), Dalmatians had been settling in West Auckland throughout the early 1900s, and by 1950 they dominated the area's vineyards and orchards. Dee (Auckland, age seventy-one) remembered an elderly Croatian couple whose grandchildren played with her son. Beth (Auckland, age seventy-two) says the old general store was run by a Croatian man and the vineyards and orchards were full of Croatian and Dalmatian families. Dee also remembered a Ukrainian refugee who, in 1968 and 1969, worked in the corner lunch bar she and her husband ran. June remembers the Chinese people that ran a Chinese restaurant her family frequented:

> We were made to go to church . . . every Sunday. And we looked forward to that because our father and mother would take us down to a little Chinese restaurant in Gray's Avenue behind the town hall, it was then. It was called the Golden Dragon. And that was the highlight of the whole week for us was going to this Chinese Dragon and having chow mein or chop suey or whatever they had.

In Dunedin, those who seemed to have had the most contact with immigrants prior to the 1980s were often associated with the city's university or hospital. Ellen (Dunedin, age sixty-five) says she has been around a reasonable number of diverse international people for decades because of her job at the university:

> Because I worked at the university for such a long time, I've always been used to people from other cultures. Working at the university we always had so many foreign students coming through to do PhDs, so you got to know them quite well over something between four and nine years depending on how long it takes.

She frequently incorporated these international PhD candidates into her social activities. Ray (Dunedin, age eighty-four) recalled working at the university with three Hungarians, who came to New Zealand as refugees after the 1956 Uprising. Paul (Dunedin, age eighty-five) explained, however, that "the university has always been a rather different case." The hospital seemed to be "a rather different case" as well. Kay (Dunedin, age eighty-three) worked as a nurse in the Dunedin hospital several decades ago and told me: "I could get on the lift and it'd be full and I could be the only white face and the only New Zealander on the whole lift. . . . We had medical staff from all over the world. . . . The hospital was very good for mingling of the masses, you know." I asked if she goes to the hospital now, for appointments or the like, if she thinks it is different or just the same as it was. She answered that now there is just "even more color."

Finally, it is also important to mention that a handful of the older New Zealanders I spoke with said that they now have *less* contact with a diverse array of immigrants than they used to, in spite of the fact that such immigrants are now more obvious and more numerous. This typically reflects the fact that some older people report simply not being out and about as much as they used to and of having a narrowing social circle in general—several particularly noted the lack of work and work colleagues, and one or two noted decreasing mobility due to health issues or lower energy levels.

This chapter has allowed older New Zealanders to describe, in their own words, just how rapidly social and cultural changes have occurred, with varying degrees of direct, personal impact. Older New Zealanders are fascinating raconteurs of immigration and the development of multiculturalism in New Zealand; they are the purveyors of how immigration policies have actually played out in everyday life and their stories bring banal population statistics to life. But just as they were able to illustrate New Zealand immigration history over the last sixty-plus years, they were also ready to express their concerns and reservations about its impact. Older New Zealanders' concerns around immigration and diversity are the topic of the next chapter.

5 · OLDER NEW ZEALANDERS' IMMIGRATION-RELATED CONCERNS

I can walk through the city sometimes and [sighs] I think, "Well, they're Polyne-sian, those are Asian students, more Polynesians. Yes, oh yes, there's an older white woman over there." "Yes," I think, "yes there's more Polynesians over there. They come from Asia somewhere" and I'm trying to work out, "would they be Japanese, no I don't think so. Maybe those ones are Korean." [Laughs.] And I find that I feel, I do, I feel almost overwhelmed at times. (Dee, Auckland, age seventy-one)

Given the amount of social and cultural change that older people like Dee have witnessed in their lifetimes, it perhaps comes as no surprise that their experiences of immigration and increasing diversity have included ample, sig-nificant concerns about these changes. Older New Zealanders' concerns include more tangible problems such as an increase in crime and the strain placed on some national resources, as well as more ambiguous concerns such as a "loss of New Zealandness." This chapter foregrounds older people's concerns as described in their own voices, and also includes some references to immigration-related popular media stories playing out in New Zealand, and the voices of other aca-demic commentators on the topic of social change and its associated challenges in New Zealand and beyond.

CRIME, SCAMS, AND SAFETY CONCERNS

Many of the older people in this study viewed rising levels of crime as, in part, a consequence of increasing immigration and diversity. They conveyed their wor-ries around crime and safety both through their own firsthand experiences and by citing media coverage of migrant-involved crimes. Patty (Dunedin, age sixty-seven) said that she follows what is happening overseas through several types of media. She described watching reports of problems that immigration had brought to other countries. For example, she spoke of the "extreme Muslim groups" in cities like Paris or "the black population in London" whom she described as being into drugs and having no hope but to join gangs. These overseas examples, she said, fueled her own and others' worries about what could happen in New Zealand as more and more diverse peoples settle here. Similarly, June (Auckland, age seventy-two) worried about the influence of overseas crimes, as viewed through television, reaching New Zealand families and exacerbating criminal behavior within New Zealand. "The young ones," she said, "what they see on television is what a lot of them imitate: 'If they can do it over there, we can do it here.'" June found it disconcerting that "overseas problems" were occurring in New Zealand—first due to television's influence and, now, in person through immigration.

Dee (Auckland, age seventy-one) felt the same way about overseas problems and crimes entering along with immigrants. She recounted a recent community meeting she attended, featuring a border patrol/customs agent as the keynote speaker. Dee was among many who listened attentively as the agent told his audience about the kinds of things that have been intercepted from people entering New Zealand. The agent brought some items with him as a display. Dee explained:

> [The agent] said how they could buy enormous amounts of ephedrine in China for fifty cents or something, so that's why it's so easy to try and send it through customs and import it. And the weapons that he'd interceded, scary scary. . . . Things like knuckle dusters with spikes all over them and horrible things, crescent shape, that they throw and it will slice you.

Several participants mentioned watching the various "border patrol" reality television shows[1] that are popular in many countries. Beth (Auckland, age seventy-two) and Dee both talked about watching the travelers and immigrants featured in these shows as they tried to bring in large amounts of food from their home countries without declaring it. This was even though some of the food was illegal under New Zealand biosecurity law:

> We watch the customs [television show] on a Monday night. Surprising what people do. . . . They signed an immigration form saying they've got no food items for immigration and customs, and they've got a suitcase full of food. . . . They've got all the excuses under the sun.

Dee also made a vague mention of "drugs" and "Internet scams" that have come with East European or South American immigrants and also cited gambling among the Asian immigrant population as a real problem. June (Auckland, age seventy-one) discussed a different type of scam, a scam involving Chinese people in New Zealand buying up large quantities of baby formula and exporting it to

China, leaving some scarcity of the product in New Zealand. This scam recently received a good deal of media coverage in New Zealand[2] and June described one of the media segments in more detail:

> I remember watching that mother they interviewed about a month ago on TV.... she was desperate for some [formula] for her baby ... and she couldn't find a thing. She went to three shops and she found one [large tin] and it was right underneath the bottom of the shelf. And they photographed all these [boxes of formula] as they were being loaded up and shipped out.... Shoving it in the back of trucks, back of vans, the tins all stacked up, 9:00 at night.... Frightening eh? And our people are missing out, our babies are missing out on that.

Many older interviewees said that immigrants have already brought change, not just to the frequency and prevalence of crime, but in the types of crime occurring. Fran (Auckland, age seventy-five) was one of many who mentioned an increase in gangs and gang activity, particularly Asian gangs or "Asian Triads."

> But now of course we're getting things like the Tongs and the gangs that are coming here and they're intimidating those that are already here and kidnapping them. The crimes against Chinese are usually done by Chinese. But they're the lazy Chinese that come here on so-called student visas and they have money chucked at them while mum and dad go home and then they get into these drug businesses.... And they kill each other.

Fran added, with some exasperation, "That's not the way to assimilate or how to thank the country that's the host country!" Later she commented on a well-publicized crime in which a nineteen-year-old Chinese student was kidnapped, held for ransom, killed, stuffed into a suitcase, and thrown into the Auckland Harbor by three other young Chinese immigrants.[3] Fran was one of several participants to recall this 2006 incident and use it as an example of the kinds of atrocities that they feared: "We've had Chinese who killed other Chinese and cut them up, put them in a suitcase, throw them in water and stuff like that. You know, that's not a New Zealand thing." Fran was incredulous and full of dismay about "the kinds of things" that previously have been "overseas problems" but are now happening in her own country.

There are several examples of media attempting to discursively link the arrival of Asian immigrants with trends in criminal offending and with particular kinds of crimes. One of the most noteworthy pieces of media to make this link was a 2006 article in a popular magazine, *North and South* (Spoonley and Gendall 2010). The article was titled, "Asian Angst: Is It Time to Send Some Back?," and the main focus was the involvement of Asians in crime. "As each week passes with news of yet another arrest involving a Chinese-sounding name, disquiet grows in heartland New Zealand about the quality of migrants we're letting through the door" (Coddington 2006, 39). There was an equally significant backlash against the article citing its racist overtones and inaccurate use of statistics (Spoonley and Bedford 2012). In New Zealand, official statistics denoting crime rates perpetrated by immigrants over time are hard to pin down. Data include a breakdown of crime offenders by ethnicity, but ethnic minority status does not equate to immigrant status. In any case, recent Statistics New Zealand data for the year leading up to June 2015 showed that crime offenders classified as ethnically Asian and Indian made up just shy of 5 percent of recorded crime offenders (Statistics New Zealand 2016).

While Elaine (Auckland, age sixty-nine) was quick to say that most of the migrants who enter are good people, she also raised her concern over gangs and the negative effect they have on personal and community safety in New Zealand. Elaine conceded that New Zealand has its own gangs among "the Māoris, I suppose, and some white people too." But she worried about both Chinese and Iranian gangs and gang-related activity happening in her country now: "They see New Zealand as somewhere they can get rid of their [drugs]. It's a good market. You don't only get *good* people coming in."

Both Fran and Elaine were two of several people who used the expression "these things just don't happen here." Fran used this phrase while recalling another well-publicized, immigrant-involved crime. According to Fran, this incident involved a Tongan family who "had a difference of opinion" with an Ethiopian family. The two families met in the middle of a park with rudimentary weapons, including a machete. Neighbors intervened and called the police. "That doesn't happen in New Zealand!" Fran exclaimed passionately. "You don't do that in New Zealand. You don't pick up your spear and go out and chase somebody!" (According to news reports, it was a young Tongan man who was stabbed after some Somalis and Pacific Peoples had been fighting.[4]) The manager of a community center in the area told me that tensions between long-term residents and newcomers, and among different ethnic or national groups, were high in the area at the time. In her opinion, this was exacerbated by the lack of public consultation when migrants and refugees were "brought into the area en masse" about twenty-five years ago. She said with some frustration that it would have been easy for the government to hold meetings and explain, "these people cook their meals, send their kids to school and sleep just like you." She felt this lack of public consultation led to some racism and anger and to this murder. While this incident was an exception to normal everyday life in the area, she said it fueled the fire of fear and misunderstanding of immigrants.

In addition to speaking of what she read or viewed in the media, Elaine (Auckland, age sixty-nine) also had a more personal story about the type of crimes and problems that can accompany some immigrants into the country:

It's a bit scary but an African girl . . . she was coming along to church and . . . well, in the end, [her husband] tried to kill her. And this is just, you see, we're not used to this.[5] Do you see what I'm staying? And it was just dreadful. . . . She was recovering from her dreadful injuries, and the police said to me . . . "How that man got into this country I don't know, he's been in jail in [his home country]." You see? With immigrants, I mean most of them are lovely, and I have a lot of friends who are from other countries, but you've got to be a bit wary. You've got to be wary.

In recent years, concerns and experiences with crime and safety, whether propagated through media or experienced firsthand, have left some older people with a growing sense of the need to "watch your back." For those who felt this way, this caution or suspicion was a new, undesired reality. Elaine, while wanting to be fair and just to most "lovely" immigrants, also wanted to convey this new reality of wariness:

As I was told by an African young lady that I used to see a lot of, we're a soft touch, we Kiwis. . . . We accept people at face value. We're not suspicious. I think we're getting more suspicious now because of things that have been happening. . . . You get so you learn to watch out for different things.

Elaine went on to explain that older people in particular were vulnerable to a new kind and level of "scheming."

I definitely feel as an elderly woman, I mean I've got a lot of help, and I just need to ask someone to get some support with something. . . . But if I didn't, I wouldn't even like to bring in tradesmen sometimes, you know? There's scheming people that are out, because elderly people are vulnerable. They'll come . . . and will ask to do a job and will ask for payment and then they might do half an hour and then go off and you'll never see them again. They prey on vulnerable people.

Elaine felt this increasing prevalence of scheming and a concomitant rise in levels of suspicion had become new attributes of life, brought about, in part, by immigration.

It is interesting to note that a few of the immigrants I spoke with have also observed an increasing amount of crime and related sense of unease over their time in New Zealand. Xui Li (Chinese immigrant) has had her Auckland home broken into, her car windscreen smashed, and her handbag stolen from her car while she was stopped at a red light. At the time of our interview, she had been in New Zealand for about twenty years and partly attributed an increase in crime to immigrants like herself. Through her daughter's translation, Xui Li explained that some Chinese immigrants "have moral conduct problems. Some of them cause crimes to happen in New Zealand—with Chinese being the perpetrators of those crimes." It is older New Zealanders, however, who can directly contrast current levels of crime and safety with "how things used to be." This, Elaine lamented, contributed to a diminishing sense of a community compared to that of her remembered youth. This sense of "a loss of community" will be expanded on later in this chapter.

THE COMPETITION FOR AND ABUSE OF RESOURCES

Broad Concerns: Abusing Resources and Privileges

Along with crime and safety concerns, older people in this study routinely cited abuse of, or competition for, limited resources as one of their main concerns pertaining to the growing number of immigrants. Concerns over resources ranged from the more trivial or annoying to the more significant and profound. Fran (Auckland, age seventy-five), for example, mentioned that a "pet peeve" or hers is when she sees immigrants abusing the Gold Card in Auckland. The Gold Card, among other things, gives those over the age of sixty-five free transport all over the city and its suburbs during nonpeak times[6]. Fran voluntarily added her photograph to her Gold Card, believing that this should be a requirement that would prevent people, namely migrants, from loaning their Gold Card to others and abusing the free transportation privilege.

> The foreigners, they don't realize this Gold Card, it's a privilege. And so when Auntie May comes over from Timbuktu, they lend her the card, she gets on the bus for free, too. Or they lend it to so-and-so from outer Mongolia who has come over to visit. And so, they get all the free perks, too.

June (Auckland, age seventy-two) provided a different sort of example of migrant abuse of resources. In this case, it was her nephew's artistic design and intellectual property. Her nephew, an artist, was designing, producing, and selling T-shirts at a large market in South Auckland. June pointed out that the market used to be "all Māori and Polynesian and that was it." Now, she says, the market also includes a large number of Asians. She recounted a recent incident in which some Chinese people wanted to photograph her nephew's designs or, in the absence of that option, wanted to buy some T-shirts. June's nephew responded: "'No, I won't sell to you because I know what you're going to do, you're going to copy them and bring them back and sell [them].'" June's nephew had recently gone to court over an incident in which Chinese migrants copied his designs and sold them for a cheaper price at the same market. Although he won the case, June says he was "disheartened" and has now moved on to pursue different artwork. "So, you see," said June, "it happens. You get people coming in from somewhere else and they take over what has been ours for so long."

Jobs: Perceptions of the Social and Economic Impacts of Immigration

June's (Auckland, age seventy-two) above account of migrant abuse of local resources in the form of artistic design and property was a unique story, but she also spoke extensively about a resource that was mentioned repeatedly by many older people: jobs. Many older participants expressed their perception of immigration as a primary cause of an overly competitive job market, or the related notion that immigrants are taking jobs away from New Zealanders. At the time of our interview, June still worked part-time and told me about the increasing number of Indian immigrant employees at her workplace:

> Even at work, I'm surrounded by Indians and my question has been to my boss, my team manager, "What's the criteria for applying for a job over here?" I said, "Because you have more Indians coming in here. We have the highest Māori population; there's not many Māori staff working over here. What's the barrier?" They say, "Well [Māori] haven't got the [certifications]."

June went on to tell me that she heard this often, that New Zealanders do not have the "white paper" (the certificate, certification, or requisite qualification) that is now increasingly required for even menial jobs. Migrants, she said, often do have the white paper and this, she bemoaned, supposedly proved an applicant's worth more than New Zealanders' life or work-related skills and experience.

June believed another primary reason why migrants often gain jobs at the expense of New Zealanders is because the migrants are accustomed to working for lower wages in their home countries and are willing to do the same in New Zealand. She explained:

> When we go into the supermarket, it used to be people who are qualified for the jobs, whether they're Pākehā, Māori, Polynesian, Chinese, or what. You go into those places now, all you see are Indians on the checkout. All you see are Indians stocking the shelves. All you see are Indians working around, picking up the trolleys. There are no Māori, there are no Polynesian, very few European, one or two. . . . I believe it's because they are used to working for low wages back home. Because we've asked, "How come the Indians behind the counter can't even speak English, some of them, and they don't know how to connect to Māori and yet they've got jobs and we haven't?" . . . Our young ones are missing out on jobs like that too whereas before they used to have jobs after school, pushing the trolleys and packing. Doesn't happen now. If there's any packing to be done, it's all by Indians.

Several older participants expressed the sentiment that "immigrants employ their own." Charles (Auckland, age eighty), to whom I spoke in an Auckland RSA chapter, felt that Pākehā New Zealanders had a history of employing whoever is best for a job, whereas contemporary immigrants only "employ their own kind." Charles's friend, sitting next to him at the club, chimed in that they both remembered "the era when things were good in New Zealand," namely, she said, when everyone had a job. New Zealand historian James Belich (2001) wrote that many experienced this time and remember it in terms of its baby boom and economic growth (particularly increased farm output, new products, and new markets). Belich described these years as a "long, slow boom," a time of growing services and public works such as roading, when "unemployment was virtually non-existent and real incomes per capita rose" (Belich 2001, 307, 314). This time of abundance had come to an end, Charles and his friend felt, mainly due to growing immigration over approximately the last four decades.

Some older participants felt that immigrants had created a lot of jobs. But others disagreed. For example, June (Auckland, age seventy-two), recalled a time when the justification for policies promoting immigration was primarily economic in nature: it was hoped that new arrivals would set up businesses and provide more job opportunities. "It didn't happen that way," June said with resentment.

> You went into any takeaways or any restaurant and you see all Asians. Where's our people? And it was talked about that "hey our people aren't getting the jobs, [the immigrants are] bringing their own families [to fill jobs]. . . ." So we definitely felt left out in the cold . . . I don't know how they're acknowledging our people for employment if no one is hiring them. So they are hypocritical of the things they're saying before they come into the country, aren't they?

Another older woman, Jolene (Auckland, over sixty-five but age unknown), had an opinion similar to June's but formed by her own experience of working in accommodation management with Chinese immigrants. Jolene was the building manager of the short-term rental complex I stayed in during one fieldwork trip to Auckland. She explained that the members of the Board of Trustees, which oversaw the physical building, were increasingly Chinese immigrants. This shift in board membership had manifested itself in a number of ways. In Jolene's experience and opinion, maintenance jobs were now routinely contracted out to maintenance businesses run by other Chinese immigrants. Jolene was no longer able to give the work to the New Zealand maintenance companies and workers she had used for years. This, in her opinion, certainly impacted negatively on the established New Zealand maintenance businesses and their employees. Jolene extrapolated this example in terms of wider societal processes. To her, this was yet another example of immigrants giving work to other immigrants, the implication of which is job losses among New Zealanders. Jolene's frustration was evident as she explained her experience of running a New Zealand business, in New Zealand, but being forced to do so in a way that benefits Chinese immigrants over established New Zealanders.

These older participants, being near or postretirement at the time of being interviewed, did not view themselves as being in direct competition with immigrants for limited job opportunities. However, their concern was for their children and grandchildren and New Zealand job seekers in general. Through their stories, they eloquently conveyed the emotional impact of the frustration, concern and resentment felt by many older people when it comes to the job market and immigrants.

Health Care: Migrants as Both an Asset and a Drain

Migrants as Healthcare Workers. In addition to jobs, health care was routinely mentioned by older New Zealanders as a specific resource that rising levels of immigration negatively impacted. However, health care proved to be a good example of the mixed feelings and seemingly contradictory notions that a topic as large and complex as that of immigration can evoke. In New Zealand, the health system is mainly funded by general taxation. It operates on a dual system of public and private providers with overview of the various regional health boards by elected members of the public. Compared with other publicly funded health care systems around the world, New Zealand's system performs relatively equitably (Hargreaves et al. 2015; Wendt et al. 2012). Two notable aspects of its operation are the removal of rights to sue for accident injury in favor of a universal coverage (Accident Compensation Corporation [ACC]) and the use of Pharmac, a centralized government funded purchaser for drugs that works to lower the costs of pharmaceuticals for New Zealand citizens while restricting access to a wider array of drugs.

The older people in this study simultaneously expressed concern that immigrants are using too large a portion of limited health care resources while acknowledging that immigrants are filling needed health care service positions. The juxtaposition of these seemingly contradictory opinions was also found in a survey by Spoonley and Gendall (2010). Two-thirds of those surveyed felt that immigrants put too much strain on already limited resources, but almost half of respondents also felt that immigrants provided skills that were otherwise in short supply (Spoonley and Gendall 2010).

Beginning with the positive effects of immigration on health care, several older participants spoke of health care staff and professionals from other countries who come to New Zealand to work. For example, many older interviewees spoke of the growing percentage of elderly, relative to the rest of the population, and the increasing need for elder-caregivers; the large numbers of immigrants filling these vital elder-care roles was acknowledged with some appreciation. According to Clare's (Auckland, age seventy) observations, many born New Zealanders, even those out of work, did not want jobs caregiving for the elderly. She also readily observed the national and ethnic diversity among nurses, stating that the nursing staff at South Auckland's major hospital are "mainly dark . . . all different races." Ellen (Dunedin, age sixty-five) agreed and felt this was because the wages were too low. Kay (Dunedin, age eighty-three), as previously mentioned, worked as a nurse in the Dunedin hospital for many years and noted that staff from around the world made the hospital a place of diversity long before the recent increase and diversification of immigrants. Diversity among hospital staff, she said, had only become more pronounced in recent decades. She recalled a recent stay in the hospital (now as a patient rather than as a staff member) and spoke about two Nigerian nurses who cared for her:

> They worked night duties on two different wards. And I can remember them because they had the softest sweetest voices . . . and they were just lovely. . . . Some nurses you think twice before you ask for help in the middle of the night. But those two, you could ask for help any time and they just seemed to be there. They're all registered nurses because everybody's a registered nurse who works in hospitals these days. But they were kind and gentle.

The older New Zealanders who recognized the contribution of migrants as health-care staff and professionals viewed this development in a positive light with one repeated caveat—language problems. Paul (Dunedin, age eighty-five) summarized this prevalent concern:

> My concern would be linguistic. Nothing else. I went to the doctor the other day . . . a woman from Sri Lanka. I didn't find anything different except that I noticed that she listened carefully to me, which was pleasing. I am well aware of the horror stories in the newspapers in the UK or New Zealand, of problems of communication in the health system and it's often blamed on migrant workers. . . . This is a problem whether it's a surgeon or a nurse aid. . . . I would be in favor of, well, more carefully devised [language] tests.

"They Come in Here with These Diseases." While immigrants were often recognized by older New Zealanders as valuable contributors to the health-care system when they worked as health-care staff and professionals, the impact of the immigrant-patient was a completely different story. Charles (Auckland, age eighty) spoke about Auckland's Middlemore Hospital and explained that when you go there, you see all migrants utilizing the services. I asked if he noticed that a lot of the doctors and nurses were also immigrants. He said yes. I then asked if he would be comfortable with immigrants caring for him in hospital. He told me that he recently had cancer-related surgery there and "you don't ask questions, you are out to lunch. It doesn't matter who is doing the surgery as long as it goes well." Charles exemplifies this ironic (and perhaps convenient) dichotomy of opinions whereby the services provided by migrant health-care professionals were routinely appreciated with no acknowledgment that the professional and

his or her family have to live their lives in the community and may well need to draw on health-care services as well.

The older people in this research routinely expressed their concern about the health-care system being "maxed out" or abused by immigrants' health-care needs. Elaine (Auckland, age sixty-nine) explained how and why she has very mixed feelings about refugees, in particular, coming into the country with intensive health-care needs. She sympathized with the plight of the refugees, but worried about the impact on the health-care system and on the New Zealanders who need services too.

> It's not really fair because they bring in these families, maybe from Ethiopia, maybe even from Iraq, and some of these children have the most dreadful illnesses where they need regular blood transfusions. Like every week or something, at such a cost to our country. But then I look at it, and I think, "well, maybe they'd die in their own country," I don't know. Our health system is very stretched, and you go into hospitals now and the waiting room is totally multicultural. . . . I was feeling a bit sort of niggly about it, I thought, "it's not really fair because they get all this treatment, and some of our own people can't get knee replacements and hip replacements. . . ." But you've got to look at it in total, I think.

Clare (Auckland, age seventy) expressed similarly mixed feelings, noting that many immigrants come to New Zealand with diseases, often made worse by not knowing how to live in New Zealand's damp climate, which can lead to damp housing and associated sickness (such as asthma) when not handled appropriately. "I don't know what the answer is really on that one. . . . If they do get sick of course they've got to go to the hospital," she said sympathetically. Then she added, "A big drain on the hospital . . . it's a big drain."

Immigrant use, or overuse, of health-care services was seen as directly detrimental to the New Zealand–born population. Fran gave the following example of such a scenario. Her corner store is run by an Indian family that she has known for about twenty years. She says she loves this family.

> But I still don't like some of their practices. One of his brother-in-laws came out and when he got here, he wasn't very well. After he had got his residency . . . they found that he needed a kidney transplant. And he'd only been here for, I think, two years. So he got a kidney transplant. You and I paid for. And the kidney that went to him could have gone to a New Zealander that's been waiting for six, seven years for a kidney.

Immigration New Zealand's web page states that an "acceptable standard of health" must be assured and that this requirement is imposed "to protect public health in New Zealand and to ensure that people entering New Zealand do not impose excessive costs and demands on our health and special education services" (New Zealand Immigration 2016b). There have been a number of high-profile cases in recent years of immigrants being denied entry or later denied residency when failing to meet certain health requirements. A most recent case involved the autistic stepson of a prestigious Auckland University mathematics professor from Belgium. Having arrived in New Zealand in 2011, the stepson was denied residency in 2016 and the family chose to leave New Zealand immediately, not wanting to live "in a country that does not respect the UN convention on human rights" (Roy 2016). Other high-profile cases (also with a good deal of international coverage) have involved highly sought-after, skilled workers being denied entry due to obesity.[7]

For some older people in this research, there was a perception and fear that those born in New Zealand do not get the care they need from a health-care system too heavily burdened by immigrants. This fear is perhaps particularly salient for older people because they are statistically more likely to require health care and health-related services at the later stages of life. Currently, an estimated 60 percent of the health expenditure on an individual is concentrated in the twelve months before death (Coleman 2006, 306).

Kai Moana and Land

In addition to the resources of employment and health care, older participants also commonly mentioned their concern that increasing immigration is causing harm to New Zealand's land and sea (particularly seafood, or *kai moana*). This topical issue has been addressed in academic literature; for example, Ip (2003a) has canvased historical accounts of Chinese immigrants from the 1980s onward who were abusing natural resources by overfishing and ignoring quotas on shellfish. This practice was hugely offensive to many New Zealanders, but, Ip argues, particularly to Māori who are often seen, and see themselves, as stewards of the land and sea, or *kaitiakitanga* (Ip 2003a). The topic has also received wide coverage in mainstream media.[8] Citing a popular reality television show that follows various inspectors as they patrol a variety of environments in New Zealand, Fran's (Auckland, age seventy-five) comments exemplified the perception that immigrants, particularly from Asia, catch and gather seafood in direct violation of rules around quotas, regulated gathering seasons, or locations:

> They come here and they don't obey the laws on fishing and stuff. The reason they've got no fish in their [homeland water] is because they don't conserve.... You watch that TV thing? That live thing about how they get caught by the inspectors? All of the sudden they can't even speak good English! ... "Oh, I didn't know. I don't speak English," you know.

Fran explained that in this episode, the Asian immigrant was catching fish that were smaller than the allowable size and the inspector issued the migrant a warning. "That's what he got. But if a Māori or a New Zealander or anybody else had done it, he'd have got a $200 fine. I think sometimes they bend over backward for the immigrants and yet he is just as capable of finding out the [rules]."

Ray and David (Dunedin, ages eighty-four and seventy-three) both mentioned their worry over wealthy immigrants (whose wealth often increases upon arrival with the conversion to New Zealand dollars) buying up large quantities of land in New Zealand, particularly large farms. Ray felt that "sort of thing has to be watched very closely." There has been unease and large national debate concerning foreign ownership of land and public spaces in New Zealand. Trundle wrote about the case of a wealthy American immigrant buying up a large amount of land in a part of the country well known for its natural beauty. She described how other immigrants distanced themselves from this immigrant and aligned themselves with "locals" by joining the discourse against the land acquisition by the wealthy American (Trundle 2010).

The sale of New Zealand land to overseas corporations is a popular media topic, particularly when the buyers are Chinese.[9] The older New Zealanders I spoke with largely did not differentiate between land being bought by foreign, overseas corporations versus land being bought by immigrants who had come to live in New Zealand or were already here. Either way, the concern seems to be the same—the land falls out of New Zealand hands.[10] Ray sited the well-publicized example of Crafar Farms in New Zealand's North Island. According to the *New Zealand Herald*, legal proceedings that featured in the media for years recently ended in a Chinese corporation purchasing the eight thousand hectares of farmland for approximately $200 million (Nippert 2015). Ray said he "strongly objects" to this sort of land sale to foreign entities and that "the regulations against the transfer of property of that kind to foreigners should be strengthened." Ray is likely to be to among those who are happy with a very recent change in the law. Passed in 2018, the Overseas Investment Amendment Bill meant that New Zealand has joined a growing number of countries, like Denmark and Switzerland, in restricting land ownership to primarily citizens (Hendrickson 2019; Parker 2018).

Concern over New Zealand land going into the hands of foreigners or immigrants was about more than simply economics and resources; it also illustrated the more abstract concern that these new landowners supposedly had no sense of attachment or emotional investment in the land or in New Zealand itself. As David said, "One of the things I'm a bit unhappy about is, there's a large part of Southland which is now owned by Chinese dairy farmers who have no particular feeling for the country other than what money they can make from growing milk." This solely economic view of the Southland landscape offended his own deep emotional attachment to the landscape, its natural beauty and rich history. An immigrant with no emotional attachment or appreciation for these things, in his opinion, was not likely to protect and conserve them.

LOSS OF COMMUNITY

Separate "Groups" of People

As Beth (Auckland, age seventy-two) drove me around her neighborhood, pointing out so many things that have changed, she whispered that she was probably a little bit racist. She found that all the different ethnic and national groupings, such as "the Islanders" and "the Asians" can be overwhelming. Many of the older people in this research spoke of a regrettable loss of community that has occurred, or that they feared will occur, due to immigration and the development of separate ethnic enclaves (or as several older people said, "ghettos"). The development of ethnic enclaves, be it geographic or social groupings of any sort, was generally seen as unfavorable, worrisome, and detrimental to a sense of community. Patty (Dunedin, age sixty-seven) remembered the division that used to exist between Protestants and Catholics when she was growing up in the 1950s and 1960s: a Protestant would not date a Catholic or vice versa. She recalled one incident in particular in which a family was totally torn apart when a young couple on opposite sides of this religious divide did go ahead and marry. Patty said, "that's not the case in New Zealand anymore." However, she feared the possibility of new forms of social division rising up to replace this old one. Speaking of Muslim immigrants in New Zealand, for example, she said: "They have a right to have a Muslim school, because we have Christian schools. But I wouldn't like to see it . . . it's part of that 'ethnic precinct' thing."

As mentioned in chapter 1, New Zealand has had a history of actively preventing and discouraging "ghettos" by prioritizing acceptance of immigrants most likely to assimilate and by geographically "pepper-potting" immigrants throughout the country to avoid the development of any enclaves (Beaglehole 2013, 15; Bönisch-Brednich 2002a). Patty gave voice to the mentality behind these immigration policies when she postulated that it is about different people needing to have contact with one another to maintain a sense of social cohesion:

> We've managed to have a society—this is probably a bit naïve—but a fairly cohesive society. . . . And so far, I guess because our society has been relatively cohesive, that's where a little bit of concern comes in because you think, "right, well we have to keep this." . . . I believe that we need to have contact with each other. We don't want little ghettos.

Many of the participants felt passionate about this topic. Fran's (Auckland, age seventy-five) comments about the perceived harm caused by ghettos illustrated this:

> They shouldn't allow ghettos. It's all very well to say, "Oh but that's the way they feel at home." Well, you know if they wanted to feel that much at home, they

should have stayed there. . . . What's your reason for being here? Is it just so you don't get shot or is it because you want to participate in the land, in the country, in the culture? You can't participate if you're sitting behind a fence over there. . . . That's not the way to get the best out of a country. . . . Immigrants, if you don't like it, go! . . . It's got to be a country that's run the way we want it to be run and not forever having to sponsor different nationalities . . . 'Cause that way nobody is going to get anything.

June (Auckland, age seventy-two) also spoke of the amount of change that has already come to New Zealand's population and her fear that the changes yet to come would include separated "pockets" of people. She told me that her grandson has an Afghani friend, but the Afghan boy's parents only allow their child to "mix with certain people." June's grandson is seemingly the only Kiwi allowed in the Afghani family's house. This, June said, makes her a bit nervous, as she has no idea what goes on in the minds of the parents and such acts of separation will potentially cause many problems "in fifty years' time."

As I spoke with Charles (Auckland, age eighty) over a beer at an RSA chapter, he explained that his chief complaint about immigrants was that they all stick "with their own kind." He explained that club membership had changed drastically in recent years. In the decades after World War II, it used to be that "you practically had to have German blood on the tip of your bayonet to get into the RSA." Now the club is open to everyone and, according to Charles, most of the current members would not have done any military service. He clearly longed for the old sense of comradery and shared experience he used to find at the club. He conveyed a sense of real grief as he relayed how a group of Iraqi men came into the RSA, sat at their own table, and spoke only to each other—"they don't even speak English." Charles and a friend both told me this change in membership has eliminated the solidarity that they once enjoyed at the club and these contemporary divisions exist against their memory of the way it "used to be."

On a side note, some of the immigrants I spoke with were well aware that sticking "with their own kind" often offended or upset some New Zealanders. Li-Na said she does not really think that most immigrants cause blatant problems in New Zealand because they tend to "live quiet lives." However, she conceded that many Asian immigrants, especially older ones, "don't mix. They don't even try to mix with other people . . . Very exclusive." She added, "even when they are doing business, it's related to Asians—Asian food shops." Although she did not think such immigrants were disruptive, she did recognize that "in a Kiwi perspective" this annoys some people who feel it does not add "value" to New Zealand.

Increasing Inequalities

As mentioned in chapter 4, many older participants cited "increasing social inequality" as either a cause or a result of the loss of community and directly tied to immigration and diversity. Kay (Dunedin, age eighty-three) demonstrated the most significant exception to this notion. In her early memories, questions such as "what high school did you go to" or "what does your father do" determined *too* much. She felt that this sort of mentality limited too many New Zealanders, not allowing them to move freely through different segments of society; she contrasted this with more equal opportunities now. But the several other older people who spoke about social equality and neoliberalism expressed the opposite sentiment: gaps in social and economic differences have grown and a new social hierarchy has appeared.

Patty (Dunedin, age sixty-seven) vividly remembered her childhood in New Zealand as a time of greater equality and cohesion. She recalled having all the essentials when growing up in state housing. "You could feed yourself, clothe yourself, have a holiday. You might own a motorcar—it might be an old one." She remembered the 1950s as being strict on "moral codes" but "quite a good time economically." With these steady economic times came a degree of social cohesion. "People who lived in state houses weren't actually poor. . . . The person next door might be earning twice as much as you but you would still have a beer over the backyard." From her state-housing youth, Patty remembers going to university and one of the first friends she made was the daughter of the dean of the dental school.

> There were people who had far more money but it didn't sort of matter. They would come to my place and stay over and I would go to their place and stay over and nobody worried. Because you could be in a state house and people around you were employed. We didn't have the sort of deprivation that you get now.

She conceded that others might have had a different experience and said a Māori friend once told her that there was indeed always deprivation in some Māori communities. But from her perspective, Patty said, a working-class family "could have a good living."

This was in contrast to current perceptions of New Zealand as a far more stratified society. Several older participants felt that this is certainly in part due to immigration—which brings in people who are at both extremes—wealthy or poor. For example, New Zealand offers "investor visas" that typically bring in wealthy investors by offering residence to those who can invest NZ$1.5 million in New Zealand for four years or NZ$10 million for three years and many requirements such as business experience, maximum age, minimum settlement funds, and English-language ability are waived (New Zealand Immigration 2016a). Although certainly not necessarily on "investor visas," June's (Auckland, age seventy-two) first memories of immigrants were seeing the large, new houses of Chinese immigrants in one inner Auckland suburb, with "pillars" and "white carpets." She contrasted this to the average standard of living she had always been familiar with. Like June, Fran (Auckland, age seventy-five) expressed wonder at the large amounts of money some migrants bring in. Fran openly contrasted this with her own reality of current economic hardship, living only on the public pension. Fran explained that she lived in a council flat for low-income elderly. She fumed that whenever there was an increase in the pension payments, it was offset with a rise in the cost of the state subsidized flat. She told me she could not eat fish more than once a week and could only buy poor cuts of meat that serve only to "flavor the vegetables." She contrasted this to many immigrants' experiences and felt there was a bitter irony: "I can't see how come the immigrants come in from outer Mongolia and they've got nothing, and then next week they've got a business and they're up and running and charging me for their bread!" She noted that another immigrant whom she knows well "has got this beautiful house, he's got these two big strapping kids that go to the best school.... They've got a lovely car. I don't begrudge them that, but I want to know how! Especially when my knees get very sore because I have to walk!"

On the other hand, Ellen (Dunedin, age sixty-five) mentioned the more economically disadvantaged migrants who come in and take up extremely low-paying jobs, creating a new, poorer, lower class. Either way, the result was the same. The presence of migrants was seen to exacerbate New Zealand's increasing gap between the rich and the poor.

LOSS OF "NEW ZEALANDNESS"—
"IF THE MIXING UP IS TOO VIGOROUS"

There was a different type of concern about immigration, too—something much harder to pinpoint than jobs or health care, something far less concrete than land and even more vague than "community" or "equality." In her seminal anthropological text, Mary Douglas (1966) spoke of "matter out of place" as that which is seen to pollute or threaten. Perceived threats associated with immigration can often be symbolic, such as the fear of losing certain values or a way of life (Spoonley and Bedford 2012) and these older people spoke about their country losing some of its essential, less tangible qualities—qualities that, in their view, made New Zealand what it is at some fundamental level. When I asked Clare (Auckland, age seventy) if she felt there were any negative consequences to immigration, after some thought, she replied, "There's quite big negatives really. I think we can lose our own identity." This reply is deceptive in its brevity; in this short statement, Clare points to the magnitude of what she and others fear will be lost or altered beyond recognition in the event of too much immigration—a nation's identity or New Zealand's "New Zealandness."

Biculturalism

Like most national identities, the ambiguous notion of New Zealandness is a flexible one. In this study, each older person defined it for him- or herself. For some, an inherent quality of "New Zealandness" that is in peril in the face of immigration is indigeneity and biculturalism. This was mentioned only by a minority of the older New Zealanders I spoke with, but it was emotionally and politically significant to those few. Patty (Dunedin, age sixty-seven) explained:

> Bear in mind that we are still on that bicultural journey. . . . Māori were always there, within their culture, when they started to lose their language. And then their Renaissance—a lot of European Kiwis find that difficult to cope with. And we're just getting that—it's not finished. We're still working on that, when you have what seems like a flood of all these different people.

As mentioned in chapters 1 and 3, one of the reasons New Zealand is such an interesting context for discussions of immigration and multiculturalism is because these social developments pose a tricky challenge to the country's framework of biculturalism (Hill 2010; Ip 2003). The shift from traditional (namely, the United Kingdom) to nontraditional immigrant source countries in the 1980s can easily be seen as a breach of New Zealand's foundational agreement—the Treaty of Waitangi—signed by Māori and the British Crown. The recruitment of non-British immigrants was a departure from this historical understanding (Spoonley and Bedford 2012). Near the end of her interview, Kate (Auckland, age seventy-four) responded to a question about whether or not she thought New Zealand was "multicultural." Initially, she answered in the affirmative, but then stopped herself and pointed out a troubling aspect of this question: "We've had this long discussion, yet we haven't mentioned the Māori. It's like their country has been taken over." Several older New Zealanders mentioned that they would like immigrants to have to go through a mandatory course where they learn about New Zealand's history and culture, where immigrants can find out, as June and Ann (Auckland, ages seventy-two and seventy-eight) put it, "what they are coming into," or "what is expected of them." These few who spoke of valuing biculturalism felt that immigrants must be educated about Māori as Tangata Whenua, the Treaty of Waitangi, and biculturalism to maintain these sacred aspects of "New Zealandness." June felt that immigrants coming into New Zealand needed to be taught the history of the country, prioritizing an awareness of Māori as the indigenous people and the presence and significance of Māori culture and language. She warned that too often migrants were coming without even knowing about Māori at all. Her concern reflected something that is often discussed in the academic literature about the complexity of biculturalism and multiculturalism coexisting: that multiculturalism is drawn on as a way of denying biculturalism and Māori's position as the indigenous people of this land (Spoonley and Bedford 2012; Walker 2004; Durie 2010).

Losing Its "Specialness"

Losing an emphasis on indigeneity and biculturalism over time was just one way older New Zealanders feared that their country could lose its uniqueness. Several older New Zealanders felt that New Zealand (and the world in general) was becoming more "mixed up" due to the "intertangling" of many different cultures and ethnicities. When I asked June (Auckland, age seventy-two) what New Zealand would be like in about fifty years, she replied:

> Probably no pure Māori, no pure European, no pure Kiwi. Could be a trickle of Māori, a trickle of Polynesian, trickle of Asian and Afghanistani or any other, could be anything! You know, but I don't think it'll be like how it is. I think it could get more, what's the word, more intertangled, eh, with the different ethnicities coming in.

Kate (Auckland, age seventy-four) verbalized a very similar fear of New Zealand losing cultural distinctiveness as people move around the world on an increasingly frequent basis. Given how significant change to New Zealand's population over the last twenty years has been, Kate felt that within just twenty more years, New Zealand could "end up like an outpost of Asia." She explained:

> I'm being very outspoken here. But I'm not quite sure how New Zealand wants to be. I mean they could say, "this is New Zealand and it's constantly changing," but, will it end up homogenized? . . . When I'm saying homogenous, I mean like all mixed-up together, like by intermarriage, we'll end up like one type of people. . . . If I went to another country, I'd like to see the people of that country. . . . If I went to Japan, I'd like to see the Japanese or Japanese things and culture, instead of when I get there I see, "oh well, they're all like Eskimos or Europeans" . . . I'm not really seeing the real Japan, which I would have liked to see! . . . And perhaps in a thousand years' time with air travel, the world will get like that. . . . I feel it's like a loss of culture and language. And I like those differences. Because it makes them special . . . New Zealand could lose its specialness.

While Kate used the word "specialness," Ray (Dunedin, age eighty-four) used the word "ethos" to identify an essential sense of New Zealandness that could be lost through immigration. "I think this whole business of immigration . . . has to be handled very carefully. . . . I think the problems occur if the mixing up is too vigorous." He further explained: "Well, if you get hordes of people coming in who are from other cultures and so on, well then, there is a danger of upsetting the whole ethos of the place." Ann (Auckland, age seventy-eight) concurred, saying a central problem with immigration is that immigrants do not know enough about New Zealand and this is unfair both to immigrants and to New

Zealanders who want certain characteristics of the country to remain constant in spite of great change. "I just wonder," Ann said, "are they doing it too quickly? Are there too many people coming? That's a bit of a worry."

"Don't Let's Be Swamped"

Several older New Zealanders felt that New Zealand can definitely handle, and indeed can assuredly benefit from, a certain amount of immigration without losing its "specialness" (as Kate would say). Immigration as a problem or as having undesirable impacts only became an issue when older New Zealanders discussed *too many* immigrants coming in, too fast. Then, the demographics of the country were seen to be shifting too fast, putting the country on track to become a completely different one. Kate (Auckland, age seventy-four) summarized: "I think we'll have more and more people coming in and then they'll all be having children and it'll get more and more multicultural. And where is the New Zealand that we knew fifty, sixty years ago? It's gone. We are a completely new place."

Population projections show that New Zealand's main ethnic minorities (Māori, Asian, Pacific) are indeed likely to grow faster while people identifying with the majority European ethnicity or "New Zealander" are predicted to decrease (as previously noted, placing "New Zealanders" in the European ethnic category is problematic and is a policy that is under scrutiny) (Statistics New Zealand 2015). The increase in the proportion of certain groups will be particularly concentrated in specific areas; for example, seven out of ten Chinese migrants, and the majority of other immigrants of Asian ethnicities, settle exclusively in Auckland (Tan 2016; Friesen 2009).

I asked two older people, having a drink in the Auckland RSA chapter, what they thought New Zealand would be like in twenty to fifty years. Both guffawed and said it will be mostly Asian and Indian with a Pākehā minority. In an interview, Elaine and Irene (Auckland, ages sixty-nine and seventy) made an almost identical remark when I asked what New Zealand will be like in twenty years: "Chinese. Asian . . . I'm not saying they'll all be, but I think it'll be very, very Asian. . . . It worries me." I asked them both what they thought about a section of Dominion Road in Auckland being proposed as a China Town. Irene answered that some older people feel as if they "are being taken over." They spoke about immigrants from Asia and immigrants of different nationalities and religions, particularly Islam. Furthermore, they mentioned their worry that too much change and too much adaptation and acceptance on the part of New Zealand could result in losing a familiar lifestyle in New Zealand:

I: I'm certainly not in favor of them changing our way of life.
E: No. No this is very, very aggravating.
I: I'm not at all. I believe they should come to New Zealand and integrate, not-

E: change us.

I:—change us. We shouldn't have to change to accommodate. Sure, yes, be more accepting, but not—.

Irene and Elaine were not the only ones to express this sentiment of a threat to national identity that could come from being too accommodating to too many immigrants. Along with this idea was the frequently voiced sentiment about immigration being something that, if undertaken too quickly, could result in the loss of essential, defining qualities of New Zealand. Patty (Dunedin, age sixty-seven) expressed the fear like this:

> I know that in Britain they've gone down the road of placatory always to people because "it's their culture and their religion." And they've gone to silly things where in kindergarten you are not allowed to say Merry Christmas. . . . Tolerance has to go two ways. I love New Zealand. I think it's a wonderful place to live. It hasn't really made any difference to me having immigrants here, it's still my country. As long as it doesn't get taken over by Muslims, or, you know what I'm saying? Or the Japanese. Or [laughs]. Because that would be very hard, anything like that would be very hard. It would change everything.

There is such a thing, according to Clare (Auckland, age seventy), as New Zealand accommodating too much to too many: "I don't think we can expect the country to cater for every need of every culture. . . . That's good that we can cater, but—don't let's be swamped." Fran (Auckland, age seventy-five) spoke with an air of exasperation about the irony of New Zealand adjusting too far in accommodating the needs and desires of immigrants: "The reason they came here [is] because it was better than where they left!" So why, she asked, would immigrants or New Zealanders want to change things too much? Ray (Dunedin, age eighty-four) said it should ultimately be up to New Zealand what to "take on board" from immigrants: "judging what is worthwhile is really for us."

The national qualities that older people felt were, or could be, threatened by too much immigration span all the issues listed above: biculturalism, safety, resources, and a degree of socioeconomic equality and social cohesion. Considering the numerous concerns and complaints pertaining to immigration that older New Zealanders so readily expressed, the next two chapters take a surprising turn. The next chapter, chapter 6, recounts how immigrants in New Zealand described older people as *more* accepting, open, and approachable than their younger counterparts. Chapter 7 then explains how it was older people who took the time to explain to immigrants the expected values and social norms that they were so fearful of losing.

6 · A SURPRISE TWIST?

Older New Zealanders as Approachable and Accepting

Older New Zealanders' "then and now" comparisons illustrate that many older New Zealanders' early lives included only very minimal exposure to diversity, particularly in relation to contemporary multiculturalism. The increase in diversity and the development of multiculturalism and even superdiversity has been, for many, a drastic and rapid change. Older New Zealanders readily expressed ample concerns and perceived negative impacts stemming from this increase in immigration and diversity. Thus, the current chapter will now move in a possibly surprising direction. By bringing in the voices of the immigrants spoken with during this research, we hear that many have found older New Zealanders to be *more* approachable, *more* accepting, and less intimidating than younger New Zealanders. This chapter begins by looking at the stereotype or assumption that older people might be more racist, before presenting many immigrants' experiences to the contrary.

STEREOTYPES AND ASSUMPTIONS OF OLDER PEOPLE AS INTOLERANT OF DIFFERENCE

Upon telling friends and colleagues roughly between the ages of twenty and forty about the topic of my research—exploring older New Zealanders' experiences of increasing diversity in New Zealand—they often immediately replied that their own grandparents could be considered racist. For example, one person told me that her grandfather inappropriately comments on the ethnicity of a person when telling a story—the Indian store owner, the Asian driver, the "dark" waitress—when it is not relevant. Another person told me with a cringe that her grandmother still readily speaks about "the Japs." Just recently, an acquaintance mentioned always telling his father, in his seventies, "not to talk like that" about most minority groups.

Many countries have various political parties more associated with the old, with racism, and sometimes, with both. In New Zealand, the political party New Zealand First[1] emerges as an arena where common, public discourse links older people with racism and/or anti-immigration sentiments. New Zealand First, and the party's leader Winston Peters, are well known for emphasizing senior citizen's issues and anti-immigration policies. Over his lengthy career, Peters' support base has been largely those over sixty years of age (Koopman-Boyden 2011b, 2011a). As a well-known politician and political personality, Peters has been known for his unwavering dedication to New Zealand's superannuation scheme and for his flagship initiative—the Gold Card (New Zealand Government 2008). The Gold Card is the discount and concession card for seniors that many older people in this research raved about. Some of Peter's political meetings and rallies could fit descriptions of Trump rallies as "a sea of gray and white"[2] (Ball 2016). At the same time, New Zealand First is equally well known for its perceived anti-immigration policies, with Peters casting himself as a "defender of New Zealand against a threatening immigrant 'other'" (Spoonley and Bedford 2012, 213). Peters targets older voters with rhetoric about a "tsunami" of immigrants "feasting on your pension pie . . . the pension pie you and other Kiwis paid for" (New Zealand First 2005; NZPA 2009).

Outside of politics, stories of older New Zealanders behaving in a "racist" manner are also occasional but popular news and media fodder, such as a case of a New Zealand man, identified as being "older" caught on video yelling racist slurs at other passengers on a Wellington bus.[3] Groups associated with older New Zealanders also sometimes have an assumed racist quality to them. For example, in another incident that created a media flurry, one South Auckland branch of the Cosmopolitan Club (originally a chain of "workingman's clubs" started in the 1950s and 1960s in New Zealand with a largely though certainly not exclusively older clientele) recently refused a Sikh man entry due to his turban (Newton 2015). Another organization with older members, Grey Power, has also been branded racist at times such as when it requested the Auckland City Council to review the number of Asian immigrants in the city in 2011. The group asked for a forum to look at the changing face of Auckland with the organization's regional director saying many members "want the country's population to remain Pacific-based and not have such a large Asian component" (Radio New Zealand 2011). An article in *The Aucklander* the following week featured a Grey Power member claiming that "many older people are concerned about the changes to their communities and to what has been familiar to them for many years." The article discusses the featured interviewee's willingness to be labeled a racist and his anger about immigrants over the age of sixty-five getting free bus rides just as New Zealanders over sixty-five do only after having paid taxes for decades (Hueber 2011).

In a final example, sociologist Paul Spoonley (a prolific, well-known New Zealand immigration and diversity researcher whose work I cite throughout this book), demonstrated the assumption that older New Zealanders are potentially more racist, or at least less comfortable with immigration and diversity, through a passing comment. The professor was interviewed for a story on a special interest show called *Close Up* (now discontinued). The story featured a "look at the reaction to the proposal to turn part of Auckland into a Chinatown." Spoonley, standing on a block of Auckland's Dominion Road, described it as "very Asian, I mean in this block here, about 80 percent of it is Asian and about 50/55 percent of it is Chinese." The reporter questioned whether this "cut out" a certain segment of New Zealanders. Spoonley replied "no," but then added, "it might do, the older New Zealander might feel a bit uncomfortable with this" before finishing with the comment, "But this is Auckland in 2011. This is multicultural Auckland." The perhaps inadvertent suggestion was that older New Zealanders might be outside of, or particularly resistant to, the area's current multicultural reality (TVNZ 2011).

This passing comment is noteworthy because it demonstrates how prevalent, but also how confused and ambiguous, the assumption of racism among older New Zealanders can be. Contrary to his passing comment, some of Spoonley's own research found that "younger people tend to be less tolerant of immigrants and less supportive of immigration than older people" (Gendall, Spoonley, and Trlin 2007, 25). This was one of the key findings of two surveys conducted in 2003 and 2006 that asked a total of 1,868 New Zealanders about their attitudes to immigrants and immigration. Although the differences by age group were primarily not considered statistically significant, respondents over the age of fifty-five routinely answered questions about immigrants more favorably. The authors stated that this was noteworthy "especially as it is commonly assumed that older (and by implication more conservative) New Zealanders are more likely to see recent changes in immigration policy and the composition of immigration flows negatively" (Gendall, Spoonley, and Trlin 2007, 26). They note that further research is needed to explore these age differences in perceptions of immigration. Using New Zealand as a kind of case study, my research makes an important, empirically derived contribution to this needed conversation about age and perceptions of immigration.

Gendall, Spoonley, and Trlin's (2007) research is in contrast to other international literature on the topic of older people and racism that has suggested the opposite—that older people are indeed more likely to be racist. For example, in addition to the international examples mentioned in chapter 1, writing about racism in Australia, Dunn et al. (2004) found that older people (as well as those without tertiary education) were much more likely to express attitudes of racism and were more likely to feel that a particular cultural group (or groups) do not belong in Australia. Their research also found that older Australians expressed stronger levels of antipathy toward Muslims. The authors suggested that this "age element" may be a part of the White Australia policy (similar to that of the

"White New Zealand" policy previously described in chapters 1 and 3) and a time when "people were socialized into a very narrow and hierarchical understanding of nation and community" (Dunn et al. 2004, 426).

Psychology researcher von Hippel boldly stated, "It is common knowledge that older people are more prejudiced than their younger counterparts" (von Hippel, Silver, and Lynch 2000, 523), but put forth a different reason for this. He and other psychology researchers have proposed that older people were more racist due to age-related deficits in certain cognitive abilities, namely, inhibitory failure when it comes to stereotypes and prejudice. Von Hippel found that elderly adults were motivated to control their prejudicial reactions but were less likely to be able to do so. Time itself, he said, "robs people of their ability to inhibit previously socialized stereotypes and prejudices" (von Hippel, Silver, and Lynch 2000, 530; Radvansky, Copeland, and Von Hippel 2010; Castillo et al. 2014). Regardless of the reason, be it socialization in earlier times of less acceptance, a reduced ability to inhibit prejudices, or something else, many older New Zealanders also described their own cohort as being less tolerant of difference and diversity brought by immigration.

Some of the older people spoken with in this research often held the assumption that members of their own age cohort are less open to ethnic and national diversity. For example, when I talked with an older New Zealand man that I met at a small music performance in Auckland, I told him that I was speaking with older New Zealanders about their perceptions of immigrants and multiculturalism. His response was, "Well, that'll be grim." An older New Zealand woman I met while we both volunteered in a Dunedin-based English language group told me that not many of her friends, if any, would do volunteer work with immigrants, but they might do other volunteer work happily. During an interview, Irene (Auckland, age seventy) told me with concern that some of her friends speak resentfully about the immigrants "taking over" New Zealand. She told me about the diverse farmer's market she goes to once or twice a week (I later went, at her suggestion). One of her friends, she explained, would *never* go there.

> She doesn't feel comfortable, you see what I'm saying? They're mostly Polynesian or Middle Eastern. Hardly a white face. Chinese . . . And my friend, she wouldn't go there, she just wouldn't. There's some of us that can't— . . . They wouldn't have a friend who is another nationality, especially not African because they are too different. . . . They'd be scared of them.

Elaine (Auckland, age sixty-nine) added to this sentiment by telling me about a woman, in her eighties or nineties, in a rest home hospital who screamed, "I don't want him!" when a black African careworker came to assist her with something. Elaine laughed uncomfortably about this woman saying such a thing, but could also understand it to a degree, as she supposed this woman had never had "anything to do" with a black African before that moment. Fran (Auckland, age seventy-five), who lives within a small, crowded complex of pensioner flats, said she knew her older neighbors would worry at the sight of some "Indian boys" coming to see her in her flat.

> I had to tell [the Indian boys], either come before half past eight or else don't come because people— ... They're big boys, and two of them are quite dark. And if they come after dark, you know, you'll have somebody looking out the window at whatever is going on: "they're breaking in" or "they're assaulting her" or whatever. And of course they're not. So when they brought me back from the hospital, those Indian boys, they all came as a group ... I had to give them all big hugs in full view of everybody. And so now ... it's alright, they're "Fran's boys." But you have to do that for [the boy's] protection.

Several older New Zealand interviewees mentioned that folks older than themselves might be more "racist" or more "challenged" by immigration and diversity's increase in New Zealand, in many cases due to memories of World War II. Christine (Dunedin, age sixty-seven) explained that her parent's generation had a "real fear of a Japanese invasion" and that some coastal residents had a plan of heading into the bush if the invasion occurred. Irene (Auckland, age seventy) told me that she was going to name her son Karl, but her mother, who had two brothers as prisoners of war in World War II, was horrified that it was a "German name." Grant (Auckland, age sixty-eight) remembers an older neighbor who had been a prisoner of war of the Japanese:

> He had seen real atrocities and had a huge hatred of [Japanese]. So he was very much against the import of Japanese cameras and Japanese cars and things because every time, "the enemy is winning the battle" ... There's a huge resentment toward that. I can understand that, that's deeply personal.

He went on to juxtapose these kinds of memories and fears with a current, everyday context, illustrating how much things have changed for some older people:

> Even though New Zealand fought with America and South Vietnamese against the North Vietnamese and the Chinese, here you are at an RSA building with a social occasion and you've got these Korean boy scouts. For a lot of our old soldiers they would just see them as Asian, they wouldn't distinguish between Korean or Chinese or whatever and they'd be against them. So it's kind of interesting to see them just as part of the scenery.

Grant, for one, says he finds this change in public attitude fascinating, but he tells me that some other older New Zealanders are simply not interested. "They just say, 'oh bloody foreigners, what the bloody hell is this?' and grumble and move on. You know they don't have the desire to figure out, 'Hey this is kind of interesting, what's happening here?'"

Kay (Dunedin, age eighty-three) said that she believes "there's a wee bit of 'us and them' still . . . among older people." She recalled overhearing a conversation recently on the bus when an elderly man said something about "putting them in a boat and sending them back where they came from." She wanted to turn around and say something but was not going to "get into it on a bus." Kay believes such a feeling lingers for some older New Zealanders when they feel that certain groups receive special treatment from the government, such as some additional social services. Clare (Auckland, age seventy) seconded this sentiment and also suggested that some older New Zealanders simply may not be around a diverse array of people of different ethnicities, nationalities, religions, and more. She explained to me that she doesn't think she herself is "typical" of New Zealanders over sixty-five, simply because she *does* engage meaningfully with many different types of people in her daily and weekly life.

Many older New Zealanders that I spoke with could speak to this subtle assumption that older people might be more likely to be "racist" and they had a sympathy for why this might be. Katherine (Auckland, age seventy) explained that in some cases the degree of change and new diversity around them can now leave some older folks more isolated:

> For the people who are experiencing complete change, particularly quite elderly people, like in their 80s', I think they find they are a little bit confined. Their friends have died, the people that come in, a lot of them, particularly Chinese, they keep to themselves . . . they can't speak English . . . It isolates you . . . I would feel that there are perhaps elderly people that are in the area that could be feeling more isolated because of the [different] cultures.

Christine (Dunedin, age sixty-seven) pointed out that the younger generations of New Zealanders might simply *think* they hear "racism" in the older generation. But, she said, you have to take into account how much change older people have seen and how far they have come in their sentiments about diverse others:

> I don't think the older generation mean to be as they are being perceived. Like, the older generation has moved quite a way, but they haven't moved far enough for the young ones. And yet they have moved quite a long way from the values, from the days, when they were brought up.

Several older New Zealander interviewees recognized that some older New Zealanders are wary of immigrants of various ethnicities and nationalities and might be deemed to be "more racist" than younger people in general.

I also spoke to a few older people who I knew would be described or perceived as "racist" themselves, including the aforementioned, self-described "racist bastard" Charles (Auckland, age eighty), who said he knew others called him
racist, too. He told me how nothing good had come from immigrants and that he
does not interact with any of them. He felt immigrants employ only each other,
do not speak English, and do not participate in the community. He believed
many of the immigrants in New Zealand are here illegally and have bad intentions. He told me in obvious and heartfelt despair that "there's hardly a Pākehā
face to be seen" around his area now and referred to all non-European races collectively as "black people."

Finally, in the course of my fieldwork, I spoke to the head of a Dunedin agency
that provides social services to older people. Hamish's previous duties had
included sending relief staff to a veteran's rest home. He told me that it was simply
a "known fact" that Japanese and German relief workers could not be sent to the
veteran's rest home because many elderly male residents had been in World
War II and "could not tolerate that." Hamish also told me that some older clients
do not want care workers of certain nationalities to come into their homes for
homecare assistance. He told me the story of an older woman who accused a
Kenyan support worker of taking a coffee mug. Hamish felt completely certain
that the Kenyan care worker did not touch the coffee mug. Rather, he believed the
older woman did not want a black person in her home and, not wanting to admit
to this, resorted to fabricating a story that would ensure a different care worker
would provide assistance the next time. Hamish said this sort of occurrence was
rare but certainly not unheard of by those in the industry. This was echoed and
validated by the head of a different Dunedin agency also providing homecare to
elderly New Zealanders. Perhaps these are the types of incidents and stories that
perpetuate the impression that older New Zealanders might not accept or be able
to "cope" with the diversity and multiculturalism that have developed in recent
decades; that they are somehow more likely to be "racist." My conversations with
immigrants, however, show a very different perception of older New Zealanders.

IMMIGRANTS EXPERIENCE OLDER NEW ZEALANDERS
AS ACCEPTING, OPEN, AND TOLERANT

Early in my fieldwork, I already had an inkling that immigrants were frequently
describing older New Zealanders as far more accepting and approachable than
the assumptions relayed above would suggest. Therefore, during a conversation
session with a Dunedin-based English for Speakers of Other Languages (ESOL)
group, I directly asked a group of about 7 migrants if they found older New
Zealanders to be more friendly than younger New Zealanders. In my fieldnotes,
I wrote that there was a distinct "murmur of confirmation." One Indonesian
woman said that the older people she encountered do not seem to mind repeat-

ing themselves or explaining something when she has trouble understanding. A young Korean woman told me that an elderly New Zealand couple next door had become dear friends of hers. She contrasted this to other, younger neighbors who were "not friendly" and to a music group for young mums and babies where the other young mums were "nice enough" but "forgot about her" as soon as the music session was over.

In a one-to-one interview with Inka (a German immigrant), the idea of older New Zealanders being more accepting of diverse peoples than their younger counterparts came up naturally when Inka told me this story about her New Zealand partner who is a builder and had a French immigrant in his work group:

> Because [the Frenchman] had such a weird name and he didn't speak English very well and then he spoke with a French accent, he was a little bit, you know, "gay." . . . He wouldn't have a chance to be accepted by the group [of New Zealand builders]. . . . I think if it was an Asian person or something, he would have really hard time. . . . In that way, I think it's much easier with older people. I think older people would accept that much more.

Inka immediately contrasted this anecdote with the following story about a rest home that she frequented as a part of her work. One day, she asked the rest home manager if the older people had responded well to the presence of an Asian immigrant nurse. The manager responded:

> "Oh the oldies have accepted her really well because she is doing a good job and she's very nice, very friendly." And I thought, "oh but, you know, there's no problem?" "Oh no, no problem at all, they've accepted her really nicely and she's doing a good job and she's perfect."

Inka contrasted this to the builder group where she felt that if "there was a really good builder from Korea or somewhere, he would have really hard time."

I continued asking both older New Zealanders and immigrants if they thought that older New Zealanders were particularly receptive to interacting with immigrants. Most of the immigrants I spoke with said, "yes," and their insights shed light on why this might be. During my conversation with Li-Na (Korean immigrant), she contrasted her interactions with her older host parents with her interactions with the host parents' daughter, spouse, and friends—all in their thirties.

> L: I've known [the daughter and spouse] for five years but still, they wouldn't talk to me. Even at the dinner table. They wouldn't ask me any single question. So I thought maybe not used to Asian people. . . . If I go to their kid's birthday party, all these people are in their like thirties, their friends. Very unfriendly.

I asked her why that might be.

> L: I feel that you have to divide: older people [are] most friendly.... Isn't it because when you get older you need more company?... Because my host dad, he doesn't really have many friends, he's kind of shy type.... So for him, having a student is like a great way for him to, like, at least talk to someone.... So, he said it's a pleasure for him to even drive students [to] school.... But for people in their 30's, they don't really have that.... They already busy with their own lives, they have kids.

Li-Na went on to say that her fellow homestay students who stayed with host parents in their thirties or forties were not as close with their host parents as those who stayed with older people. Host parents in their thirties and forties are "busy with kids. And you are just another extra one. They don't pay extra attention, you're just like one of them. 'My kids and you.'" Again and again, the positive interactions that I uncovered between older people and immigrants seem to come down to this idea of time, pace of life, and *not* being as busy as other segments of the population may be.

More Time and a Slower Pace

In a study on urban incivility in Melbourne, Australia, Phillips and Smith (2003) found that while younger people, and younger minority people in particular, are often singled out in research as the perpetrators of incivility, it is actually more often middle-aged and older adults. In gathering examples of incivilities (which they defined as commonplace actions and interactions that are perceived to be rude or inconsiderate), Phillips and Smith (2003) found that older people were more likely to be mentioned as perpetrators than other groups such as minority youth or drug users. In direct contrast to this and the aforementioned rhetoric and statistics citing older people as more racist, in my research, immigrants often described older New Zealanders as receptive and pleasant in their interactions with the migrants themselves. When I relayed this finding—that migrants often described older people as more pleasant to interact with—to my older participants, some were not surprised and others were initially surprised but, upon reflection, felt this made sense. Some older New Zealanders suggested one reason immigrants might find older people to be more open: because older people are often moving through daily life at a slower pace. This slower pace can mean some older people are more amenable to engaging with, for example, the newcomer at church or the stranger on the bus.

Fatima (Iranian immigrant) told me that church had played a major role in her settlement into New Zealand. Twice she told me that the older New Zealanders at her church were the first ones she communicated with upon arrival in New Zealand because they were more patient: "The first people I started to communicate with was the older people. Normally younger people, it's true, it's really hard for them to make a communicate and they are not much patient." Fatima, in her thirties, has become close friends with a New Zealand woman in her seventies, referring to this older woman as her "best friend." While many older people have helped Fatima to improve her English through patient communication with her, this particular older woman has also taken ample time to help Fatima with her university assignments. Fatima jokingly said she will share her degree with her older friend.

Xui Li (Chinese immigrant) told me that it is the older people she encounters who allow her the time to translate in her head before speaking. Diah (Indonesian immigrant) expressed a similar sentiment about the time that older people take in communicating with her:

> I like to interact with older people because they don't speak really fast. Like in the shop when I serve them, they speak quite slow so I can understand really well. Because young people, like, really fast. . . . It happens in every country like that. Young people always busy. . . . Sometimes if I want to say something, then [older New Zealanders] want to listen. Because, uh, my English is not really good . . . but the older people always asking, "What do you mean dear? Sorry I don't understand." And then I explain again.

During our first interview, Inka (German immigrant) mentioned that older New Zealanders overall seemed to take more time in speaking with her, but she struggled to put her finger on why that might be. During our second interview where we looked at the photos she had taken as a part of the optional photovoice task, I asked if she had thought any more about this. Inka had thought about it and felt that older New Zealanders had more time and an inclination to just "enjoy the situation—it might be talking to me. Whereas young people are always on a mission and, you know, busier."

When I told Iris (Auckland, age ninety) that several immigrants felt more at ease communicating with older people, she was initially surprised. But upon thinking it over, her thoughts resonated with Inka's observations. She talked about how younger New Zealanders are not very patient with themselves or each other. She felt this was due to computers, television, and other technology that encourages young people to live through quick "little sound bites." Older people, she felt, might not only have more time but also have less pressure on how that time and attention is divided. Patty (Dunedin, age sixty-seven) echoed this very sentiment: "I guess a lot of people don't have time, if they are young people, are working. . . . But they work very hard, nowadays. People work, they carry their work home with them in their laptop or their cell phone." I mentioned to Ellen (Dunedin, age sixty-five) that many immigrants found older people to be more approachable and willing to engage in small talk. She agreed, saying "that's probably very true."

Ellen pointed out that when she takes the bus, she herself finds that "it is quite nice to have a nice conversation with somebody."

Sometimes older New Zealanders' interactions with immigrant strangers certainly go beyond the fleeting chat on the bus such as when older people end up volunteering with or alongside immigrants. Every two years the New Zealand General Social Survey conducted by Statistics New Zealand asks respondents whether or not they volunteered in the last month and breaks the answers down by age group. In 2012, people aged 65 to 74 reported volunteering the most (38 percent). Thirty-one per cent of 55- to 64-year-olds reported volunteering, 34 percent of 45- to 54-year-olds, 30 percent of 35- to 44-year-olds, and just 25 percent of 25- to 34-year-olds (Volunteering New Zealand Incorporated 2015). Ellen's (Dunedin, age sixty-five) observations were in line with these statistics and she pointed out that it is often older people who have time to do volunteer work that then brings them into contact with immigrants. I asked Ellen, who is a volunteer English-language partner, if that particular type of volunteer work was a good fit for older people. She answered that it was because older people have the time and the flexibility in their schedules to accommodate "the learner's" (the immigrant's) schedule. "Sometimes the learners have got specific time requirements, like they want a time when their husband is not there and the children are in school . . . you've got to have perhaps time in the middle of the day to do that." She carried on to say that it is not just having available time, but putting less pressure on how that time is spent and allowing others, immigrants, to take *their* time.

> A lot of the older retired people our age are actually really patient, too. So we don't rush with anybody saying, "oh you've got to learn this, you must know this." . . . Sometimes young people assume that everybody learns at the same rate that they do and when you are older, you realize that no, that's really hard.

If older New Zealanders have more time and attention to offer an immigrant, this goes hand in hand with their willingness, according to many immigrants, to engage with immigrant strangers in small, passing ways, like simply making small talk. Li-Na (Korean immigrant) said that older New Zealanders are good at "small chattering . . . like if I'm in an elevator, I don't know what to talk [about]. I just wouldn't say anything." But any older people in the elevator, she said, will "just chatter away." Inka (German immigrant) mentioned the same sort of approachability of older people through their willingness to engage in small talk:

> I think it's very easy, or easier, to speak with older New Zealanders than youngers. You know to make first contacts and have a chat, just as a chat. I feel comfortable, or it's just going easier. Which I notice that quite often . . . with old people, we just talk about something—nice flowers and this and that—but you have a connection.

Whereas with young people, it's much harder I think, to just have a chat or make small talk.

A few immigrants mentioned that older New Zealanders are not always warm immediately and could be rather standoffish at first. However, the immigrants who described this still said they found older people to be receptive and friendly if the immigrant made the initial approach. Maria (Filipino/American immigrant) said the older New Zealanders at her church tend to stick to their own small groups when a cup of tea is offered after the service. She noticed that when there is a newcomer, "only one or two will talk to them." However, while the older congregants "won't go out of their way" to talk to a newcomer, Maria realized that if she took the first step, she was warmly received: "I guess for my part, I have learned to try to talk with them and you know, they will talk to you. They're very nice." Li-Na (Korean immigrant) had a very similar experience with the older New Zealanders at her church in Dunedin, as well as the rest home where she volunteered. She felt the older people might initially be reserved around her because they had never "interacted with Asians" and they often assumed she did not speak English. But once she made the initial approach, she found the older people to be friendly, "genuinely nice," and interested in her, asking all sorts of questions. Inka (German immigrant) mentioned her observation that some older New Zealanders are a bit too reserved and polite to ask a stranger or newcomer too many questions; they are just "a bit scared to be nosey." But when contact is initiated, they are often warmly receptive.

A Familiar Role

Several immigrants mentioned that they also found interactions with older New Zealanders to be familiar and comfortable because they could fall back on social rules that govern their interactions with older people in their own home countries. Whereas interacting with younger New Zealanders can feel like unknown and unstructured territory, with no known guidelines for doing so appropriately, interacting with older people involves the same, familiar rules as it would back home, making it more predictable. In my first interview with an immigrant, I asked Helen (Asian immigrant[4]), if she thought that she interacted differently with older New Zealanders than she did with younger ones. I wondered if this was a poor question—too broad and vague. I was surprised when she did not hesitate to respond.

> I interact different . . . it's because of age. For the Asian, we Asians, we respect elders. So when I interact with older New Zealanders, probably I more polite and nice and try to help. And when I offer help, they are more accepting. So I feel more comfortable with that. But young New Zealanders . . . it's quite harder to approach. When I interact with young Kiwi, probably I have more self-protection.

I'm more conscious of what I'm saying and what I'm doing. But when I interact with older New Zealanders, I'm more relaxing.

She added that she becomes "more submissive" with older people in New Zealand just as she does in Korea, so in a sense she knows what to do. Diah (Indonesian immigrant) said she is more polite to older New Zealanders, just as she would be to older people in her home country, Indonesia. She, too, suggested that she is more submissive, out of respect, even though she sees that younger New Zealanders are typically not afraid to disagree or "debate" with their elders. Diah gave me an example of interacting with her ESOL conversation partner, Henry, a New Zealand volunteer in his seventies. "Henry has 'A' opinion and I have 'B.' So, I'm not speaking my 'B' because it is quite rude for me. 'The better is this one.' I didn't say that."

Li-Na (Korean immigrant) lived with her grandfather for years as a child in Korea and upon moving to New Zealand, she missed the company of older people. So she sought out older New Zealanders by beginning to volunteer in a rest home. This way she could also gain needed English language practice. She noted that choosing a rest home for volunteer work was, perhaps, unusual for an immigrant in her twenties.

I mean my friends would be like, they would prefer work at a shop rather than going to rest home. . . . But for me, it was easier, I guess, and I enjoyed it. I knew that I was going to enjoy talking to them. . . . So that's how I have this bond, with like older people. To me it's easier.

This handful of stories about immigrants interacting with older people according to the same social norms that would govern such interactions in their home countries resonated with some of my own fieldwork observations. One afternoon in Auckland, I was approaching an intersection on foot. Due to construction, the crosswalk was redirected and the new path required pedestrians to step off the curb, down onto an uneven section of road. I watched as an older New Zealand woman approached the crossing and hesitated at the edge of the curb. As I stood there wondering whether or not to offer assistance, a tall, middle-aged man with a large, black turban rushed out of a store, approached the older woman, and helped her off the curb and across the uneven surface. They chatted politely (I noted his thick accent) and she thanked him and continued on her way. Other numerous times, I watched older people board the public buses and noticed that when all seats were full, it seemed to be young Asian passengers who were the first to jump up and offer their seats. This being a fleeting moment with, for example, no chance for me to eavesdrop on conversation and accents, I have no way of knowing if the Asian passengers were immigrants, but several older New Zealanders also mentioned this phenomenon.

In contrast with the other immigrants, two immigrants told me that the same social rules that govern their interactions with older people back home *do not* apply in New Zealand. Fatima (Iranian immigrant) said that older people in Iran are more conservative and she must worry about how she dresses and behaves. She does not have this concern with older New Zealanders. Xui Li (Chinese immigrant) felt that older people in New Zealand are, on the whole, more educated and polite than older people in her homeland of China. In spite of the different nature of these interactions with older people in New Zealand as compared to their homelands, both Fatima and Xui Li emphasized that they nonetheless find older New Zealanders easier and more comfortable to interact with than younger New Zealanders.

Fatima (who is in her thirties) also mentioned that while she does have "more fun" with younger New Zealanders, these interactions can be laced with uncertainty. It is, after all, her younger New Zealand friends who are also the ones who are more likely to tease her.

> Even my close friend, when I say some things by mistake and she's laughing and laughing and mocking me . . . Or sometimes when I don't know the meaning of a word, they mocking me . . . And one of my close friends said to me, "sometimes you embarrassing me when you say the word wrong." Poor her. I say, "Sorry". (Laughing.)

She went on to tell me that in one of her classes at the university, the other students called her "Nuclear Atomic Girl" because she is Iranian. "Oh it's fun," Fatima explained. "They are teasing me, I'm just laughing. But sometimes you can see little things." While younger New Zealanders can be "a little bit hard to deal with," older New Zealanders "are very careful . . . They are more mature, so they know how to act, how to talk . . . Polite and caring about you, for instance if you are sick or upset, their understanding is really higher." So, while Fatima can have "more fun" with her younger friends, they also upset her more often and she appreciated the maturity typically inherent in her interactions with her older New Zealand friends and contacts.

Li-Na (Korean immigrant) explained the same phenomenon about being "teased" by younger New Zealanders, but in Li-Na's case, it was downright racial abuse. Nearly every Friday night while walking home from work at a Dunedin restaurant, cars of younger New Zealanders would drive by and yell, "Learn English!" or "Go home!" Li-Na felt this behavior was often fueled by alcohol. She believed that most younger New Zealanders are "fine" but because of this upsetting, repeated experience, she felt unsure about the kinds of interactions she might have with younger people. She appreciated that there is a higher degree of social safety in the predictably polite interactions with older New Zealanders. Even though she has found many older people "are not used to Asians," she knows they will be friendly if she interacts with them. In other words, she told me, it was not the older people who were drunk and yelling racist remarks from their cars on a Friday night.

Older People Are More Distanced from Some Concerns

In some fascinating interview excerpts, some older New Zealanders described how their own middle-aged children were far less open to interacting with immigrants than themselves. Elaine (Auckland, age sixty-nine) and Irene (Auckland, age seventy) spoke about this observation in their own families, though they struggled to find an explanation for it.

ELAINE: My family, especially my son, they are not really wanting to include.... They're not really genuinely welcoming. I don't often take any [homestay/exchange] student around to their place.

IRENE: No, I feel the same way.... Yet they are always very polite to them.

ELAINE: Oh, they're always very polite, but I know underneath— ... It's different than us.

IRENE: ... I mean I would love nothing better for Christmas than to ask strangers to my house for dinner, New Zealanders or any nationality that needed. But my children have a certain resistance to that, so I just don't.

ELAINE: Yes, I agree.

IRENE: I don't think it's a cultural thing so much, it's just—.

ELAINE: I don't know, perhaps not wanting to bring an outsider in, I don't know.

While Elaine and Irene struggled to identify why their middle-aged children were less "welcoming" to immigrants, several immigrants and older New Zealanders both suggested that younger New Zealanders may have particular reasons for being more conflicted about immigrants. Jobs and job competition with immigrants were mentioned a few times as a possible source of contention within the younger New Zealand population. As mentioned in chapter 5, June (Auckland, age seventy-two) spoke extensively about her feeling that immigration has negatively impacted job opportunities for many New Zealanders, particularly Māori. June's worries rest mainly with the decreased opportunities for young Māori such as the young people in her area who can no longer get jobs bagging groceries after school as they have in the past because the positions have been filled by immigrants. Ellen (Dunedin, age sixty-five) said her daughter has "a different point of view entirely" than her own view, due to her experience competing with and working with immigrants. Ellen said she felt that lower-paid occupations such as cleaners or garage hands often have a higher concentration of migrant people. Ellen told me that her daughter, who works as a health aid, said "'All these migrants, they've got to stop bringing so many in, they're getting all the jobs. I'm sometimes the only New Zealander on the shift.'"

Inka (German immigrant) said her husband (a New Zealander in his forties) certainly expressed this concern that "younger" New Zealanders might have—that there are "too many [immigrants] coming" for the number of available jobs. Inka's husband also worried about the increasing cost of living and limited affordable housing, but at the same time did not want natural areas being taken over by building homes (or other structures). Ellen felt that younger New Zealanders, trying to get their lives going with jobs, housing, and family, might have more of these various concerns and conflicts with immigrants. An older person, she said, is "just that little bit removed perhaps" from such things. This in turn, allows them to be "more accepting."

Ellen continued to say that while there will always be some "biased" people, she suspected that many people over sixty-five are "probably quite relaxed and more prepared to accept different points of view and different cultures and things." Helen (Asian immigrant) felt older people can certainly be more relaxed about different situations and contexts because they simply have more life experience. Inka (German migrant) expanded upon this idea saying that older people are sometimes "wiser about the world . . . not in a rush to experience new things and not so focused on themselves. . . . They are kind of above it and they just want to enjoy."

But with a laugh, Inka also raised the possibility that sometimes older New Zealanders might just be "more polite" than their younger counterparts and simply opt to "hold back their comments and opinions" one way or the other. I took this idea to Eve (Dunedin, age ninety-six) and asked if she thought it was possible that older New Zealanders were sometimes more approachable and willing to have a chat with an immigrant stranger simply because they were more polite. Initially, Eve said that she "wouldn't have any idea." But then, illustrating the possibility that some older New Zealanders place high value on politeness, she added that she herself has "always felt that politeness is a way of life." But Iris (Auckland, age ninety) suggested that older people who are more accepting or willing to interact are not doing so out of mere politeness. She harkened back to New Zealand's less diverse history that has been described in chapters 1 and 4, and suggested that older New Zealanders' background in this era of greater homogeneity (Ward and Lin 2005; McMillan 2004; Ip 2003a) has actually made them less suspicious or wary of others and more inclined to interact with whoever is standing next to you. "Fifty years ago," she said, "everybody was more or less, not completely, but on the same footing as it were. So we didn't sort of have to—we just didn't stop and think, 'Oh dear, who's that?' We would just talk to people and share life with them." When I asked if this was a generational difference, she replied "yes."

Symbiosis

This chapter has focused on providing a powerful set of examples about how some older New Zealanders and the immigrants with whom they have inter-acted have found multiple points of connection across difference. To conclude this chapter, I will discuss how these social relationships can be beneficial to both the older New Zealander and the new migrant, both of whom may occupy a position of marginality relative to the wider society. To do so, I return to the previously mentioned and most prevalent theme among interviewees regarding why immigrants often have their most congenial interactions with older New Zealanders: that older New Zealanders often simply have more time and atten-tion to offer to immigrants. I then suggest that many migrants also have more time and a need for social connection. This shared position of "more time" (per-haps due to their shared position of marginality) has led to some social relation-ships that are mutually beneficial.

As Christine (Dunedin, age sixty-seven) explained, if immigrants come into contact with a language group, a church group, a mother's group or just a friendly person who begins to chat on the bus:

> It is likely to be the older person who has time to slow down and speak more slowly maybe, and all the rest of that. The volunteer population is mostly sixties-plus simply because we are the people who have a bit of time to do it. So a lot of migrants probably come into contact with someone older than themselves— who may or may not be a trained volunteer—but who is able to give them time and not rush them.

Many of the immigrants in this study also described having an ample amount of time themselves for things like volunteer work, club membership, church com-mittees, spontaneous small talk, and more. Immigrants often come to these social and volunteer roles as a way to meet other people, get involved in their new community, or practice English. These interactions could be beneficial to both parties.

In many countries, loneliness has been identified as a key issue of concern for older populations. In the United Kingdom, loneliness has been identified as a key issue for older people with estimates that 10 percent of those over sixty-five are lonely most or all of the time and the number of isolated older people at risk for loneliness is much larger (Bolton 2012). In New Zealand, Statistics New Zea-land found that those over sixty-five reported the lowest levels of loneliness compared with other age groups, at 11 percent (Statistics New Zealand 2010). However, Age Concern New Zealand has noted that Statistics New Zealand's grouping of "those over sixty-five" does not reflect the possibility that loneliness might increase sharply after age eighty as it has been shown to do in the United

Kingdom (Age Concern New Zealand 2016; Bolton 2012). Furthermore, another study of 332 older New Zealanders showed a different picture—that approximately 8 percent of the respondents were severely lonely but an additional 44 percent were moderately lonely (La Grow et al. 2012). Even just a quick look at the websites of some New Zealand organizations for older people reflects the prevalence of the discussion or problem around social isolation.[5]

In terms of immigrants, a range of studies have found that many immigrants also experience social isolation in New Zealand (Ni Bhroin 2012; Maydell-Stevens, Masggoret, and Ward 2007; Ho et al. 2003; Flores-Herrera 2015). One study considered migrant women in particular noting that many migrant women felt "intensely isolated . . . because migrating had stripped them of their former sources of support" (Longhurst, Johnston, and Ho 2009, 341). They elaborated that a lack of driving skills, English-language proficiency, and paid work, all compounded by lack of a social network, leave many women essentially confined to their homes and domestic chores (Longhurst, Johnston, and Ho 2009).

This was certainly reflected in the firsthand observations of the director of a Dunedin migrant settlement service, Vonnie. Vonnie told me that it is female migrants who struggle the most to settle into their New Zealand surroundings and society. Castles and Miller (2009) have written about the "feminization" of migration, meaning that women are increasingly becoming the primary immigrant—the person in the family who acquires a work visa and instigates the family's migration (often to host countries looking for nurses, caregivers, and health aids for an aging population) (Hochschild 2000; Castles and Miller 2009). From Vonnie's perspective, however, it is still most often men who have a work visa, job offer, or some connection upon entering the country, meaning the women largely come to accompany their husbands. In this situation, women can struggle to find social and personal connections and are left somewhat isolated while their husbands are at work (and any children are at school). While the male might already speak English or be able to learn "on the job," the female must search for other language acquisition opportunities. While the man makes social connections and learns local norms at work, the woman has to seek out social and cultural inclusion. Thus, it is often female migrants who join English conversation sessions, who volunteer, who might join groups more readily, and who might have more flexible schedules or free time. According to Vonnie, women's struggle to settle in happily and find life satisfaction in New Zealand is the biggest barrier to immigrant families successfully and permanently settling. In her opinion, helping the female migrant find her footing and a new sense of belonging in New Zealand was the single most important factor to ensuring that immigrant families settled well and benefited from their move, as well as ensuring that the local community benefited from having them come.

As has already been noted, the immigrants I spoke with in this study were overwhelmingly women and all formal migrant interviewees were women. While acknowledging the limitations of this sample, it also reflects the image described above and I routinely met migrant women who were somewhat socially and professionally isolated with a reasonable amount of spare time on their hands. At a Dunedin migrant women's group that I attended regularly for more than a year, I met numerous women who signed up to volunteer in rest homes or to be a companion through Age Concern. I witnessed the women spreading information about these types of volunteer opportunities to other migrant women. For many women it was a way to "help out" locally and thus to "serve a purpose again." For some, it was also a chance to practice English one-to-one with a New Zealander, in this case, an older New Zealander interested in receiving a volunteer visitor for company and conversation.

Inka (German immigrant) and Jane (British immigrant) volunteered at the Botanic Gardens and the Stroke Foundation, respectively. Both described their fellow volunteers as primarily older New Zealanders. As mentioned already, Li-Na (Korean immigrant) volunteered as a visitor in a rest home, engaging older New Zealanders in conversation. Maria (Filipino American immigrant) worked full time as a nurse and sought out further social connections through social gatherings and committees at church where most of the other members were older New Zealanders. Isa (Papua New Guinean immigrant) worked as an aide in a rest home after starting out as a volunteer. I watched as she advised the members of the Dunedin migrant women's group to seek out similar work in the high-demand field of elder care through first volunteering. (The group of migrant women, including myself, celebrated with Isa when her contract progressed from volunteer to casual aide to permanent aide.) A few weeks after a conversation with Isa, a Nigerian woman told the group she had obtained a trial volunteer contract to be a conversation partner at a rest home. With pride she said that she was thoroughly enjoying speaking to one particular older New Zealand woman about art.

With these examples, I argue some immigrants have the same type of free time and desire for social contact as some older New Zealanders. These crossovers of time and situation can foster symbiotic relationships—whether fleeting or substantial. When Inka (German immigrant) worked as a caregiver in elderly people's homes, she always arrived full of questions—"it's so interesting to me! I ask about how they went to school, where was the school, how was life." She appreciated hearing the local history through the older New Zealanders she worked with. And she knew they appreciated her company and conversation while she assisted them. This was also the case for the already mentioned example of Li-Na (Korean immigrant) who volunteered in a rest home and did so because she missed the company of her grandfather and because she needed to practice English. But she was very aware that the older people benefited from her presence too:

Because most people there, their kids would never visit them. Only like Christmas. So what do they do? . . . Gradually, they want me to come to their room, they show me how to knit, they would tell me their stories.

Clare (Auckland, age seventy) spoke about the mutual benefits that both she and her immigrant homestays gained from their relationships with each other:

> We like them to experience our life; we're older but they still seem to want to come. We run a singing club once a month and they come to that, they think that's fun. And they come to the orchestra. . . . From these other countries, they all seem to have an instrument, so that's interesting. We take them on special trips to various places. . . . It enriches us, I mean we could just sit here and be boring old you-know-what's, but at least it keeps us on our toes for a while. I've learnt a few things about the other countries.

The idea that similar experiences of time and pace enabled symbiotic relationships between immigrants and older New Zealanders was verified in an unexpected way. While talking with Diah (Indonesian immigrant) she began to explain that she did not interact with very many older people in her home country. In fact, she avoided them:

> It sounds silly, sounds not respectful. Usually in Indonesia [older people] don't have other work and then want to talk a lot. And then sometimes if we keep close to them, we keep talking. And I have so many things I have to do!

Diah continued to say that she was far busier in her life in Indonesia and that many young people there might avoid conversing with older people for the same reason. I pointed out that it sounded like Diah, as a migrant in New Zealand, was in the same situation as older people—with a bit more time on her hands. She laughed and agreed with the point I was making, "so we have the same position, situation. . . . I think that's good thinking. Yeah, I think because I am not so busy here, I, yeah—. The same."

The free time she found on her hands in New Zealand, as well as the social isolation while her husband worked and her son attended school, put her in a position similar to that of some older people. Whereas at home she did not, in New Zealand, she had the time and desire to chit chat, to volunteer. This put her in frequent contact with older New Zealanders who also, she felt, had the same kind of time and desire to interact in this way. Diah mentioned one of the volunteers at the English conversation group she goes to, an older New Zealand man. He told Diah that it is "very rewarding" to talk to immigrants in the group because he "could be lonely" otherwise and this is something that "keeps him going." In other words, it was definitely a mutually beneficial means of social interaction. In some cases, these mutually beneficial interactions between immigrants and older New Zealanders could also be seen as providing a new role for older New Zealanders—that of "Mentor of Kiwiness." This is the topic of the next chapter.

7 · MENTORING "KIWINESS"

This chapter explores older people's experiences of increasingly diverse surroundings by examining one specific type of interaction some of the older New Zealanders in this research had with the immigrants they now routinely encountered: that of "mentor of 'Kiwiness.'" Many older New Zealanders in this research freely and casually shared historical knowledge and narratives, little lessons that immigrants reported as unfolding exponentially into helpful boosts to their understanding of New Zealand and their sense of belonging in their host country. Be it deliberately or subtly and unknowingly, these older New Zealanders helped immigrants demystify the often ambiguous and invisible (but nonetheless very strong) parameters of an "ethos" of "Kiwiness." Some older New Zealanders also helped immigrants navigate bureaucratic systems and expected social norms by suggesting what to do and what not to do, according to their own knowledge of "Kiwiness." During the interview coding, "mentor of 'Kiwiness'" emerged later in the process as a theme that encapsulated many of the other codes. Uncovering older New Zealanders as "mentors of 'Kiwiness'" provides a concrete example of the mundane ways that these two segments of an aging and diversifying population actually interact and coexist.

As mentioned in the previous chapter, interactions between older New Zealanders and immigrants can be symbiotic or mutually beneficial. Mentoring immigrants in "Kiwiness," as it will be explained in this chapter, can be a source of some satisfaction for some older New Zealanders and also be of tremendous practical and emotional value to immigrants. It is important to note, however, that one of the only other research articles I found about retirees (often white) engaging with migrants and refugees cited the inherent power imbalance in this interaction. Erickson (2012), spoke about the shared liminality and mutual benefit occurring when older people volunteer with refugees, but also advised being wary of an imbalanced relationship that may result in perpetuating social inequalities and older people forcing hegemonic ideas of the "worthy citizen" onto a migrant (Erickson 2012).

Also within the limited literature about older people interacting with immigrants is a small body focusing on migrant caregivers caring for older residents.

In this scenario, older people are the recipients of care and assistance. In the numerous countries facing population aging, "workforce issues may prove to be the greatest challenge facing health systems in the future" (Cornwall and Davey 2004, 79). New Zealand is just one of many countries that has looked and will continue to look overseas to help fill its need for health-care workers (Cornwall and Davey 2004; Badkar, Callister, and Didham 2009). In many countries, this scenario—of a pinched health-care system seeking overseas health professionals and caregivers to tend to the needs of the growing elderly population—migrants are part of the solution. Immigrant/older person interactions can be complex, especially in formalized or institutional settings (Bourgeault et al. 2010; Kiata and Kerse 2004). Nonetheless, immigrants can be seen as rescuers or saviors to a stretched elder-care industry. This chapter presents a different perspective of the interactions between older people and immigrants—one in which the older people are the *givers* of assistance, rather than the receivers; one in which older people subtly but significantly aid immigrants in important, everyday ways. This view of older New Zealanders as "mentors of 'Kiwiness'" is in accordance with an approach to aging that is purposefully outside the paradigm of aging as loss or deficit but demonstrates instead how the old are active, reflective members of changing societies.

MENTORING THE PERCEPTIONS OF NEW ZEALAND "NORMS"

It is important to point out that even just within this study's small sample, older New Zealanders' understanding of "Kiwi" social norms and expectations vary according to their own life experiences. One place this was most evident was in the informal daily English conversation groups organized and hosted by an older New Zealand man, Alan (Dunedin, age eighty). The majority of immigrants who came to these conversation groups were female and most were in their twenties, though some were older. As mentioned in chapter 3, I participated in these conversation groups for months, shifting between the role of fellow immigrant and that of "Kiwi host" as a white, native English speaker and a "Western" migrant assumed to have fit into Pākehā New Zealand easily. Alan routinely positioned me as a "New Zealander" for the purposes of these conversation groups and explicitly looked to me to provide further evidence for the migrant women of behavior that he proposed was typical for young New Zealand women.

On one occasion, Alan explained that New Zealand men tend to have the power/authority in relationships. As an attempt to verify this, he asked me who had the power in my marriage. I replied that I thought it was basically equal, or at least that my husband and I both worked toward a power balance. Alan seemed a bit flustered with my answer and he then opened it up to the group for discussion, asking the others in the room, all women and one man, "Who has the power in your relationships?" The answers varied greatly as each person explained a little bit about his or her unique, individual relationship. Sometimes country of origin or cultural background and expectations were mentioned, but not often. Alan seemed a little taken aback by this. On another occasion, he talked about how his wife, as a married New Zealand woman, would *never* be seen in public without her wedding ring on. Again, he looked to me to verify that a married New Zealand woman would and should always wear her ring to mark her marital status. I explained that I had a different experience—that I had not had a wedding ring for the first six months of my marriage and that I often took it off for outdoor activities. The other young immigrant women in the group began to chime in; some said they found wearing their wedding band to be very important, while one said she had forgotten to put her wedding band on for the last several days and was not wearing it at the meeting; this was inconsequential to her. Shortly thereafter, as Alan headed outside for a cigarette break, he instructed the all-female group to ask me about American or New Zealand weddings and for us all to discuss boyfriends, because, as he said, young women always want to discuss weddings and boyfriends. As soon as Alan left the room, the women exchanged a few knowing looks and then some proceeded to chat about university studies while one woman asked me questions about obtaining a New Zealand driver's license.

Sometimes I worried that Alan seemed to be passing on gender roles from an earlier version of New Zealand or just a New Zealand reality that he knew but that I did not. Because he framed many topics as "how things are done in New Zealand," I felt some responsibility to share my different perspective of young women's lives in New Zealand. (This, it is interesting to note, seemed more in line with these migrant women's perspectives, who represented numerous countries and cultural backgrounds.) As the other women spoke, however, I came to realize that they understood the subjectivity and possible generational differences in what they were hearing, in spite of any language barriers or cultural differences. They seemed to know Alan well enough to be a little suspicious of some of what he was saying, but to also respect and enjoy him enough to carry on. (It is important to note that hosts can, knowingly or inadvertently, reinforce social inequalities and hegemonic norms when interacting with immigrants {Erickson 2012}).

In contrast, Patty's (Dunedin, age sixty-seven) version of New Zealand women's roles and realities was much different, but she too directly mentored her values and expectations. She openly made a point to tell young female immigrants about the historical development of women's rights in New Zealand as a central tenant of "New Zealandness." She explained to migrant women that she encountered in various community groups and particularly the daughters in a Jordanian family that she had become close with, that New Zealand was the first self-governing country to give women the right to vote in 1893 and that many feel that women's suffrage became and remains a central part of the nation's self-image. Memories of participation in New Zealand's feminist movement of the 1960s and beyond were particularly important to Patty, personally and politically. She explained (to the young, Jordanian, Muslim women in particular) that she herself worked very hard for progress toward equality and viewed it as a fixture in New Zealand society that cannot and should not be taken for granted. Speaking of a variety of issues, such as underage marriage, Patty said: "I feel very hot under the collar. . . . I don't care what culture you come from, what your religion is, you obey our laws. And we fought hard . . . our female ancestors fought, and we fought for equal rights and for girls, for the age of consent to be sixteen." She explained that she feels "very very strongly" that New Zealand laws on human rights, women's rights, and gender equality must be protected. Alan and Patty's variations on gender roles and women's social norms in New Zealand society demonstrate that the social norm or concept of "Kiwiness" was unique to an individual's perspective and life experience. Thus, this research notes when consistencies in these concepts occur, but does not aim to pinpoint or verify generalized notions of New Zealand "norms." Rather, it describes older New Zealanders mentoring younger immigrants in social norms and expectations *according to their own perspectives.*

RECOUNTING WHEN IMMIGRANTS BREAK VALUED NORMS

Older New Zealanders' various understandings of "norms" or an "ethos" of "New Zealandness" sometimes became evident when they told me about upsetting occurrences of immigrants breaking these norms. These stories of immigrants breaking New Zealand norms were relatively common and ranged from little mistakes deemed barely worth mentioning through to immigrant behavior perceived to be significantly transgressing core New Zealand values. Like "home" is often noticed and defined most easily when it is left (Chaudhury and Rowles 2005), so too is it often easier to define social norms and expectations when they are transgressed. Thus, when older New Zealanders recounted stories of immigrants who transgressed their ideas of New Zealand norms or values, they revealed their mundane expectations of daily life; incidents that seem almost insignificant can become very important and even emotionally charged when broken.

Paul (Dunedin, age eighty-five), for example, told me about an immigrant at the bottom of his street who routinely broke what even he admitted to be "a trifle" that doesn't "impinge upon us much." However, he mentioned it three separate times through the interview.

We notice that there's a lady, I suppose Indian, perhaps from Fiji, down at the bottom of the road, who has come in to live there. And she puts all her washing in the front of her house, which almost nobody in Dunedin does. She even strings a line to the lamp post and it's there every day; does a lot of washing. And

FIGURE 4. Photo exemplifying "a typical Kiwi." (Photo by John B. Turner, 2005)

I'm just wondering if anybody is telling her that this isn't done. . . . Maybe there's no washing line at the back, in that case the landlord has failed to put one there. But it could cause people to perhaps mark you out as different and not trying to at least respect some of the local ways.

While admitting it is a small matter and showing concern for the immigrant's well-being and fitting in, Paul's anecdote also illustrates that breaking assumed norms, even small ones, can be anything from annoying to offensive.

In fact, not hanging washing in front of the house is related to a part of "Kiwi-ness" I heard repeatedly mentioned by some of the older New Zealanders interviewed: that of keeping a neat or tidy lawn and garden. This point was really driven home when I asked John (Auckland, age sixty-eight) if there was such a thing as a typical "Kiwi." John, a photographer, used several photographs to visually aid his answers to my questions (in line with the complementary photo voice aspect of this research project). This photo, he felt, was one excellent depiction of "a typical Kiwi" (see figure 4).

Several older New Zealanders verbalized what John presented visually: that keeping a tidy lawn and garden is appropriate "Kiwi" behavior. Elaine (Auckland, age sixty-nine) also explicitly explained that it is an expectation not being met by immigrants and the lack of tidy gardens has changed how her neighborhood looks and feels.

This suburb used to be totally Kiwi . . . But now there's Africans and Chinese, they're lower socioincome bracket. And Middle Eastern too and different, other people, many others. There's nothing wrong with them living here except that because they don't have places like we do in their own countries, they don't keep the outside of their houses tidy.... They've probably lived in apartments, so they've got no clue.... They [are] just in the house and leave the grounds. When I say it's changed, it's changed in that no longer do people mow their lawns regularly, keep their places tidy.

Elaine demonstrates that this aberration from what she views as a valued Kiwi norm—the keeping of a tidy garden—is an emotionally charged manifestation of the neighborhood's changed ethnic makeup. New Zealand sociologist Claudia Bell (1996) specified that maintaining a tidy garden is a valued norm relating back to colonial ties with England and is important specifically for Pākehā New Zealanders. As early as the 1850s, cottage gardening was flourishing in New Zealand: "Suitable climate and soil conditions here, along with the cultural tradition of 'do it yourself' have made gardening both a popular pastime and a serious industry" (Bell 1996, 168). "Prescription gardening," Bell explained, with a distinct style to follow, has often helped ensure that gardens "look English" and that properties are "attractive" (Bell 1996, 168).

Not maintaining a tidy garden is perhaps a seemingly small transgression but is a symbol of immigrants failing to adhere to a larger, enduring Kiwi value— tidiness in general. A well-known national slogan extends the mandate for tidiness beyond the private garden: "Be a Tidy Kiwi."[1] Be A Tidy Kiwi is an iconic brand that has been around in various forms since the 1960s, claiming to bring New Zealanders together as kaitiaki, or guardians, of the country's clean, green identity (Be a Tidy Kiwi 2019). The value placed on being a "Tidy Kiwi" through, for example, maintaining tidy gardens and not littering, is a part of New Zealand's national image of being "Clean and Green." Egoz (2000) explained that "New Zealand's 'Clean and Green' image is central to New Zealanders' collective psyche"—be it in images of sublime, untouched, and untainted wilderness or of a neatly cultivated and productive landscape (Egoz 2000, 63; Bell 1993). The "Clean and Green" image is heavily invoked as a marketing measure to tourists, with one of the latest national tourism campaigns being "100% Pure New Zealand" (Bell 2008, 346). Within New Zealand, there has been significant criticism of this image *not* being a reality in New Zealand's actual environmental and tourism policies. For example, Egoz (2000) wrote that organic farming, while contestably far better for the environment, is actually in conflict with New Zealand's desire for "Clean and Green" landscapes because organic gardening and farming is aesthetically "messy" and disruptive of the valued "orderly landscape" (67).

Returning to private gardens, the importance of keeping a tidy garden was highlighted in a study on aging in place in suburban New Zealand. Keeling (1999) found that within a predominately Pākehā, middle class, retirement community near Dunedin, New Zealand, the manageability of their gardens factored largely into some older New Zealanders' decisions about where to live in old age.

For example, one older woman explained that her choice and ability to stay in her family home was facilitated by hiring others to trim the hedges, weed the garden, and cut the grass. Others, however, frequently discussed their decision to move to a smaller property in relation to their need for "minimal garden responsibilities" (Keeling 1999, 8). So valued was a tidy garden among the older people in Keeling's study, that the inability to maintain one signaled that it was time to downsize from the family home. These same older New Zealanders might be among those who find it disconcerting, then, when immigrants break this value of tidy gardens.

The New Zealanders over sixty-five in this research provided many other examples of social norms of "Kiwiness" that were, from their perspective, being broken by immigrants. Ann (Auckland, age seventy-eight), for example, was one of several who mentioned her experience of immigrants frequently breaking the unspoken rules of moving aside to share space when walking along the footpath. Ann explained that Chinese and other Asian immigrants in particular do not move aside to allow easy passing on the footpath.

> When we used to go out on Queen Street, they just didn't seem to have any manners. They'd walk all over the pavement and wouldn't get out of your way. And I got to the stage where I'd just walk straight into them and if they didn't move, tough. Because we were brought up that you walked on one side of the road, of the pavement, and leave the other one clear. . . . I suppose Asians, because of their numbers in their own home cities, just have to be, they have to be pushy to get anywhere, don't they? I've really noticed that . . . they're just brash, somehow, you know?

Politeness in New Zealand is strongly related to the value placed on egalitarianism (a perceived New Zealand value previously discussed in chapters 1 and 5) (Holmes, Marra, and Vine 2012), or at least the facade of egalitarianism (Bönisch-Brednich 2008). Pākehā notions of egalitarianism tend to derive from an intolerance of self-promotion and settlers' early rejection of a class-based system left behind in Britain. Māori values of egalitarianism, however, derive more from reflecting subjugation of the individual to the group. Despite the different roots, Holmes and colleagues argued, the result is a high valuation by many New Zealanders of egalitarianism and collegiality (Holmes, Marra, and Vine 2012). For Ann, it is possible that this lack of moving aside to share the sidewalk equally among all present was a breach of her notion of egalitarianism and associated basic politeness.

A few older New Zealanders shared brief stories about immigrants breaching another perceived social norm by taking things that the older New Zealanders considered to be either communal and not to be taken by one person (such as paper towels in a public toilet or salt and pepper shakers in a lunch bar) or as being private property (such as flowers from one's garden). Privacy can be characterized as "bound to cultural, political, economic and technological change" (Blatterer, Johnson, and Markus 2010, 1). As such a dynamic and contextualized value, differences in notions of privacy can easily create conflict. Valuing privacy is to value important aspects of the conditions needed for individual and collective flourishing (Blatterer, Johnson, and Markus 2010); thus, perceived breaches of privacy can take on great emotional and social significance. A few older New Zealanders told stories that illustrated a difference between their notions of privacy (particularly pertaining to their homes and gardens) and some immigrants' apparent notions of privacy. While one or two of the interviewed older New Zealanders expressed great joy in having an open home with people, especially family, coming and going freely, several other New Zealand interviewees expressed valuing the private space of one's home and the important sense of safety that comes from that boundary. Elaine (Auckland, age sixty-nine) explained how some immigrants have a far different idea of houses as more communally approachable. Some older New Zealanders, she explained, specifying particularly those of English descent, find that distressing.

> I learned this from my little African friend, they live in communities over there, this is poor people. She told me that they would just go in and out of each other's houses. We New Zealanders, or from English descent, we tend to be, we invite somebody to come. . . . You don't just pop in and out of your neighbors' places. But with the Africans, they're very different, they just wander in and out of each other's places. So we had a time here, which is a bit scary for some elderly people, and this little African girl just wandered into someone's unit [in her retirement village]. Opened the door, walked in. . . . Well my friend had the same circumstance, just down in this area of units and this little African girl just walked in and [my friend] said to her, "Would you mind going!" She got such a shock! . . . But you see this is the difference. . . . There's all these vast differences.

Fran (Auckland, age seventy-five) provided another example of breached privacy. An older New Zealand friend had to call the police when several "African immigrants" were climbing her tree to pick the fruit. "Well, they thought it was perfectly alright for them to go and help themselves, strip the tree. [Her friend] had to get the cops in, not just for her safety, but to explain to them, 'This is New Zealand! We don't do that!'" These last two examples also reflect the perceived undesirable impact of immigrants on the highly valued attribute of "safety" in New Zealand as discussed in chapter 5.

One of the most powerful examples of the significance and emotional impact of some more mundane norms of "Kiwi-ness" being broken came from my encounter with Charles (Auckland, age eighty) at an Auckland RSA chapter. We spoke at some length, a fascinating conversation that swayed back and forth between his current experiences of living in what had quickly become one of Auckland's most diverse areas and his memories of "how New Zealand used to be" dating back to World War II and the 1950s. Charles had many concerns about the impact of immigrants in New Zealand, from job competition to education to safety, all of which he elaborated on in tones of exasperation. However, he punctuated this discussion with what was, for him, the strongest point of all: "They don't play sports. They don't *even play rugby!*" As I noted in my fieldnotes: "this was an unspeakable breach to Charles. It was a personal affront. He was nearly in disbelief and he said this as if it alone validated all of his concerns and dislike of immigrants." I recalled Charles looking at me with wide, teary eyes. I heard the same sentiment, that immigrants do not play rugby, in at least two formal interviews as well.

Although not spoken of with quite the same emotional intensity by the other interviewees, the repetition of this theme illustrates that participating in sports, particularly rugby, is at the heart of what "Kiwiness" is all about according to some older New Zealanders. After the 2011 Rugby World Cup, which took place in New Zealand, there was some talk among academics and in the media about rugby as a surrogate or substitute religion in New Zealand. In an interview, Professor Peter Lineham (who has researched the link between sport and religion) explained that New Zealand's colonial society was built on "hard-working, sweating heroes," and this image is still a striking feature of rugby. Thus, rugby is "linked with nation building" in New Zealand (Massey University 2011). Sociologist Paul Spoonley, however, wrote an article for the Asia New Zealand foundation about the talent pool and support for rugby inevitably changing as New Zealand becomes more diverse. Sports like football, he said, will become more significant with immigrants from around the world having more knowledge of, access to, and involvement with football far more than rugby (Spoonley 2014; Edens 2017).

Grainger (2009) wrote that Pacific rugby players in New Zealand, like former All Blacks captain Tana Umanga, demonstrate that when immigrants play and excel at rugby, they are embraced as "part of mainstream New Zealand" (2347). (In this case, it is actually about the son of immigrants—Umanga was born in New Zealand to Samoan immigrant parents.) Grainger argued that this is a false, superficial, and "unstable" acceptance of Pacific peoples, especially those born outside of New Zealand, as "fully-fledged Kiwis" (Grainger 2009, 2335, 2343); however, it demonstrates that immigrants (and indeed Māori and New Zealand—born Pacific Peoples) who play and excel at rugby are "good" immigrants and "good" minorities. Pākehā New Zealanders in particular, Grainger argued, can claim color blindness and a society based entirely on meritocracy and unity when Pākehā, Māori, and overseas and New Zealand–born Pacific Peoples play and succeed in rugby together. For some older New Zealanders, like Charles, this shift in sporting interest, whereby immigrants do *not* partake in rugby, is a threat to these perceived national values, unity, and identity.

OLDER NEW ZEALANDERS AS "MENTORS OF 'KIWINESS'"

Stories of immigrants breaking perceived New Zealand norms were often retold easily by older New Zealanders in this research and fit Bönisch-Brednich's idea of "ready-mades" or key narratives that are polished, drawn upon often, and ready for presentation at any time (Bönisch-Brednich 2002b, 70). However, while older New Zealanders had ready-made stories to illustrate immigrants breaching New Zealand norms, they also simultaneously engaged in *helping* immigrants to learn and to abide by New Zealand norms. In other words, many of the older New Zealanders in this research were knowingly or unknowingly working toward the amelioration of their own fears and complaints surrounding immigration by taking the time and opportunity to mentor immigrants in expected or desirable behavior. This is what I have come to call "mentoring 'Kiwiness.'"

This mentoring of "Kiwiness" takes place in a variety of both official and unofficial capacities. For example, a few older New Zealanders in this study are trained English conversation partners and are paired with learners through volunteer organizations. Others have official volunteer roles through churches— welcoming immigrants, hosting English conversation sessions, or providing other services. Several older participants either have recently or currently taken on "homestays" through both formal and informal means, teaching all sorts of social rules and subtleties in their own homes. These older New Zealanders assume the role of mentor (though none called it that) deliberately and are able to verbalize their reasons for doing so. Elaine (Auckland, age sixty-nine) has hosted homestay students formally for years and now houses two migrant women connected to her through informal channels. She views herself as having an important role in teaching "Kiwiness."

> I feel that we are giving them a look at Kiwi life and Kiwi culture. And that's why they are with us. . . . For instance, I know that one certain race, they're very interested in how much your house is worth, various questions that we as Kiwis, we would never ask somebody, even our friends. . . . I just say, "look, we don't ask those questions in our culture." . . . And with eating, too—if I see them doing anything—I don't want them to go out somewhere else and really embarrass themselves by eating the wrong way. They might choose a knife to eat or they might not know the right manners and some things some of them do could be quite offensive to other people.

In many cases, however, mentoring "Kiwiness" often took place in the informal, casual realm, such as while having regular lunches with an immigrant coworker or helping a migrant neighbor with gardening. Older people also frequently assumed an informal mentoring role in fleeting moments, such as Iris (Auckland, age ninety) did when riding in a taxi driven by an immigrant driver. Iris recalled how she had spoken with her Indian taxi driver that very morning, teaching him a bit of New Zealand history as he drove her past a local memorial on the way to her destination:

> I was telling him about the Savage Memorial and the Depression in the 1930s, because I was a schoolgirl then. Then when Mickey Savage came and he became, oh 1935 I think, he became prime minister and the Labour Party came into being. And they started building state houses and all sorts. And people, well, the work force, had a lot more work to do. I can't remember all the things that used to happen, but I remember the Depression very well.

Whether formal or informal, sustained or fleeting, older New Zealanders passed on their knowledge and "tuition" in "Kiwiness." The following section gives a few more examples of what this mentorship looked like.

ROLES/EXAMPLES OF MENTORING "KIWINESS"

Purveyors of History

The older New Zealanders in this study seemed to take on several roles as "mentors of 'Kiwiness,'" with purveyors of history being one of them, as demonstrated above by Iris during her taxi ride. Evidence of older New Zealanders as purveyors of history can be heard in their interviews, recounted from my own interactions, witnessed throughout my fieldwork, and even further validated by some immigrants. Several immigrant participants described learning about local or national history, gaining much more insight about and grounding into New Zealand, through their interactions with older people. Some older New Zealanders might not even have been aware that they were offering immigrants a valuable path of connection to New Zealand; however, some immigrants in this project were very conscious and appreciative of this type of exchange. Inka's (German immigrant) first job in New Zealand, like many new immigrants (especially females), was as a homecare assistant for elderly people based in their own homes. She stayed in this job for several years and explained how her interactions with the older people whom she helped care for gave her great satisfaction:

> I was just cleaning for these people so they still can stay home. And do little chores for them, like going shopping. . . . But I thought it was really great to meet these old people. It was just when I had arrived here and I didn't know much about New Zealand and it was a great way to get to know the history. [New Zealand] history is not that long and these people have kind of experienced it all. The old people were always happy when I came in, you know, we had a cup of tea most of the time and then started talking . . . their grandfather bought the land

and the huge farms, it's so interesting to me! And I ask how they went to school and where was the school and how was life.

The phenomenon of older New Zealanders sliding into a role of purveyors of history for new immigrants is all the more interesting when considering that immigrants' lack of local, historical knowledge is of concern to older New Zealanders. In chapter 5 some older New Zealanders discussed their discomfort with immigrants' poor knowledge of New Zealand history and context. When I attended a community meeting for a group that aims to create positive relationships between New Zealand and China, Iris (Auckland, age ninety) said she was bothered that immigrants do not know New Zealand political history. A lifelong political activist and Labour Party supporter, Iris said she regretted that so many immigrants supported John Key (the National Party leader and prime minister at the time of our interview) because "he smiles nicely." The group talked about what had been good or bad under various party leadership over the last several decades and suggested that immigrants do not know all of this political history and precedent but vote only according to what is presented to them at face value at the moment. (I noted, in my fieldnotes, that as I sat there listening to this group discussion, I exemplified the problem—a new immigrant who could not participate much in this discussion due to my unfamiliarity with some of the political history they were discussing.) Even in this environment, within a group formed to support positive international ties and immigration from China, lack of historical, political knowledge was still strongly felt as a troubling attribute of the immigrant population.

As previously mentioned, Patty (Dunedin, age sixty-seven) worried about young immigrant women not knowing and valuing the women's rights movements in New Zealand, while June (Auckland, age seventy-two) was greatly troubled by immigrants' lack of knowledge of Māori, historically and currently, in New Zealand. June elaborated:

> I'm talking about those that do manage to come into the country, need to attend classes of the history of Aotearoa . . . to understand there is another language in New Zealand, there is another race in New Zealand—not only the white race but Polynesian race. Too often some of them come into the country, don't even know who we are. . . . I think that can cause a lot of misunderstandings. . . . So it's really asking them to be a bit more mindful of the cultures; it's important that they understand the country that they are coming into.

Other literature shows this same trend in and beyond New Zealand—that immigrants' lack of knowledge and attachment to their host country can be threatening to local, long-term residents. For example, Demuth (2000) wrote that "degrees of attachment" (25) to a place typically are related to the amount of time passed in a place. It can be disturbing to those who are quite attached to a place, over years and decades, to see newcomers who are not as attached (Demuth 2000). In a globalized world, today's immigrants often exemplify transnationalism and have interconnected worlds and multiple loyalties. This can be unsettling to long-term local residents who can feel that multiple loyalties held by immigrants threaten national coherence (Grillo 2010). In fact, Grillo has argued, transnationalism and globalization can trigger fear among the locals about a fragmented society where difference and diversity are seen as ungovernable and unmanageable (Grillo 2010). This can actually engender, then, a strong nationalist response of one nation, one culture, or in the case of New Zealand, possibly, two cultures. An influx of immigrants who do not share an established resident's knowledge and appreciation of past events, and who do not, therefore, have the same type of investment in and attachment to this place, are a collective threat.

Whether done knowingly or not, then, when older New Zealanders share their historical perspectives and knowledge about the neighborhood, city, or nation, they may be acting to lessen the threat of immigrants who do not understand or appreciate the historical, political, and cultural context they have come to. For example, June (Auckland, age seventy-two) demonstrated how she actually worked, one micro interaction at a time, to ameliorate her fear and concern about new immigrants knowing nothing about Māori. She still worked part-time in a large office setting and recounted her interactions with her immigrant coworkers.

> I have this friend at work—we try to encourage Te Reo[2] with a lot of them—and he can give his *whakapapa*.[3] He can say his name in Māori and where he comes from and the plane that his ancestors flew over in. And he's quite proud of that achievement. Then we've got another Indian, he can do the same thing too, all in Māori. So he said, "There, June, did we pass?" And I said, "yeah, you pass." And it's just the closeness of communication again, when you acknowledge one another. So I asked them to share with me their *whakapapa*.

June also expressed her interest in beginning to volunteer with refugees coming into the country to be able to help them in a variety of ways, including facilitating this sort of cultural knowledge acquisition.

Several immigrants seemed very aware that their lack of local, historical knowledge might mean they are at least perceived to be less attached to some things held dear in New Zealand. For example, Fatima (Iranian immigrant) knows this might be considered a negative aspect of immigration:

> [Immigration] has disadvantages because, to be honest, when the country is not your country, you do not care about the country as much as the New Zealander might. I love New Zealand but I'm sure, a person who is from New Zealand, more care about her country than me. About nature, about conservation, all these

things. . . . They are caring to look after all the, you know, local trees or, many things. But maybe I don't.

But again, it can be the older New Zealanders who help new immigrants "care more" and connect with New Zealand through historical knowledge. I experienced these lessons in history and "Kiwiness" many times myself. For example, upon wandering into an Auckland RSA chapter one afternoon, I met Ed (Auckland, age seventy-three). Ed was retired New Zealand Army and we chatted easily and good rapport came quickly. Ed began to show me names, carved into the walls, of people from the area who had served in World War I and World War II. I noticed that a lot of the streets in the area were named after these veterans. I later wrote that in that moment:

> I was an immigrant gaining a new understanding and connection to a piece of New Zealand through talking to an older person and gaining some historical insight that I might not otherwise get. To Ed, every one of these street names had meaning. Migrants might not, probably would not, have any idea why those streets are named, what they are. Of course, neither would most younger New Zealanders!

For Ed, and seemingly many of the older people sitting around the RSA that day, enjoying a beer and some conversation, the names on the walls held deep meaning and the names of the local streets referred to actual people who came from this very neighborhood, not long ago. The personal meaning attached to these street names and these former local boys was obvious in Ed's reverence as he explained the names to me and pointed out the handful of photographs of young men in by-gone military uniforms. Ed's passing history lesson had an immediate impact on me—in this case, the new, unattached immigrant. Suddenly the nondescript, suburban, traffic-filled arteries that I had been wandering through in that area of South Auckland took on new significance.

Again and again, I found myself fascinated with older New Zealanders recounting how things "used to be." At times, I have struggled to make a connection to New Zealand—the landscape, the cities, the national ethos—and have found that the historical perspective gained from older people's casual conversation has helped me form a more meaningful relationship with my host nation. I now know about the ladies who made the famous tapestry inside the cathedral forty years ago and about the family that started a local, popular retail business in the 1950s. I can recount how the pubs used to close at 6 P.M. and nothing was open on Saturday or Sunday. Through their stories, I have become a bit more tied into my adopted surroundings as I go about my daily life. In the course of conducting these interviews, I was being mentored in "Kiwiness"—from subtle lessons like being given Kiwi food (Afghan biscuits, sandwiches of ham on white bread, and countless cups of tea) to more explicit instructions like being told to familiarize myself with a local historical figure I had not heard of: "If you live here, you should."

These moments of being mentored often took on great significance for other immigrants, helping them form a connection, an understanding and a sense of belonging in their host country. For example, Inka (German immigrant) spoke further of the lessons she had learned about older people's individual lives while she helped care for them, and how that translated into the current local "Kiwi" culture she experienced and into some aspects of New Zealand national identity that she could now fully appreciate, such as the "Kiwi bloke"[4] and "Number 8 Wire."[5]

> Meeting all my oldies, that really gave me understanding of New Zealand, a really deep knowledge and really feeling for it, how old people must feel and what is it to be a New Zealander in that way. Like to have claimed that land and that's their farm, and they have worked with their own hands . . . I think all this hopes and dreams is probably in them and they succeeded and they did it and so they are proud of that. . . . On TV you see the ads and they tell you about the "Kiwi bloke" and the "Number 8 wire attitude" and all that. You can really see how it grew.

Inka's newfound appreciation for certain valued characteristics of "New Zealandness" sounded like just the kind of thing many older New Zealanders in this study wanted new immigrants to know, understand, and respect. The older New Zealanders were the ones, knowingly or unknowingly, sharing these historical "lessons" with immigrants, and helping—little by little—to ameliorate the "problem" of immigrants lacking attachment and awareness of local history.

Assisting with Daily Life

Protectors. Beyond purveyors of history, older New Zealanders take on other roles within a mentoring relationship as well, roles that were evidenced through fieldwork observation and from interviews with both immigrants and New Zealanders over sixty-five. Older New Zealanders in this study seemed to sometimes act as protectors of immigrants. I witnessed this frequently in the informal English conversation groups hosted by Alan (Dunedin, age eighty). At one session, a middle-aged Korean woman explained to the group that she had a negative and upsetting experience when repairing her car. She recounted paying the bills but not getting a receipt and not understanding what was going on or what the charges were. Alan, who was already familiar with her situation, said she was being ripped off and that he was aware of the "despicable behavior" from this particular car repair business. He warned the rest of the Korean, Chinese, and Indonesian immigrants present that they should never go to this business; several of those present seemed very familiar with this warning from Alan.

Other than Alan, the other consistent volunteer English conversationalist in this Dunedin group was Jerry (Dunedin, age seventy-three). One day, Jerry and Alan introduced me to Sara, a young woman from China, and told me she was their most regular attendee. They spoke with great pride about how much Sara's English had improved—from speaking no English at all upon her first attendance at the group to now speaking clearly and with humor. Jerry and Sara seemed to have a warm relationship. The following is an edited excerpt from my fieldnotes:

> Sara was telling me that she had been yelled at while walking along the main street in Dunedin at night, people driving by yelling things like, "Go Home!" As Sara told me this, Jerry made the motion of shooting a gun. Sara said jokingly, "Are you talking about hunting?" Jerry said he wanted to shoot the people who said things like that to Sara and others like her. Sara paused, then looked up and said, "Would you?" And they both laughed.

In a final example of older New Zealanders acting as protectors of immigrants by looking out for their well-being, Clare (Auckland, age seventy) recounted the advice she and her husband gave to their homestay students: not to come home late at night, be as careful as they would in their own country, and ring Clare if they thought they were in trouble. "I say, 'it's safe, but who knows?' . . . You have to be sensible."

Practical Assistance. Older New Zealanders acted as mentors with very practical advice as well. They aided in filling out paperwork, navigating bureaucratic systems like registering a car, catching a bus, or putting out rubbish for collection. Ellen (Dunedin, age sixty-five) was a volunteer English language tutor through a formal agency but the role of the tutors goes beyond language. She told me: "We're actually concerned with teaching English *and* resettlement, our organization. So we're always teaching people little things." When I asked if she thought that retired and older New Zealanders were particularly good at being tutors and mentors she replied:

> Yes . . . they generally have got plenty of time. . . . And older people know where everything is in Dunedin and they know who to go to if you've got a problem and they are quite happy to perhaps go with somebody. I've taken at least one learner and enrolled her at the library. All sorts of advice you can give to people about how to sort out a problem—that you know because you've lived here all your life.

Ellen explained that often times the things immigrants need help with might be small and something a New Zealander would take completely for granted. She provided another example of this: helping one of her "learners" with acquiring firewood for home heating over winter:

She'd been buying her firewood from the supermarket or the garage because she thought they were the cheapest places around. And I said, "Oh no they are actually the dearest places. You want to ring up and get it delivered." "They will deliver it?" She'd been driving every week to buy one sack or something. And so, got out the phone book and showed her how to ring up and order some. And they brought it to her house and she's so pleased; it's a lot cheaper, too. There's all sorts of things like that.

These are perhaps the seemingly small things that can make a huge difference in an immigrant's settlement and quality of life. This research has demonstrated it can often be older people who have the time to help with the "small" but significant things. Simply through informal neighborhood networks, Fran (Auckland, age seventy-five) has been called on to help immigrants write CV's and prepare for interviews. In another example, Christine (Dunedin, age sixty-seven) has helped immigrants pass the Food Handling Certificate test required for anyone wanting to work in a restaurant.

Mentoring Social Expectations and Guidance on Daily Living. As Elaine (Auckland, age seventy) mentioned earlier, older New Zealanders can also act as mentors of "Kiwi" behavior and small social rules. Paul (Dunedin, age eighty-five) commented that he feels he should not change his ways to accommodate immigrants *because* he recognizes their need and desire to learn "Kiwi" ways. He had a small, informal music and singing group whose members met at his home once a week. Several of the members were from China and he believed, "one of the reasons they come [to the group], I'm sure, is not just for the fellowship or the music but for the socializing for the, the cultural, acculturation." Clare (Auckland, age seventy) provided a strong example of teaching one valued aspect of Kiwi behavior in her opinion—not littering. In another strong example of the previously mentioned value of being a "tidy Kiwi" (as well as the significance of immigrant transgression of this value), she described her reaction to witnessing an immigrant woman littering:

> There's a shop down the road ... [and a woman] from maybe Pakistan, not sure actually, she went out the front and just threw her food, rubbish, in the gutter. And I said, "No! Dirty! Very dirty!" Fancy me saying that! I said, "No, no you don't do that in New Zealand. Very dirty." But you see, that's probably, they do it at home.

Clare said the woman did not pick her rubbish back up, but she doubts the woman will do it again. While some might find Clare's reaction a little harsh, she felt that she needs to protect certain values of "New Zealandness" and also that this immigrant needed to learn some of these behaviors for their own good and safety in the country.

In another example, Christine (Dunedin, age sixty-seven) told me she has learned from her English-language learners that many immigrants are greatly perplexed by New Zealanders' "concentration on the weather" as a topic of conversation. Immigrants, she had realized, find the focus on the weather to be a small, Kiwi, social nicety—a "rather odd" one that they just "don't get." So Christine had taken to explaining her perspective on why New Zealanders discuss the weather so much: its unpredictability. But she went further; she also explained to her learners that being ready and able to discuss the weather is a valuable skill for those trying to acquire some "Kiwi" ways: "it is most people's small talk." Knowing this, she said, will help immigrants to interact with New Zealanders in casual conversation, which in turn could help them with significant hurdles like obtaining work.

From explaining that school playgrounds are for public use outside of school hours, to providing a taste of "Kiwi" foods such as pikelets, to "translating" Kiwi phrases such as "Good on ya, mate," the examples of older New Zealanders sharing little tidbits of useful information with immigrants were numerous and varied. On occasion, mentoring and advice on small social rules was amusingly "outdated," such as the advice that thirty-four-year-old Fatima's (Iranian immigrant) eighty-something New Zealand "parents" gave her about dating. Quickly realizing that their well-intentioned advice was completely inappropriate for her current situation, Fatima sought out advice from New Zealanders in their twenties instead.

Kinship That We Choose

Older New Zealanders sometimes seemed to move beyond giving practical advice, or even lessons in local history, and would sometimes take on the role of local family—as a parent or grandparent—to an immigrant with whom they had a closer relationship. June (Auckland, age seventy-two) had Indian neighbors across the street with young children who came over and called her "Nan" or "Nana." June laughed briefly as she recalled some of the looks this raises from others. She was one of several older New Zealanders who mentioned being called "Kiwi mum" or "Granddad" by certain immigrants.

The immigrants spoken to in this research reiterated the existence of this type of relationship. As mentioned just above, Fatima (Iranian immigrant) is close with a New Zealand couple in their eighties. She lives with this couple, whom she met through an informal church network.

> When I came here, always I was missing my parents a lot because I was so close with mum and dad. But as long as I am with this couple, it's a good thing. . . . They always treat me as, like my parents, you know always caring a lot about me. . . . Always I am calling them "Kiwi Mum and Dad."

Helen (Asian immigrant) said an elderly couple on her street in a diverse Auckland neighborhood was also like her local guardian parents. Helen explained that this casual relationship formed and took on some meaning to her after her own parents visited from her home country. Her own parents were always outside, tending to her yard and garden. The elderly New Zealand couple next door (perhaps endeared with Helen's attempt to keep a tidy garden) became quite friendly with Helen's parents, even with no common language. When Helen's parents left, she felt the older local couple generally keeping an eye on her and her well-being, always waving a friendly hello in passing and sometimes coming over to offer gardening tips.

Many times, I witnessed a bond between an older New Zealander and immigrant who had become somewhat close with one another. In one of Alan's (Dunedin, age eighty) English conversation sessions, I asked a young Hungarian immigrant how she heard of Alan's conversation groups. She explained that her father had immigrated to New Zealand fifteen years ago and had participated in Alan's "lessons" at that time with great appreciation. This Hungarian man referred his daughter to Alan's groups as well when she recently joined him in New Zealand. In addition, several female immigrants brought their babies along to Alan's sessions now and then. Alan was always thrilled to see them; I witnessed him meeting two new babies of his group members for the first time since their birth—he took such pride in them and the migrant women obviously took some pleasure in bringing their babies along to meet Alan. And so it seemed Alan was involved, at times, with more than one generation of an immigrant family.

Alan and several other older New Zealanders told me they had been overseas to attend the weddings of immigrants they had met or hosted in New Zealand. Serving as local family, "nana or granddad, mum or dad," to younger immigrants often seemed to please these older New Zealanders as their own children and grandchildren were often spread throughout New Zealand and overseas. However, this role of fictive or chosen kin was equally if not more beneficial for the immigrants in this study who explained that some older New Zealanders, especially those they got to know well, gave them a sense of family connection in their adopted country.

Be it via helping an immigrant to order firewood, to obtain a library card and to learn to talk about the weather, or by teaching an immigrant pieces of New Zealand history and culture, or perhaps by being a Kiwi parent or grandparent, these older New Zealanders aided new immigrants in gaining footing in New Zealand. This portrayal of older people as givers and proactive shapers of formative societal relationships is in direct contrast to more common depictions of older people as recipients of help and passive members of society. The immigrant voices in this chapter validate that this assistance from older New Zealanders and the relationships with them were appreciated and meaningful to the immigrants on the receiving end, sometimes almost immeasurably so. The next chapter goes on to argue that in this context, older New Zealanders actually exemplified the qualities of cosmopolitans and that it was their slower pace of life—their cadence—that often allowed them to do so.

8 · COSMOPOLITAN CADENCES

For many older people in New Zealand and beyond, the development of contemporary multiculturalism has become so marked a social change that even those who have not moved themselves now have regular, everyday contact with difference. Thus, while this book began as a story about aging and time, it is clearly also a story about difference. It is the story of how older people are living with and within difference, as it has manifested around them with the development of globalization, migration, and multiculturalism. A helpful lens to analyze this experience is provided by the concept of cosmopolitanism. Whereas cosmopolitanism was addressed in chapter 3 as a methodology, here cosmopolitanism is introduced a second time as a framework for an exploration of the productive engagement with difference and grounded expressions of hospitality to strangers that were revealed in this research project. In this chapter, I engage with some of the current debates in cosmopolitanism, namely, discussions of cosmopolitan consciousness and the call for a critical cosmopolitanism. I explain that while the older people in this research had ample and potent concerns about immigration and accompanying social changes, these concerns were largely on a macro scale, while their micro interactions with immigrants often exemplified cosmopolitan ideals. The chapter concludes by returning again to the idea of time as I claim that older New Zealanders' cadence facilitated cosmopolitan interactions with the immigrants whom they now routinely encounter.

GLOBAL MOVEMENT → MULTICULTURAL SETTINGS → LOCAL CONTACT WITH DIFFERENCE

Global movement has had a pervasive impact socially, economically, and politically, resulting in rapid ethnic and cultural diversification and new sites of coexistence with difference. The social sciences have taken a number of approaches to encounters with difference over the last several decades, with one early, well-known contribution, for example, coming from social psychology: contact theory. In the early 1950s, Allport (1954) proposed that people are uncomfortable with the unknown and anxious about encounters with difference. He proposed that contact is essentially a prejudice reduction strategy—it "lessens feelings of uncertainty and anxiety by producing a sense of knowledge or familiarity between strangers, which in turn generates a perception of predictability and control" (Valentine 2008, 324). But his theory was largely concerned with majority prejudice. The focus of social science research on contact with difference then shifted instead toward the experiences, rights and recognition of minority groups (Glick-Shiller and Fouron 1990; Becker 2003; Burns 1993). Considerations of contact with difference are now shifting again to focus on connections and coexistence across difference, especially in urban settings (Valentine 2008; Baumann 1996; Wessendorf 2014a).

As an anthropological study of "social differentiation" in "complex social environments" (Vertovec 2015a, 14), this book identifies and locates the macro forces of transnationalism, globalization, and migration within the personal and social lives of individuals—in this case, older New Zealanders. Although the focus of this study is older New Zealanders who themselves have not moved, it is still a story about migration and migration's pervasive effect. It is thus in line with anthropological studies of migration that work at a micro and meso level of analysis while engaging with macro level factors like the structural and historical context within which people chose to migrate (Brettell 2003). In studying the interaction between macro structure and individual agency, anthropological studies often illustrate individual and local stories, richly represented within larger, impersonal systems of political economy (Brettell 2000, 2003). This research on older New Zealanders' experiences of the growth of multiculturalism in their country has paid similar attention to contextual global forces as lived through local individuals and the micro scale of their everyday interactions with difference. Cosmopolitanism has emerged as one way of discussing the reality of and the potential for living together with difference and is the framework this chapter will utilize to discuss globalization and multiculturalism as manifest in older New Zealanders' resulting mundane encounters with difference.

The concept of cosmopolitanism is itself a "diversity of related conceptualizations" (Glick-Shiller and Irving 2015, 1), but its roots are typically traced back to the Enlightenment notion that every human has equal worth and ought to have an allegiance to human-kind beyond kinship or country (Cheah 2006; Rapport and Stade 2007). The concept's recent resurgence is commonly traced back to Kant's view of a stranger's right not to be treated with hostility (Cheah 2006). Cosmopolitanism is routinely used both as a description of the contemporary, globalized world—with its mobility (Sheller and Urry 2006), transnationalism (Glick-Shiller, Basch, and Blanc-Szanton 1992), and superdiversity (Vertovec 2010a)—and as an argument for transforming the world into a better one by moving beyond national thinking to a global integration, a "new universalism," and cosmopolitan law (Kahn 2003; Glick-Shiller and Irving 2015; Beck and Sznaider 2006). Recent approaches to cosmopolitanism have included its manifestation as moral philosophy (Rapport 2012), ethical project (Appiah 2006), research methodology (as discussed in chapter 3), and as an argument in support of humanitarianism and an approach to human rights (Tan 2016).

Cosmopolitanism has its critics, many citing its idealism and untenability. Valentine (2008), for example, sought to remind us that tolerance is still about those in power choosing to be tolerant or not; the discourses of cosmopolitanism can be dangerous, she said, in their celebration of "the potential of everyday encounters" while the "knotty issue of inequalities" are ignored (Valentine 2008, 333). Other critics have pointed to war and fundamentalisms (often unleashed by nationalism and religion) as living, robust contradictions to cosmopolitanism (Glick-Shiller and Irving 2015), with some suggesting that colonialism, empire, slavery, capitalist exploitation, and the Holocaust have basically curtailed the cosmopolitan project, at least in its earlier renditions (Prakash 2015).

Multiculturalism itself has recently been subjected to some very similar proclamations of its "failure" or its unfeasible utopianism, with some saying a backlash against multiculturalism is characterizing the early twenty-first century. The framework of multiculturalism emerged as a type of middle ground that resisted both exclusion and assimilation by instead offering simultaneous membership and recognition of difference (Castles and Miller 2009; Grillo 2010). Since the mid-1960s, national norms were increasingly perceived as heterogeneous and a multicultural framework was thought to be able to accommodate a certain amount of diversity and a new pathway of incorporation (Grillo 2010). A "retreat from multiculturalism," however, has gained momentum as new security concerns arise in tandem with an emphasis on national values and loyalty (Castles and Miller 2009, 14). In Europe, for example, a moral "panic" is reframing difference as a threat to social cohesion (Grillo 2010, 20). In Australia, an ideology of cultural homogeneity undermines official multiculturalism (Dunn et al. 2004). Politically, multiculturalism has recently been seen as inadequate for addressing concerns around cultural division and "the desire for social cohesion" (Noble 2009, 46). In February 2011, British prime minister David Cameron spoke of multiculturalism as a "failed policy" where segregated communities have behaved completely "counter to our values" (Wright and Taylor 2011). At the same time, former French president Nicolas Sarkozy claimed France had been too concerned for the identity of immigrants and not enough with the identity of the country: "if you come to France, you accept to melt into a single community" (Agence France Presse 2011). As discussed at the opening of this book, both Trump and the Brexit "Leave" movement found support in promising to dramatically reduce immigration (Wilson 2017). In New Zealand, as previously mentioned, the rhetoric against multiculturalism (or at least the rhetoric around the challenges of it) has been, in part, about the difficulty of fitting multiculturalism within or alongside the country's bicultural framework while maintaining the place and rights of indigenous New Zealanders (Hill 2010; Spoonley and

Bedford 2012). For some, multiculturalism represents an inherent danger to Māori (Walker 2004).

In light of the criticisms of cosmopolitanism and in such an era of backlash against multiculturalism, a fundamental question of cosmopolitanism has been asked: is "such a project of humanist universalism ... dead dogma?" (Rapport 2012, 10). Castles and Miller (2009) suggest, however, that it is the rhetoric against multiculturalism that has changed more than the reality of it, while Kymlicka (2012) adds that this rhetoric mischaracterizes the multiculturalism experiment, its future prospects, and its progress (Kymlicka 2012). After all, most people in settings of diversity continue to coexist in daily life. "The massively apparent fact" is that diverse peoples in cities "do talk to one another as customers and shopkeepers, passengers and cabdrivers, members of a bus queue, regulars at cafes and bars" (Laurier and Philo 2006, 353). Noble wrote that to avoid a romanticized view of cosmopolitanism and to move away from abstract rhetoric, we can look at sites of "unpanicked multiculturalism" or spaces of cultural complexity where difference and intercultural cohabitation are negotiated in everyday lives (Noble 2009, 50). It is such coexistence of difference in daily life that this study of older New Zealanders considers.

This research on older New Zealanders' experiences of increasing diversity joins discussions of a cosmopolitanism that addresses the impact of global mobilities and other manifestations of globalization that facilitate *daily* encounters with difference. This type of everyday, lived cosmopolitanism has been called "quotidian" (Nava 2006) and "mundane" (Nowicka and Rovisco 2009b); an "actually existing cosmopolitanism" (Robbins 1998), "working class cosmopolitanism" (Werbner 1999), "vernacular cosmopolitanism" (Werbner 2006), "banal cosmopolitanism" (Beck 2002), and more. As anthropologists have approached cosmopolitanism as an object of study, they have attempted to, in part, identify a social category of cosmopolitans (Rapport and Stade 2007). In 1990, Hannerz differentiated between "locals" and "cosmopolitans" with the latter exhibiting openness toward divergent cultural experiences and cultivating skills in navigating foreign terrains (Hannerz 1990). Sometimes referred to as "neoliberal cosmopolitanism," this view of cosmopolitanism focuses on lifestyle and "elite travelers" with a taste for "the Other" (Glick-Shiller and Irving 2015). However, anthropologists have since thoroughly problematized any dichotomy of mobile, elite, assumedly "open" cosmopolitans placed in contrast to tradition-bound, ethnocentric "locals" (Glick-Shiller and Irving 2015). Travel, transnational lifestyles and a high degree of mobility, after all, certainly do not automatically constitute a cosmopolitan "openness" (Ong 2002), while at the same time, as this chapter argues, being more stationary does not negate cosmopolitan encounters. As has happened with so many older people worldwide in their lifetimes, the world has come to them. When the world has come to you, mobility is not required to regularly encounter difference.

This research on older New Zealanders joins that which has approached cosmopolitanism ethnographically (Werbner 1999; Wardle 2000; Falzon 2009a; Kennedy 2009) and have found it is less an elite category or ideology and more a reality for many who live an "actually-existing" (Robbins 1998) or "mundane" cosmopolitanism (Nowicka and Rovisco 2009b). In these views, cosmopolitanism does not operate somewhere in elite circles or in the abstract. Instead, cosmopolitanism is embedded in involuntary confrontation with "the Other" in ordinary people's everyday lives (Nowicka and Rovisco 2009a) as they live successfully side by side, inevitably offending one another but recognizing the need to associate peacefully (Kahn 2003; Kant 1974).

In this view, cosmopolitanism governs everyday interactions in settings where globalization has eroded the borders of previously separated common people and their life-worlds. As multiculturalism is a local, daily reality in cities and neighborhoods across the world, a certain cosmopolitanism simply exists in the actions and interactions of individuals and groups living in these settings (Kahn 2003). Older people are among those who, without being hypermobile or elite, now coexist with difference manifest in the immigrants who now live next door, assist them at the bank and volunteer alongside them. It is during some of these fleeting interactions, as well as within some more sustained relationships, that the older New Zealanders in this research often exhibited cosmopolitan ideals.

Valentine would warn that the sort of claim that I am making here might be a "worrying romanticization" and "naïve assumption" that contact with others translates into respect for difference (Valentine 2008, 325). Simple bodily copresence, after all, does not necessarily lead to reflexive, conscious cosmopolitanism (Werbner 2006). Nor does politeness; strangers do generally behave in courteous ways in public, guided by normative modes, contextual expectations, or "urban etiquette." Such mundane enactments of ritualized codes, Valentine argued, are *not* indicative of personal values (Valentine 2008, 329). Thus, some theorists caution that such contact should not be automatically "scaled up" as indicative of a cosmopolitan consciousness or an intentional openness and engagement with difference and "the Other" (Valentine 2008, 325). My data suggest, however, that it is far more complicated than whether or not these interactions can be "scaled up." This study demonstrates the need for a view of cosmopolitanism that is more plural and contextualized and accounts for the complexities and ambiguities of everyday life in settings of diversity. In the following section, I present the contradictions inherent in the older New Zealanders' responses to immigrants, multiculturalism, and difference, before moving on to explain how these older New Zealanders contribute to the debates of cosmopolitan consciousness and the call for a critical cosmopolitanism.

CONTRADICTORY COSMOPOLITES

Fran (Auckland, age seventy-five) did not stray far from home anymore and was known to openly complain about immigrants, be it, in her opinion, their abuse of New Zealand resources, their lack of hygiene, or their many other undesirable qualities. Nonetheless, she talked equally openly about her appreciation of meeting and interacting with immigrants because doing so "helps you see further than the end of the table." Hard of hearing, Fran used a teenage Pakistani girl as a "secretary" to help her place calls. This young migrant woman clearly shared an amiable relationship with Fran, evident when she helped arrange Fran's interview for this research. Although Fran complained about her Indian neighbor's wealth and fancy new car in comparison to Kiwis with more restricted means, Fran spent her afternoons helping an eight-year-old Indian boy, new to English, with his school assignments. While Fran enthusiastically delivered tirades about the ample annoyances and wrongdoings of immigrants, she set her evenings aside to open her home to three migrant Muslim women for an exercise group so they could get some exercise in their culturally required private, female-only environment.

Older New Zealanders' experiences and discussions of the daily diversity now around them were often filled with contradictions. To provide a few more examples of these contradictory sentiments, I return to the voices of the older interviewees. Elaine and Irene (Auckland, ages sixty-nine and seventy) recalled the mid-1980s as the time when more and more immigrants from more countries began arriving in Auckland and they remembered feeling "as if we were being invaded." During the course of their interviews, both commented, with some resigned disapproval, that New Zealand will be "Chinese" in just another twenty years' time. Indeed, Irene said, nowadays it is "very hard to find a Kiwi" when you step on a public bus and that the immigrants she encountered once on board sometimes failed to follow expectations of politeness and were "rather pushy." She hated the way some immigrants spat in the streets. As mentioned in chapter 5, both Elaine and Irene openly worried about the amount of health-care resources going to immigrants, with Elaine feeling, in spite of her humanitarian consciousness, that this was unfair to New Zealanders. Both worried about new and increasing migrant-related crimes, bemoaning that some migrants arrived with blatantly poor intentions. Both felt concern about the impact of Islam, as brought by immigrants, in New Zealand. They particularly worried about how some Muslim women were treated and hated the idea of New Zealand being "influenced" by it. Elaine explained, "I suppose in some ways we don't like to see this. It's more the religion coming into our country, trying to, it's trying to take us over." All of this suggested a strong resistance and opposition to immigrants in New Zealand.

Elaine's worry about Islam's influence, however, "wouldn't stop me from being friends with them," she said, adding that she did indeed have Muslim

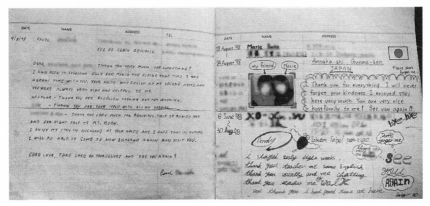

FIGURE 5. Irene's visitor book. (Photo taken by the author with interviewee's permission; all identifying details blurred by Les O'Neill)

friends. Irene agreed, "I wouldn't go along with [Islam] but I do accept that they are people." As mentioned earlier, over three decades both Elaine and Irene have hosted almost countless exchange students or new immigrants in their homes from many nations, cultures, and religions. Irene brought her "visitor's book" to our interview, which she showed me with interest and pride, pointing out all the different nationalities and languages on its pages. This prized book was filled with messages from her various homestay students and immigrant guests. (See figure 5.) "The more you have to do with them," she told me, "the more you get to love them." Elaine concurred.

At the time of our interview, Elaine was hosting one young Middle Eastern woman and maintained a close friendship with another. "I love keeping up with all their goings-ons. Boyfriends and all the lovely, interesting things. It's gorgeous." At different points during her interview, Elaine explained that she loved going to church because she'll see a new, foreign family and, wondering where they are from, go and speak with them. "As I've seen it," she said, "people are the same. If you're smiling at them, they know that you're kindly towards them." Elaine spoke of her willingness "to get involved in other people's lives," namely, immigrants, to lend a hand.

At a different point in the interview, however, Elaine's tone changed once again as she shared her opinion that, actually, most people understand and prefer their own culture while being "wary" of others. Thus, she confessed she "wouldn't deal with an Indian businessman" because "their ways are so different. . . . Even Chinese . . . you've got to know the way they do business or you'll be taken in." She continued that she would much prefer to go to "a Kiwi for most professional things" like a lawyer or a dentist. Immediately after this statement, however, she revealed that, actually, her dentist *is* a foreign migrant. And her doctor? He is an Indian immigrant, "a lovely man . . . very clever."

MACRO CONCERNS VERSUS MICRO INTERACTIONS

Elaine and Irene's narratives demonstrate how many of the interviews frequently included contrasting sentiments about diversity in New Zealand; excerpts from one individual's interview often appeared to be from two persons with two dramatically different opinions on the matter—one, from a person open to and engaged with difference and the other from an intolerant person who might even be labeled racist. Such seemingly incompatible sentiments about diversity in New Zealand were frequently found on the same page of an individual's interview transcript. While many aspects of immigration overall might be worrisome or even just bad, the immigrant next door or working in a favorite café might be lovely, good, and even beneficial. Older New Zealand participants' contradictory thoughts often fit a pattern: expressing macro concerns about some large-scale, undesirable impact of immigration while simultaneously exemplifying cosmopolitan ideals in their micro interactions with individual migrants.

To provide another example of this pattern, we can return for a moment to June's (Auckland, age seventy-two) substantial worries about the negative impacts of immigration that were described in detail in chapter 5. June was the most verbose respondent on the topic of the commonly expressed concern that immigrants were taking jobs from New Zealanders. She questioned why immigrants "have got the jobs and we haven't." She spoke about the long-term harm coming from extended periods of unemployment, with young New Zealanders losing motivation and becoming angry and frustrated. June also spoke of her concern that Māori are being ignored and overlooked by immigrants and by the government as it turned its attention toward those immigrants; she feared biculturalism was losing "any meaning." Yet in spite of these substantial misgivings about jobs and nonexistent recognition of indigeneity, June told me of her interest in becoming a volunteer host to a refugee family once she had fully retired. She had also considered, "getting involved with that English as a second language [program]" and becoming an English-language partner. She had great sympathy for the refugees who come to New Zealand "scared" and "not knowing what they are coming to." She explained that "taking on an immigrant family and helping them" would be a "wonderful opportunity . . . to get to know another race and to help that race." As mentioned in the previous chapter, June is the one who delights in the little Fijian-Indian boy next door calling her "Nan" and goes out of her way to teach her migrant coworkers how to create and recite their *mihimihi*, a Māori introduction that explains your ancestry and where you come from as well as your connections to others. June's very real and redolently expressed "macro" concerns pertaining to immigration exist right alongside her genuine micro cosmopolitan interactions with individual migrants.

As a final example of this pattern, I return again to Charles (Auckland, age eighty), the self-described "racist bastard" with whom I spoke at an Auckland

RSA chapter. Charles told me, with sincere exasperation, about the undesirable damage done by immigrants and the total lack of benefits coming from increasing immigration. He bemoaned immigrants for not interacting in the same ways, for "stealing" jobs and causing the extinction of local traditions. I asked (with part curiosity and part provocation), "Like that guy over there?" and I pointed to a young man sitting near us in his clubroom bar, a young man who appeared to be both foreign and an ethnic minority. "Who that?" Charles questioned as if I was being ridiculous. "That's just Sam," he said in a pejorative tone, making *me* feel racist for even implying that Sam exemplified one of these immigrants that Charles was complaining about. Sam was a totally different matter, an individual in whom Charles recognized individual humanity easily, in spite of Sam being a part of a larger change that Charles found truly regrettable.

Empathy for, appreciation of and openness to migrants and diversity were sentiments sometimes immediately juxtaposed with the kinds of seemingly intolerant comments that feed the stereotype that older people are racist. These older New Zealanders' complaints about the large-scale impact of immigration do not necessarily imply that the smaller, convivial interactions are insincere or constitute unmeaningful contact. Rather, these older people simply remind us that people's experiences of their environments are complex; they hold strong, contradictory opinions simultaneously and often do so while still recognizing the humanity in the person having a pint next to them at the club.

CONSCIOUS COSMOPOLITANISM, CRITICAL COSMOPOLITANISM

Nowicka and Rovisco (2009a) suggested that cosmopolitan consciousness occurs when a mode of self-transformation occurs; when people become more reflexive about their experiences of others and rework their boundaries. A reflexive, conscious cosmopolitanism could be described as having a basis in political or ethical reasoning with a desire to engage with humanity outside of established categories (Skrbis and Woodward 2013). This is in contrast to "tactical" or "de facto" cosmopolitanism, for example, where a person engages with "the Other" when and where it is to their own benefit rather than out of any openness or recognition of shared humanity (Skrbis and Woodward 2013, 108). Older New Zealanders certainly demonstrate this de facto cosmopolitanism from time to time. Some described their social circles shrinking to varying degrees and found it was in their best interest to engage with difference personified in the people around them at church or living next door. For some older New Zealanders, children have moved to other cities or countries and friends and relatives have died while their own retirement or mobility limitations have limited their personal contact in general. Longtime neighbors and friends may have moved away to join adult children elsewhere or to enter an assisted living facility across town. It is immigrants who have since bought and moved into those vacated houses. To *not* engage with immigrants would mean, for many, that their social circles would shrink further. Furthermore, some older New Zealanders engaged out of necessity with the difference personified at the hospital or medical clinic, such as one older New Zealander who asked me, when we were discussing situations like that, "What choice do I have?"

Each individual encounter between an older New Zealander and a migrant will vary and each individual older New Zealander may shift in and out of openness. For anyone, including older New Zealanders, one encounter with difference may very well be tactical or de facto or be a routine performance of politeness while the next might be a conscious, moral decision to engage with "the Other" respectfully and as an equal. Often, intentions and meaning will shift with the context, and over time. A "conscious cosmopolitanism" is neither foreclosed nor a guaranteed outcome of contact (Nowicka and Rovisco 2009a, 7; Glick-Shiller and Irving 2015). The older people in this research demonstrate that constant meaningful engagement with difference may not be possible in today's urban environment where we are "continuously exposed to and immersed in diverse cultural experiences mostly without thinking, reflecting or feeling the need to engage" (Skrbis and Woodward 2013, 99). For older New Zealanders, for whom contact with diversity may be new and their current diverse surroundings may be so very different from the ones they grew up in, it may be particularly true that cosmopolitanism is not a fixed state but is continually being generated and reworked through social interactions. They demonstrate the reality that cosmopolitans come from many kinds of social positions and situations.

The older New Zealanders in this research also show us that in spite of great misgivings about larger, macro issues (in this case those associated with rapid population diversification) engendering cosmopolitan ideals in many daily interactions is still possible, and indeed is happening. In doing so, these older New Zealanders problematize the "paradoxical gap" that Valentine has warned us about (Valentine 2008, 325). Valentine is particularly skeptical of a discrepancy between people's celebrations of tolerance compared with their actions of indifference or even bigotry. She warned that this discrepancy is at best an "uncomfortable" and "paradoxical gap" between people's proclaimed values in relation to their actions (Valentine 2008, 335, 325). People may adhere to cosmopolitan ideals in theory, she said, while not taking any action accordingly in practice. Older New Zealanders, however, rather than speaking in cosmopolitan overtones and doing nothing to action their own words, are often doing the opposite: they are speaking openly about their resistance to and concerns about an "excess of alterity" (Grillo 2010, 20) while engaging in cosmopolitan micro interactions, recognizing the humanity in the immigrant next to them. Myers (2007) argued that everyday residents of quickly changing nations should be able to ask difficult questions without being labeled racists, questions such as, Will admitting so many immigrants endanger our country as we know it? (Myers 2007). Older New Zealand-ers, especially given the amount of change they have seen, are perhaps entitled to long for a traditional Kiwi roast while fretting about immigration's impact on increasing social inequalities and the need to lock their doors these days. They can do and feel these things all while giving baked goods to the new Jordanian neighbor or welcoming a Taiwanese mother into their singing group.

These older New Zealanders remind us that we must account for the fact that in practice humans find themselves struggling with conflicting demands and navi-gating settings that are local microcosms of a complex world. Thus, this research with older New Zealanders supports the call for a critical cosmopolitanism that recognizes that "it's complicated," that personal, historical, and geographical con-texts are not irrelevant and that openness is not a permanent state of being nor sustainable as a sole mode of sociality (Stacey 2015; Glick-Shiller and Irving 2015). A critical view of cosmopolitanism is being increasingly employed by some to "signal a rejection of the universalizing narratives of cosmopolitanism" and instead recognize human openness as socially situated, processual, and aspirational (Glick-Shiller and Irving 2015, 5). This stance allows for uncertainty to coexist with shared understanding while also recognizing the always-present and impor-tant role of context. A critical cosmopolitanism, then, is not just about belonging to the world, but belonging to it in a particular way and accounting for the com-plex contexts of individual lives. A critical cosmopolitanism recognizes the social processes and moral shifts that are necessary for moments of mutual recognition and relationality to emerge (Glick-Shiller and Irving 2015). These older New Zea-landers show us that cosmopolitanism can emerge within and alongside internal contradictions and complex contextual influence.

Rapport wrote that in spite of cosmopolitanism's flaws, "a valid project remains" as does his continued imagining of cosmopolitanism insights "emanci-pating the individual . . . from symbols and structures that collectivize, homog-enize and totalize" (Rapport 2012, 13–14). Similarly, Glick-Schiller and Irving wrote that in spite of cosmopolitanism's "baggage" (including its utopianism), and though many of its proponents share a sense of "uncertainty, uneasiness and ambivalence," the concept continually resurfaces and ultimately endures (Glick-Shiller and Irving 2015, 8). We can salvage a vision of cosmopolitanism as unten-able and utopian by pluralizing it (Prakash 2015). Ramadan (2015) recently reminded us of Diogenes's claim that human virtue and morality are better revealed in someone's everyday actions than in abstract terms or philosophical theory. Cosmopolitanism, then, is "steeped in the ordinariness of human life" (Skrbis and Woodward 2013, 107). If we are to do as Ramadan suggested and apply and judge any theory, including cosmopolitanism, in terms of our lived experience of daily life, including the tensions that lie within it, then it is these older New Zealanders' mundane, micro actions that clearly exhibit the ideals of cosmopolitanism.

It is migrants that are typically assumed to be cosmopolitan, through their global movement and contact with difference based on mobility. Migrants have developed a cultural or cosmopolitan competence (Vertovec 2009) or a cosmopolitan "toolkit" (Glick-Shiller and Irving 2015, 2) that they bring on their journey as they migrate from one place and/or culture to another. But older people, like these older New Zealanders, remind us that many of those who have "stayed still" now require a cosmopolitan toolkit as they move through their daily lifeworlds. Many of the older people in this research have acquired this cosmopolitan toolkit "at home" and in spite of their "mixed feelings," namely, their macro level reservations about the diversity that now characterizes parts of their country. Sometimes their cosmopolitanism may be de facto, but this does not negate a cosmopolitan consciousness at other times and genuine enactments of Appiah's (2006) "kindness to strangers." Of course, small encounters, or even more sustained ones, don't always or automatically constitute deep engagement with cosmopolitanism; however, underestimating acts of everyday encounters, as we risk doing by assigning them labels such as "mundane" or "banal," unnecessarily demotes their possibilities and potential. Demoting the impact of everyday cosmopolitanism obscures the impact and weight these interactions might have on people's lives (Skrbis and Woodward 2013). As we heard from the immigrants in chapters 6 and 7, even fleeting positive interactions with older New Zealanders unfolded to help migrants in a variety of significant practical and emotional ways. If the immigrants are the measure of these "mundane" encounters with older New Zealanders, they count these interactions with older people as appreciated, significant, and even formative moments true to the nature of cosmopolitanism.

A COSMOPOLITAN CADENCE

Nearing the end of this book, it seems appropriate to once again engage with the concept of time and its relevance to aging. Time "is at the very root of what makes us human" (Adam 2006, 119); it is pervasive, an "inescapable dimension of all aspects of social experience and practice" (Munn 1992, 93). Time is therefore central to older peoples' experiences of increasing diversity. Many older people have witnessed substantial sociocultural change; thus, it is time's passage on a grand scale that is evident, over decades and through a lifetime. Chapters 1 and 4 both spoke to the degree of change that older New Zealanders in this research readily described witnessing and experiencing in their lifetimes, including the change at the heart of this book—sociocultural change related to immigration and increasing diversity. Older New Zealanders' perspectives of change over time, often relayed through "then and now" comparisons give form to what can otherwise be time's omnipresent but invisible force.

Time has also emerged in this research as a rhythm of daily life that shaped some interactions between the older New Zealanders and migrants. Chapters 6 and 7 engaged with time in this sense of daily routines and a pace of moving through everyday life. It is this second aspect of time that I engage with again here, further developing the finding that older people sometimes have a slower, less distracted pace or a cadence that facilitates cosmopolitan interactions with the immigrant stranger.

In chapter 6, immigrants identified older New Zealanders as those who allowed them time to translate in their heads or who took the time to explain certain small but important social norms or historical contexts. One immigrant explained that older "host parents" were more friendly and invested than younger or middle-aged ones who were busy with their own children, their jobs, and/or their own aging parents. As described in chapter 6, immigrants had many examples of older New Zealanders pausing for a chat in the supermarket or helping them with their university assignments. In chapter 7, I cited my own ample observations of older people doing seemingly small things to aid immigrants in emotional or practical ways, which I called "mentoring 'Kiwiness.'" It was here that I first suggested it was older people's cadence, their free time and unhurried, less distracted pace of daily life, that allowed them to converse with immigrants at a slower pace, to act as protectors by offering advice about bad businesses or by supporting an immigrant who had been subjected to racial slurs recently. It was these older New Zealanders' cadence that allowed them to help an immigrant obtain firewood for home heating or get a food handler's certificate required for a job. It was one older New Zealanders' cadence that prompted her to take the time in a corner shop to explain, to a confused immigrant owner, a euphemism that the previous customer had used while rushing out the door.

Older New Zealanders may be more removed from what Adam (2006) called "clock time," or a time that has become independent of natural processes and applicable anytime, anywhere. It is invariable, standardized, quantified, and universalized. In many cases, clock time has become synonymous with "machine-time." Living systems, she argued, must adapt to machine time these days and the cumulative effects of machine time requirements have begun to register on both health and sustainability (Adam 2006). Within machine time, and systems that abide by it, elderly are undervalued (along with children, the unemployed, carers, and subsistence farmers). Adam argued that machine time is closely associated with money; when time is money, faster is better. Here, she mentioned the important role of information and communication technologies (ICTs), which keep so many of us linked into the processes of machine time, all the time. ICTs, she said, compress time into constant instantaneity and simultaneity, leaving many of us "everywhere at once and nowhere in particular" as we move through daily life (Adam 2006, 124).

Perhaps due to their greater distance from this contemporary commodification of time (Munn 1992) and the pressures of wage labor society (due in part to being fully or semiretired), the older New Zealanders in this study largely sat outside this dominant paradigm of machine time. Perhaps because of this peripheral status in relation to machine time, and perhaps simply because older New Zealanders came of age in an era that predated ICTs, far fewer older New Zealanders seemed to be preoccupied with their portable screens or with using ear phones in public. At different points in this thesis, a few older New Zealanders talked about how they considered that they were far less preoccupied with ICTs than younger New Zealanders (though a few were certainly very technically savvy). As previously mentioned, Patty (Dunedin, sixty-seven) said she has really noticed how cell phones and laptops mean people take work home and on vacation; Iris described how television and cell phones have made younger people live their lives in disjointed little "soundbites." Rather than being "everywhere and nowhere," older people might just be more "here."

The older New Zealanders in this study thus exemplified an exception to Amin's (2002) characterization of urban contact as a matter of "parallel lives" and transitory moments that do not even count as encounters (Amin 2002, 326). For example, less "controlled" by machine time, as Adam would say, many of the older New Zealanders featured here were more likely to have and to take the time to chat with a stranger, have a cup of tea with a neighbor, linger after church. They were less likely to be rushing or multitasking and more likely to strike up a conversation while waiting in a queue or, as witnessed several times in the course of this fieldwork, while riding on a public bus. More often removed from the pressures of raising a family or propelling a career, older New Zealanders often had and spent more time than their children or grandchildren attending to strangers, chatting with a passerby or conversing with a taxi driver (perhaps rather than interacting with a smart phone!). As the immigrants in this research further explained and verified, some older New Zealanders were far more approachable than their younger counterparts because they often had, and offered, more time.

Though the purpose of this book has been to focus on the experiences of older New Zealanders, in chapter 6 I explained that sometimes immigrants, especially migrant women with whom I conversed, were also not as fully entrenched in the height of familial and professional demands on their time as other contemporary urban dwellers can be. As some New Zealand research has suggested (Longhurst, Johnston, and Ho 2009; Aye and Guerin 2001) and as Vonnie, the coordinator of a Dunedin migrant settlement service said in chapter 6, migrant women can often experience social isolation. In the course of this research, I observed that this sometimes translated into migrant women both having more time for, and sometimes actively seeking out, some community activities and contact. This was the case, for example, for Diah (Indonesian immigrant) who was in Dunedin to support and accompany her husband while he undertook four years' worth of postgraduate study. With her limited English, and a young but school-aged child to tend to, Diah did not work in New Zealand. She described having far fewer commitments and engagements in her host country than in her home country. While it was older New Zealanders who hosted informal English language chat groups that migrants (such as Diah) attended, it was then migrants (such as the women in the Dunedin migrant women's group) who often provided "home visits" to the elderly through Age Concern, seeking a chance to make a local contribution. Time and again during the course of this research, the two categories of older New Zealanders and immigrants were seen to overlap—at church functions, community music groups, volunteer driven organizations, or simply as two visitors at the local botanical gardens with a bit of time to spare.

Older New Zealanders' cadence not only enabled moments of urban contact to be less parallel and more meaningful but also facilitated interaction with immigrants in what Amin (2002) would call "spaces of interdependence" or "micropublics" (Amin 2002, 969). These are something in between fleeting urban moments and more formalized spaces. These are the uniquely local spaces that have been mentioned throughout this thesis—workplaces, community centers, clubs, communal gardens, churches, and more—where people from different backgrounds come together with strangers in the name of a common activity or interest, allowing new patterns of social interaction to take place. Micropublics are settings where more meaningful (and sustained) contact and interactions might happen, where crucial acts of reconciling and overcoming ethnic cultural difference can take place (Amin 2002).

Amin placed micropublics in contrast with fleeting public spaces and encounters that, he claimed, are "not naturally serving of multicultural engagement" (Amin 2002, 967). He wrote of the limitations of public spaces to facilitate intercultural dialogue and described some urban settings as, in reality, being rather ambiguous and falling short of "inculcating interethnic understanding" (969). Relative to these fleeting spaces, Amin suggested it is instead micropublics that are "ideal sites for coming to terms with ethnic difference" because "prosaic negotiations are compulsory" (969). Micropublics are effective in placing people from different backgrounds into new settings where shared interest in a common activity "disrupts easy labelling of the stranger . . . and initiates new attachments" (970). When established as a local, bottom-up type of engagement rather than a prescribed, top-down arrangement (at a national or policy level) (Williamson 2016), micropublics constitute more than just sites of copresence but a chance to create a habit of practice where interchanges across difference are effective and lasting.

This book has presented evidence that is both in conflict and in agreement with Amin's (2002) above work. In conflict with Amin's work, this research has demonstrated the presence of cosmopolitan interactions in fleeting urban life. In the case of the older New Zealanders in this research, who often moved through daily life at a different cadence—slower, on the periphery of machine time and less influenced by ICTs—fleeting urban spaces can and do sometimes facilitate meaningful engagement across difference. As Ellen (Dunedin, age sixty-five) explained, she was the only person on her street without an automatic garage door opener. When she got out of her car to open her garage door manually, she typically chatted with the immigrant family next door. All the other younger New Zealand neighbors, she said, only drove in and out in a hurry.

In support of Amin's notions of micropublics as more effective spaces for sustained meaningful interaction, this research has demonstrated that this is indeed the case for older New Zealanders and immigrants in workplaces, schools, churches, clubs, community interest groups, and more. Often these meaningful and more sustained interactions across difference are facilitated again by the cadence of older New Zealanders and occasionally the similar cadence of some migrants, too. In this research, it was both migrants and older New Zealanders who spent some of their time as volunteers—for Greenpeace or the Stroke Foundation and more. It was both migrants and older New Zealanders who sat as classmates in arts and crafts courses or as club members in a music group. It was older New Zealanders and immigrants who sometimes lingered after "official" gathering times ended—one perhaps waiting for a taxi while the other looked for an opportunity to interact with a local. It was their overlapping cadences that brought them into what was often symbiotic contact with one another.

In spite of more and more evidence that cosmopolitanism often exists in ordinary, everyday encounters, the original legacy of a cosmopolitan as an elite social type (Noble 2009) means that qualities such as good education, extreme geographic mobility, and access to modern technologies are still often assumed to constitute cosmopolitanism. Businesspeople, diplomats, journalists, IT professionals, and frequent flyers typify much of what we associate with cosmopolitanism (Skrbis and Woodward 2013). This is in contrast to Eve (Dunedin, age ninety-six), who when asked if she got out much replied that in recent years she had developed "a policy of 'don't go.'" Such an image of an older person—who perhaps no longer drives, let alone flies, and may only go out to the corner shop, a medical appointment, or a local social engagement—is not the image conjured up in discussions of cosmopolitanism. And yet, uncovering the older New Zealanders in this research as unlikely cosmopolitans is exactly what I have aimed to do. If we embrace a critical cosmopolitanism, older New Zealanders, without ever needing to stray far from home, and with all of their substantial misgivings about immigration, personify cosmopolitan ideals in many of their daily interactions. They have, and take, the time to do so.

9 · CONCLUSIONS

This book opened with a broad narrative sounding around the globe—that older people are resistant to the diversity that globalization and migration have brought to their surroundings. We see this narrative through statistics whereby younger people in Organisation for Economic Co-operation and Development (OECD) countries, for example, are more favorable to immigration than older people (Heath and Richards 2018). We see this narrative in analysis and commentary around two of the defining political events of our time, Brexit and Trump's 2016 election, where older people and anti-immigration sentiments seemed to coexist and the desire "to bring back the 1950's" (Ball 2016) has now redirected global destiny. We see this narrative in movies, podcasts, comic strips, and YouTube clips: older people are often racist. We see it in media headlines that proclaim, "The data are in! Young people are definitely less racist than old people" (Kenny 2017).

This book has taken a much needed closer and more personalized look at how older people have experienced a changing world. This conclusion first places older people's experiences of aging amidst accelerated sociocultural change outside of any simplified views or ready-made paradigms of aging as "loss" or as "successful." This research feeds and supports the growing notion of aging in place where "place" is dynamic and ever-changing. Specifically, it has made a substantial and needed contribution to aging in place in cities impacted by global movement. When locating older people at the center of such settings of contemporary multiculturalism, aging in place can only be conceptualized as a process that involves continual change and adaptation.

Furthermore, these older New Zealanders have shown us that place not only shapes but is shaped by older people (Sharlach and Moore 2016; Andrews et al. 2007). I conclude this book by proposing that through fleeting micro moments, small encounters, and informal relationships—that would easily be missed by any scale of "activity" or collection of statistics—these older New Zealanders were subtle, hidden and unexpected "agents of social change" (Lamb 2009, 9).

CONTESTING POLARIZED VIEWS OF AGING

Polar opposites are often resorted to when viewing aging and the old - oscillations "between hope and fear, between negative stereotypes of old age and positive elixirs that promise . . . overcoming time and aging itself" (Moody 2009, 68). This research has purposely shied away from narrow reductions of "aging-as-loss" on the one hand or "successful aging" on the other. This exploration of older New Zealanders' contact with diversity and difference depicts something far more complex and nuanced than either of these polarized depictions. Instead, this research presents a view of aging that certainly includes loss but also adaptation, novelty, growth, and a view of older people, as I will argue in this conclusion, who are often (overlooked) contributors to modern societies rather than sitting outside of them, or worse, draining resources from them.

This research joins a growing body of contemporary anthropological studies that contests "the aura of inevitability and loss deeply associated with aging, particularly in Western societies" (Graham and Stephenson 2010a, ix). Early gerontological studies of aging formulated aging as a universal process of biological, psychological, and social decline. For example, as mentioned in chapter 2, disengagement theory proposed that normal aging is a mutual withdrawal between the aging person and others in the social system to which he or she belongs (Cumming 1963). Within this paradigm, the memberships of old age—kinship, friendships, perhaps church and other areas of socialization—are all assumed to be marked by a high level of agreement among members and many explicit common values with little deviation from a common viewpoint. Thus, as an older person disengages from a variety of roles, he or she is less likely to take on new roles (Cumming and Henry 1961). This view is in line with, and has perhaps fed, a commonly accepted notion of old age as a "sociocultural state in which significant changes are neither generated nor welcome" (Hazan 1984, 568). This research with older New Zealanders suggests, however, that in many contexts these days, the assumption of "sameness" in older people's social worlds is no longer accurate (if it ever was). Rather, neighborhoods, shops, medical clinics, churches, buses and more, are often, at the very least, peppered with difference and diversity and older people are engaging with these new social environments in ways that make sense to them.

Many constructions of time, particularly Western or industrialized constructions, have also placed aging on the trajectory of loss. When time is construed as linear and as a commodity—a left-to-right trajectory where "time is money" and productivity is measured accordingly—then aging is constrained to "loss" and "decline." Particularly in biomedicine and some areas of gerontology, a view of aging has too often aligned with a linear model of acquired losses, ultimately leading to the loss of life. Furthermore, aging is linked to loss and decline in a science and an economy that value "newness" (Graham and Stephenson 2010a, xii). In chapter 8, we saw this described in a slightly different manner as "machine time" (Adam 2006, 119). In machine time, in which time can be "saved" and time ultimately "runs out," aging is irreversible and the time of the elderly is undervalued (Stephenson 2010). This book has, instead, illuminated a different manifestation of time: a cadence offered by older people that facilitates interactions, kindness to strangers, and sometimes the creation of novel social roles.

This research on older New Zealanders refutes another negative rendition of aging in common discourse: the current, international rhetoric of "population aging," which is the latest manifestation of aging-as-problem. In New Zealand, the construct of aging as a demographic problem began with its colonization. After white settlers began to arrive in the new pioneer settler society, the sentiment that "older workers are less productive" began to take hold. At the same time, New Zealand's settler population was still overwhelmingly male—and unmarried. Older men with few resources and no family to care for them were considered a growing social threat. Older men were then cared for as those suffering from an "illness" rather than, perhaps, someone who just needed certain types of social or practical assistance. Since then, the state's response to aging has contributed to aging being defined as illness (Saville-Smith 1993). This rhetoric of aging as disease can have terrible repercussions for the elderly, who, as their numbers grow, are by inference "part of a contagion" (Stephenson 2010, 6). Now, discussion of the aging population in New Zealand, as elsewhere, presents the demographic phenomenon as a dire state of affairs and perpetuates the construction of older people as an economic and social problem.

On the other hand, the pendulum has swung far to the opposite extreme with discussions and paradigms of "successful aging" or "the third age." These movements strongly reject aging as a time of disengagement, withdrawal, and loss, and present later life instead as a fulfilling and involved time. However, anthropologists such as Lamb (2014) suggest that the "flourishing of scientific research and public discussion on how to age well" has led to a "moral and political obligation—to make our own aging successful" in the midst of neoliberal values and the panicked rhetoric of population aging (Lamb 2014, 41). The successful aging movement has been criticized for conflating ideas of health retention and vigor with success thereby merging successful aging far too easily with not aging at all (Stephenson 2010). As Andrews put it, creating the moral imperative to be the eighty-year-old on skis and not in a wheelchair, denies "the old of one of their most hard-earned resources: their age" (Andrews 1999, 301).

Lamb (2014) argued that a goal of aging successfully, of "declining to decline" sets people up for failure (Lamb 2014, 42). In speaking with her informants in Boston, Lamb wrote that she certainly began to see the appeal of lifelong vitality and longevity. Yet she argued that the "popular and scientific model of successful aging would be enhanced—more productive, helpful, realistic and perhaps even inspiring—if it were to incorporate the realities of change, decline and mortality"

(Lamb 2014, 49). Lamb argued for recognizing "meaningful decline" as a valid dimension of aging, not incompatible with a vibrant later life (Lamb 2014, 48). Others have argued that an undervalued aspect of so-called successful aging is adaptation—adaptation to some decline and to other changing personal and social circumstances (Moody 2009; Rodriguez-Galan 2013; Counts and Counter 2001). Lamb's (2014) notion of meaningful decline and other current studies of aging as adaptation create a space for older people to remain relatively stationary, or "moored," yet actively adapting to changing circumstances (in this case socio-cultural change) in varying, meaningful ways.

An older person's participation in life and society might very well include significant loss and might not look like the "successful aging" poster of an eighty-year-old on skis. But it might mean chatting to a new migrant at church or inviting another to join your music group. It might mean engaging beyond "the call of duty," so to speak, when a young Tongan boy knocks on your door while doing a school project about the types of gardens in the neighborhood—giving him a tour of your garden and a cup of tea and a good deal of your time. It might mean then accepting the invitation when that boy's family asks you to a potluck bar-beque at their house. These micro interactions with older New Zealanders were of substantial value to the immigrants on the other side of these interactions and I propose are also of benefit to the multicultural societies in which they live. Yet these micro interactions can be all-together missed amidst "deeply rooted" assumptions of the old as "inflexible and resistant to change" (Hazan 2000, 15), perceptions of aging as loss, or the rhetoric of the old as a collective liability.

OLDER PEOPLE AGING IN PLACE:
MOORINGS IN THE SEAS OF CHANGE

As a project positioned intellectually at the intersections of aging and diversity, this research has recognized older people as members of diverse, contemporary, multicultural settings and now suggests that as they age in place, they are like "mooring posts"[1] as the tide of change comes in around them. In many con-temporary settings in this "age of migration," even staying still involves experi-encing great change and new contact with difference. As life expectancies increase, a greater extent of change may be experienced within a single life span. Even people remaining in familiar places find the nature of their relationship to the place may be "ineluctably changed" and the "illusion of a natural and essential connection between the place and the culture broken" (Gupta and Ferguson 1992, 10). While remaining tethered through time to primarily one locale, many older people now live in a very different country than the one of their memories. The older New Zealanders in this research remind us that change and the need for adaptation are not avoided by aging in place.

The older New Zealanders in this research fit definitions of aging in place. Barret, Hale, and Gauld (2011) define aging in place as the support to remain living in one's long-term family home. Sometimes aging in place is defined more broadly as remaining living in the community with some level of independence rather than in residential care (Davey et al. 2004). Schofield et al. (2006), emphasize a "choice" element to aging in place, defining it as "promoting the ability of older people to remain living in the residences and communities of their choice" (Schofield et al. 2006, 275). Most of the older New Zealanders in this research were still in their own long-term, family homes, some were in more recently acquired homes or flats, and two were in a retirement community but living completely independently. All were in the same areas where they had lived for decades. With one possible exception, all could be described as living in the housing situation of their own choosing. None were in assisted living or residential care. Some had varying degrees and types of assistance to continue to live in their current situations.

Policy-based aging in place discussions frequently focus explicitly on older people remaining within their own homes and creating the means to do so through practical measures. Discussions of this sort often include things like the nature of in-home personal and medical assistance and beneficial physical adaptations such as railings along stairwells and easy-to-turn taps. Claims of people's preference to age in place abound with policymakers and health-care providers often favoring aging in place's cost-saving measures compared to institutional care (Wiles et al. 2012).

Social scientists, however, are considering the more complex personal experiences of remaining in one's own home—for example, the pitfalls of one's home becoming a site of care (Barret, Hale, and Gauld 2011). Furthermore, aging in place is increasingly being recognized as much more than a maintained presence in one's home but as a complex, ambiguous process. This research with older New Zealanders highlights the importance of viewing aging in place as a process—a continual negotiation with identity, social, political, cultural, and personal change (Wiles et al. 2012; Andrews et al. 2007). These older New Zealanders have shown us that aging in place is to age among a web of connections to neighborhood, community, and even nation. The experience of aging in place does not stop at the property line; a home setting operates at both a personal and structural level (Wiles et al. 2012), with national and even global circumstances permeating individual lives.

When an older person's social and community surroundings are accounted for while aging in place, experiences of environmental change cannot be denied. More research is needed on aging in place in cities (Phillipson and Scharf 2005) and these older New Zealanders provided a needed window into aging in cities shaped by global movement. Even for those who do not move, who stay and are aging in place, change and novelty related to world migration trends and local manifestations of multiculturalism both permeate the so-called border of the private dwelling and abound in the broader community.

Even if we assume the narrowest view of aging in place and speak only of an older person's physical dwelling, the new diversity in many areas still crosses the threshold of the older person's doorstep and enters their private space—be it in the form of a home caregiver from the Philippines, Samoa, or Nigeria, or the volunteer home-visitor from Malaysia or Korea who stops by to have a chat, or the neighbor's Iraqi music wafting in through the windows, or the Chinese meal brought home from the ubiquitous takeout shops. Furthermore, if we broaden our definition of aging in place to include many aspects of community (as older people themselves do [Wiles et al. 2012]), then the changes and difference that older people now encounter multiplies tenfold to include all the "foreigners" on the buses, the multiple languages now offered at the church service, the changing restaurants and shops, the multitude of ethnicities manifested in the doctors and nurses encountered at the medical clinic or in the staff at the post shop. Aging in place may mean much stays familiar for an older person, especially when compared to shifting to a totally new location and situation (such as a rest home near family or a retirement community abroad). However, with this research I propose that a view of older people as "moorings" reminds us that their surroundings are far from static and that change and difference flows around even that which stays still.

LIABILITY . . . OR ASSET?

It takes some sifting through the rhetoric of the old as intolerant and resistant to change to find a different, hidden narrative. When you do, you find stories that zero in on older people, dotted around the world, embracing difference at the individual level. Like the retired French couple who have offered up their spare room to refugees and have had a young Sudanese man with them for a year and a half. Like a few of the older New Zealanders in this research, the older French couple also referenced their adult children (who, if headlines are to be believed, might be less racist based solely on their younger age) not being keen on their parents taking in refugees (Baron 2018). In locating our hidden narrative of older people positively engaging with difference, we can also land at a monastery in Arizona where retirees, some "wearing hearing aides, some who appeared to have suffered strokes and others who had endured hip replacements" are welcoming migrants released from border detention (Jordan 2019). Here, retired physicians offer a walk-in clinic and other older volunteers sort donated clothes, serve chicken soup, or offer art activities to children.

In Ottawa, a seventy-three-year-old retired civil servant who chairs a refugee sponsorship group explains that a number of retired volunteers are "driving refugee families to the dentist . . . instead of playing golf" (Dixon 2016). Across the

Atlantic in Germany, refugee organizations are seeing an increase in older volunteers, like sixty-seven-year-old Georg who has taken in a sixteen-year-old Syrian refugee boy (Tomkiw 2016). And back around the world closer to the site of this book, a group old older people in Melbourne, Australia, dubbed "the Fiesties," have gone out of their way to make it known that the refugees who are being housed in the spare units of their retirement community are welcome (Donovan 2018; Welcome to Eltham 2016). In these around-the-world examples of older people engaging with a diverse array of migrants, like this book, many of them talk about the precious commodity that older people sometimes possess: time. Some agencies view retirees as a largely untapped resource and are seeking out retirees to volunteer. One refugee agency coordinator in Germany explained that along with their time, older volunteers often bring a valuable patience to their interactions with refugees (Tomkiw 2016). In societies "that often marginalize seniors' experiences," some older people get a valuable sense of fulfilment from being able to offer their time (Macaraeg 2018). Such is the case for a ninety-three-year-old woman in Memphis: when she moved into a retirement community and gave up her car, she thought her life of volunteering and activism was behind her. At her retirement community, however, she and other older residents now run an English Second Language group with the expressed intent of helping eleven refugees pass their naturalization test (Macaraeg 2018).

These international examples and the older New Zealanders in this research sometimes made a point of welcoming strangers in formalized ways—through church programs, settlement services, or volunteer agencies. In addition, facilitated by urban ethnographic methods, the value of this New Zealand research is in revealing that older people often offered informal, micro gestures of hospitality, too. They did this through their daily interactions, sometimes even unknowingly: the passing conversations on the bus, the chats after church, the gardening help at the neighbor's place. These more fleeting, hospitable interactions with migrant strangers were facilitated by their time and their cadence—a slower pace of living and a less fractured presence.

Without a doubt, the older New Zealanders in this research had complicated, mixed feelings about immigration and the changes that diversity has brought to their daily surroundings. This includes real fears and significant loss, such as a diminishing sense of community, a fading feeling of familiarity, a disappearing assumption of safety, a vanishing guarantee of access to resources. Yet some of the immigrants who encountered them found older New Zealanders to be open, approachable, and hospitable—central tenants of cosmopolitanism. Some older New Zealanders even demonstrated that they were taking on a new role in their new surroundings, by sharing bits of history, explaining social norms, or providing practical assistance to a newcomer.

Over fifty years ago, one of the original authors of disengagement theory argued that older people must find or be given roles "that young people cannot fill" (Cumming 1963, 30) to avoid a harmful degree of disengagement. This research proposes that it is specifically older people that are the "mooring posts" as they age in place and the tides of change and waves of mobile people flow in around them. It is often older people who have a slower, less distracted pace of life that facilitates cosmopolitan interactions with newcomers representing difference and diversity. When we step outside a notion of linear time, where aging is constrained to loss and even "wasted time," to instead an "unhurried experience of living" then "a greater veneration of old persons" arises (Stephenson 2010, 14). In this New Zealand–based research, and echoed anecdotally in places as varied as Memphis to Melbourne, it is older people's unhurried cadence that often enables the subtle but valuable interactions with stranger-migrants, interactions that exemplify cosmopolitan ideals of recognizing and tending to the humanity of "the Other." Engaging with immigrants through fleeting chats, longer relationships, and sometimes the informal role of "mentor of 'Kiwiness,'" moored older New Zealanders are already filling a role only they can fill: micro agents of social change and adaptation in multicultural settings. If integration of immigrants or a degree of cohesion, or both, is essential for the success of today's growing sites of multiculturalism, perhaps older people are not social or economic liabilities but rather are an unexpected resource, a hidden but significant asset.

ACKNOWLEDGMENTS

I would like to thank all of the participants in this research—the older New Zealanders and immigrants who spoke with me either in passing conversations or in formalized interviews. Thank you for giving a stranger the gift of some of your time and your thoughts.

Doing a PhD is a process that affects every aspect of one's life for years. I thank my husband for his unwavering support and I thank the three beautiful children who entered this world during this process, giving me perspective, humility, and time-out for blowing bubbles. I thank my mom, as always, for instilling in me a love and appreciation of learning and for giving me wings. All of my family and friends played a part in supporting this endeavor in too many ways to list here. I am lucky.

I have been extremely grateful for the University of Otago Doctoral Scholarship and specifically the Social Anthropology Programme, which was my academic home for the majority of this process. To Dr. Cyril Schäfer, thank you for your kind, genuine encouragement, the chocolates on your office table, and the chats about balancing serious medical conditions with academia. You are sorely missed. Finally, to Professor Ruth Fitzgerald, without whom neither this research nor my professional achievements to date would exist—thank you for somehow simultaneously offering attentive guidance along with autonomy and trust. You continue to be a true mentor well beyond the confines of official supervision and I am so grateful.

Thank you to the anonymous reviewers of my thesis and of this manuscript whose feedback resulted in improving this text. Many thanks to Sarah Lamb for the opportunity and support to publish in this series. And thank you to Jasper Chang at Rutgers University Press and all who walked me through the many details of publication.

NOTES

1. AGING IN TIMES OF GREAT CHANGE

1. https://i.pinimg.com/originals/09/16/c4/0916c4bdc26ba31db5a6dce2f220b71e.jpg.
2. This research was approved by the University of Otago Ethics Committee, approval number 11/088.
3. The italicization of words in Te Reo Māori follows the general academic style to italicize non-English words. I recognize, however, that Te Reo Māori is the indigenous language of Aotearoa New Zealand and one of the country's three official languages and therefore is not a foreign language in the Aotearoa New Zealand context.

4. "THEN AND NOW": NARRATIVES OF CHANGE

1. A short video has been created to illustrate the degree of neighborhood change Leonard and Ann have seen. The video features their voices as they shared memories of what their area of Auckland used to be like. Their voices overlay images and video footage of the same area as I saw it in 2012. See https://youtu.be/P2XewJPU1L0.
2. "Dairies" are small corner convenience shops.

5. OLDER NEW ZEALANDERS' IMMIGRATION-RELATED CONCERNS

1. See, for example, *Border Patrol*, http://tvnz.co.nz/border-patrol/index-group-5071690, and *The Inspectors*, http://tvnz.co.nz/the-inspectors/index-group-5764378, accessed 25 March 2016.
2. See the televised report June is referring to here, "New Zealand Baby Formula Nabbed by 3rd Party Exporters," Campbell Live Newshub, 17 July 2010, http://www.newshub.co.nz/tvshows/campbelllive/nz-baby-formula-nabbed-by-3rd-party-exporters-2012071717#axzz42XtadhhI, accessed 25 March 2016.
3. See "Chinese Police Alerted over Suitcase Murder," *New Zealand Herald*, 21 April 2006, http://www.nzherald.co.nz/nz/news/article.cfm?c_id=1&objectid=10378224, accessed 25 March 2016.
4. See Geoff Cumming, "Racial Melting Pot an 'Explosive' Brew," *New Zealand Herald*, 19 January 2002, http://www.nzherald.co.nz/nz/news/article.cfm?c_id=1&objectid=786966, accessed 25 March 2016.
5. It is imperative to note that domestic violence actually occurs at a high rate in New Zealand. One in three ever-partnered New Zealand women report having experienced physical and/or sexual intimate partner violence in their lifetime. When psychological/emotional abuse is included, that number jumps to one in two (Fanslow and Robinson 2011). Twenty-nine percent of women and 9 percent of men report experiencing sexual assault in their lifetime (Mayhew and Reilly 2009). (See also New Zealand Family Violence Clearinghouse, Data Summaries, snapshots at: https://nzfvc.org.nz/our-work/data-summaries/snapshot accessed 2 May 2021.) The persistence of domestic violence in New Zealand and its chronic underreporting are reinforced by informal social sanctions against women who report domestic abuse (Giles and Adamson 2005).
6. See https://www.supergold.govt.nz/, accessed 25 March 2016.

7. For one example, see Kathy Marks, "Obese Migrant Told to Lose Weight before Making Move," 17 November 2007, http://www.independent.co.uk/news/uk/home-news/obese-migrant-told-to-lose-weight-before-making-move-400723.html, accessed 15 May 2016.

8. For two sample stories, see Ann Clarkson, "Hefty Fine for Blackmarket Crayfish, Paua Dealer," September 4, 2015, http://www.stuff.co.nz/national/crime/71753936/hefty-fine-for-blackmarket-crayfish-paua-dealer.html, accessed 25 March 2016, and Rodney Times, "Concerns for Shellfish," *Auckland Now*, 3 April 2014, http://www.stuff.co.nz/auckland/local-news/rodney-times/9896571/Concerns-for-shellfish, accessed 25 March 2016.

9. See the following stories: "Who Is Really Buying New Zealand?," May 2, 2012, http://www.stuff.co.nz/national/6368089/Who-is-really-buying-New-Zealand, and "Chinese Biggest Buyers of NZ Land in 2014," *New Zealand Herald*, 29 January 2015, http://www.nzherald.co.nz/business/news/article.cfm?c_id=3&objectid=11393727, accessed 25 March 2016.

10. See also Christopher Adams, "Crafar Dairy Farms Deal Finally Settled," *New Zealand Herald*, 1 December 2012, http://www.nzherald.co.nz/business/news/article.cfm?c_id=3&objectid=10851202, and "Chinese Buy More Farms—Peters," *Newshub*, 4 February 2014, http://www.3news.co.nz/politics/chinese-buy-more-farms—peters-2014020419#axzz3SFBGWKN8, accessed 25 March 2016.

6. A SURPRISE TWIST? OLDER NEW ZEALANDERS AS APPROACHABLE AND ACCEPTING

1. See New Zealand First's website at www.nzfirst.org.nz, accessed 5 April 2016.

2. See, for example, this image from New Zealand First's website, https://web.archive.org/web/20171105033021/http://www.nzfirst.org.nz/superannuation.

3. See "Racist Bus Rant Caught on Video," News Hub, 26 March 2015, http://www.newshub.co.nz/nznews/racist-bus-rant-caught-on-video-2015032612#axzz44QgSjSxb, accessed 5 April 2016.

4. Helen was very concerned about confidentiality and I have opted not to reveal her specific country of origin.

5. See, for example, Super Seniors, "Preventing Social Isolation," New Zealand Ministry of Social Development (2016), https://www.superseniors.msd.govt.nz/health-wellbeing/preventing-social-isolation/index.html, accessed 15 May 2016, and Age Concern New Zealand, "Key Information on Loneliness and Social Isolation" (2016), https://www.ageconcern.org.nz/ACNZ_Public/Loneliness_and_Social_Isolation_Research.aspx,accessed 15 May 2016.

7. MENTORING "KIWINESS"

1. See https://beatidykiwi.nz/.

2. Te Reo Māori, or the Māori language.

3. Ancestry, lineage, or genealogy.

4. The Kiwi Bloke is not a featured entry but is mentioned throughout *Te Ara: The New Zealand Encyclopedia* as the archetype of a strong, silent, independent, no-nonsense, hardworking man. See http://www.teara.govt.nz/en, accessed 21 March 2016.

5. No. 8 Wire is a particular gauge of fencing wire that has been "adapted for countless uses in New Zealand." It has become a symbol of Kiwi ingenuity and invention. See http://www.teara.govt.nz/en/inventions-patents-and-trademarks/page-1, accessed 25 March 2016.

9. CONCLUSIONS

1. In making this claim, I borrow and reinterpret Hannam, Sheller, and Urry's (2006) vision of "moorings" as "special, infrastructural and institutional moorings that configure and enable mobilities" (Hannam, Sheller, and Urry 2006).

REFERENCES

Adam, Barbara. 2006. "Time." *Theory, Culture & Society* 23 (2–3): 119–138.

Age Concern New Zealand. 2016. "Key Information on Loneliness and Social Isolation." Age Concern New Zealand. Accessed 10 January. https://www.ageconcern.org.nz/ACNZ_Public/Loneliness_and_Social_Isolation_Research.aspx.

Agence France Presse. 2011. "Multiculturalism Has Failed, Says French President." Agence France Presse, 11 February 2011.

Ahmed, Anya. 2015. *Retiring to Spain: Women's Narratives of Nostalgia, Belonging and Community*. Bristol, UK: Bristol University Press.

Allport, Gordon. 1954. *The Nature of Prejudice*. Reading, MA: Addison-Wesley.

Amin, Ash. 2002. "Ethnicity and the Multicultural City: Living with Diversity." *Environment and Planning A* 34 (6): 959–980.

Amit, Vered. 2000. "Introduction." In *Constructing the Field: Ethnographic Fieldwork in the Contemporary World*, edited by Vered Amit, 1–18. London: Routledge.

Andrews, Gavin J., Malcolm Cutchin, Kevin McCracken, David Phillips, and Janine Wiles. 2007. "Geographical Gerontology: The Constitution of a Discipline." *Social Science & Medicine* 65 (1): 151–168.

Andrews, Molly. 1999. "The Seductiveness of Agelessness." *Ageing & Society* 19 (3): 301–318.

———. 2009. "The Narrative Complexity of Successful Ageing." *International Journal of Sociology and Social Policy* 29 (1/2): 73–83.

Antonio, Jason G. 2019. "Immigrant Workers Sought to Replace Retirees and Fill Vacant Jobs." *Moose Jaw Today*. Accessed 8 March 2020. https://www.moosejawtoday.com/local-news/immigrant-workers-sought-to-replace-retirees-and-fill-vacant-jobs-1507896.

Appiah, Anthony. 2006. *Cosmopolitanism: Ethics in a World of Strangers*. New York: W.W. Norton.

Atchley, Robert. 2000. "A Continuity Theory of Normal Aging." In *Aging and Everyday Life*, edited by J. Gubrium and J. Holstein, 183–190. Hoboken: Blackwell.

Auckland Litter Prevention Steering Group. 2016. "Be a Tidy Kiwi." Accessed 21 April. http://www.beatidykiwi.nz/.

Aye, Alice, and Bernard Guerin. 2001. "Astronaut Families: A Review of Their Characteristics, Impact on Families and Implications for Practice in New Zealand." *New Zealand Journal of Psychology* 30 (1): 9–15.

Badkar, Juthika, Paul Callister, and Robert Didham. 2009. *Ageing New Zealand: The Growing Reliance on Migrant Caregivers*. Wellington: Institute of Policy Studies.

Badkar, Juthika, Paul Callister, Vasantha Krishnan, Robert Didham, and Richard Bedford. 2007. "Gender, Mobility and Migration into New Zealand: A Case Study of Asian Migration." *Social Policy Journal of New Zealand* 32: 126–154.

Ball, Molly. 2016. "Trump's Graying Army." *Atlantic Monthly*, 25 October 2016. https://www.theatlantic.com/politics/archive/2016/10/trumps-graying-army/505274/.

Baron, Clementine. 2018. "Retired French Couple Take Sudanese Refugee into Their Home." United Nations High Commissioner for Refugees. Accessed 8 March 2020. https://www.unhcr.org/news/stories/2018/6/5b179f3c4/retired-french-couple-sudanese-refugee-home.html.

Barret, Patrick, Beatrice Hale, and Robin Gauld. 2011. "Social Inclusion through Ageing-in-Place with Care?" *Ageing & Society* 32 (3): 1–18. doi: 10.1017/S0144686X11000341.

Bartley, Allen, and Paul Spoonley. 2005. "Constructing a Workable Multiculturalism in a Bicultural Society." In *Waitangi Revisited: Perspectives on the Treaty of Waitangi*, edited by Michael Belgrave, Merata Kawharu, and David Williams, 136–148. Auckland: Oxford University Press.

Barusch, Amanda Smith. 2008. *Love Stories of Later Life*. Oxford: Oxford University Press.

Baumann, Gerd. 1996. *Contesting Culture: Discourses of Identity in Multi-ethnic London*. Cambridge: Cambridge University Press.

BBC. 2018. "Brexit: Too Many Older Leave Voters Nostalgic for 'White' Britain, Says Cable." In *Politics*, 11 March 2018. https://www.bbc.com/news/uk-politics-43364331.

Beaglehole, Ann. 2013. *Refuge New Zealand: A Nation's Response to Refugees and Asylum Seekers*. Wellington: Otago Press.

Beausoleil, Emily. 2014. "Embodying an Ethics of Encounter." eSocSci Network, multi-campus e-conference, 10 April 2014.

Beck, Ulrich. 2002. "The Cosmopolitan Society and Its Enemies." *Theory, Culture & Society* 19 (1–2): 17–44.

Beck, Ulrich, and N. Sznaider. 2006. "Unpacking Cosmopolitanism for the Social Sciences: A Research Agenda." *British Journal of Sociology* 57 (1): 1–23.

Becker, Gay. 2003. "Meanings of Place and Displacement in Three Groups of Older Immigrants." *Journal of Aging Studies* 17: 129–149.

Bedford, Richard, and Elsie Ho. 2006. "Immigration Futures: New Zealand in a Global Context." *New Zealand Population Review* 32 (2): 49–63.

Belich, James. 2001. *Paradise Reforged: A History of the New Zealanders from the 1880s to the Year 2000*. Auckland: Penguin Press.

Bell, Claudia. 1993. *Rural Way of Life in New Zealand: Myths to Live By*. Auckland: University of Auckland.

———. 1996. *Inventing New Zealand: Everyday Myths of Pakeha Identity*. Auckland: Penguin Books.

———. 2008. "100% Pure New Zealand: Branding for Backpackers." *Journal of Vacation Marketing* 14 (4): 345–355.

Bell, David. 2016. "Plenary Session." British Society for Gerontology Annual Conference, Stirling, 6 July 2016.

Blatterer, Harry, Pauline Johnson, and Maria Markus. 2010. "Introduction." In *Modern Privacy: Shifting Boundaries, New Forms*, edited by Harry Blatterer, Pauline Johnson, and Maria Markus, 1–6. Basingstoke: Palgrave Macmillan.

Blinder, Scott, and Lindsay Richards. 2020. "UK Public Opinion toward Immigration: Overall Attitudes and Level of Concern." In *Migration Observatory Briefing*. Oxford: Migration Observatory.

Bolton, Margaret. 2012. *Loneliness: The State We're In: A Report of Evidence Compiled for the Campaign to End Loneliness*. Oxon: Age UK Oxfordshire.

Bönisch-Brednich, Brigitte. 2002a. *Keeping a Low Profile: An Oral History of German Immigration to New Zealand*. Wellington: Victoria University Press.

———. 2002b. "Migration and Narration." *An Electronic Journal of Folklore* 20 (May 2002). http://www.folklore.ee/folklore/vol20/brednich.pdf.

———. 2008. "Watching the Kiwis: New Zealanders' Rules of Social Interaction." *Journal of New Zealand Studies*, nos. 6/7 (October): 3–15.

Bourgeault, Ivy Lynn, Jelena Atanackovic, Ahmed Rashid, and Rishma Parpia. 2010. "Relations between Immigrant Care Workers and Older Persons in Home and Long-Term Care." *Canadian Journal on Aging* 29 (1): 109–118.

Brettell, Caroline. 2000. "Theorizing Migration in Anthropology: The Social Construction of Networks, Identities, Communities and Globalscapes." In *Migration Theory: Talking across Disciplines*, edited by Caroline Brettell and James Hollifield, 97–135. New York: Routledge.

———. 2003. *Anthropology and Migration: Essays on Transnationalism, Ethnicity and Identity.* Walnut Creek: AltaMira Press.

Brooking, Tom, and Roberto Rabel. 1995. "Neither British nor Polynesian: A Brief History of New Zealand's Other Immigrants." In *Immigration and National Identity in New Zealand: One People, Two Peoples, Many Peoples?*, edited by Stuart Greif, 23–49. Palmerson North: Dunmore Press.

Buffel, Tine, Chris Phillipson, and Thomas Scharf. 2013. "Experiences of Neighbourhood Exclusion and Inclusion among Older People Living in Deprived Inner-City Areas in Belgium and England." Special issue, *Ageing & Society* 33: 89–109. doi: doi:10.1017/S0144686 X12000542.

Burns, Allan. 1993. *Maya in Exile*. Philadelphia: Temple University Press.

Caldwell, Melissa. 2010. "Moscow Encounters: Ethnography in a Global Urban Village." In *Urban Life: Readings in Anthropology of the City*, edited by George Gmelch, Robert Kemper, and Walter Zenner, 55–72. Long Grove, IL: Westgate.

Callister, Paul. 2004. "Seeking an Ethnic Identity: Is 'New Zealander' a Valid Ethnic Category?" *New Zealand Population Review* 30 (1–2): 5–22.

Campbell, Alexia Fernandez. 2018. "Why Baby Boomers Need Immigrants to Fund Their Retirement, in 2 charts." *Vox Media*, 23 October 2018. https://www.vox.com/2018/8/1/17561014/immigration-social-security.

———. 2019. "Want to Save Social Security? Let in More Immigrants." *Vox Media*, 24 April 2019. https://www.vox.com/2019/4/24/18514306/social-security-immigration.

Candea, Matei, Jo Cook, Catherine Trundle, and Thomas Yarrow. 2015. "Introduction: Reconsidering Detachment." In *Detachment: Essays on the Limits of Relational Thinking*, edited by Thomas Yarrow, Matei Candea, Catherine Trundle, and Jo Cook, 1–34. Manchester: Manchester University Press.

Cassidy, John. 2018. "Why the United States Needs More Immigrants." *New Yorker*, 22 June 2018.

Castillo, Jose Luis Alvarez, Alfredo Jimenez Equizabal, Carmen Palmero Camara, and Hugo Gonzalez Gonzalez. 2014. "The Fight against Prejudice in Older Adults: Perspective Taking Effectiveness." *Revista Latinoamericana de Psicologia* 46 (3): 137–147.

Castles, Stephen, and Mark Miller. 2009. *The Age of Migration: International Population Movements in the Modern World*. 4th ed. New York: Guilford Press.

Chase, Susan. 2002. "Narrative Inquiry: Multiple Lenses, Approaches, Voices." In *Handbook of Qualitative Research*, edited by Norman Denzin and Yvonna Lincoln, 651–679. Thousand Oaks: Sage.

Chaudhury, Habib, and Graham D. Rowles. 2005. "Between the Shores of Recollection and Imagination: Self, Aging and Home." In *Home and Identity in Later Life: International Perspectives*, edited by Habib Chaudhury and Graham D. Rowles, 3–18. New York: Springer.

Cheah, Pheng. 2006. "Cosmopolitanism." *Theory, Culture & Society* 23 (2–3): 486–496.

Chu, Ben. 2016. "Brexit Is One More Example of the Older Generation Financially Bankrupting the Young." *Independent*, 28 June 2016. https://www.independent.co.uk/voices/brexit-eu-referendum-financial-economic-impact-older-generation-bankrupting-young-a7107666.html.

Clark, William. 2007. "Assimilation, Multiculturalism and the Challenge of Marginalized Groups." California Center for Population Research On-Line Working Paper Series.

Coddington, Debrah. 2006. "Asian Angst: Is It Time to Send Some Back?" *North & South Magazine*, December 2006, 38–47.

Cohen, Robert. 1978. "Ethnicity: Problem and Focus in Anthropology." *Annual Review of Anthropology* 7: 379–403.

Coleman, David. 2006. "Population Ageing: An Unavoidable Future." In *The Welfare State Reader*, edited by Christopher Pierson and Francis Castles, 298–308. Cambridge: Polity Press.

Cornwall, J., and Judith Davey. 2004. "Impact of Population Ageing in New Zealand on the Demand for Health and Disability Support Services and Workforce Implications." Wellington: Ministry of Health.

Counts, Dorothy Ayers, and David Counter. 2001. "Over the Next Hill." 2nd ed. Peterborough, Ontario: Broadview Press.

Cumming, Elaine. 1963. "Further Thoughts on the Theory of Disengagement." *International Social Sciences Journal* 15: 377–393.

Cumming, Elaine, and W. E. Henry. 1961. *Growing Old*. New York: Basic Books.

D'Alisera, JoAnn. 2004. *An Imagined Geography: Sierra Leonean Muslims in America*. Philadelphia: University of Pennsylvania Press.

Danely, Jason, and Caitrin Lynch. 2013. "Transitions and Transformations: Paradigms, Perspectives and Possibilities." In *Transitions and Transformations: Cultural Perspectives on Aging and the Life Course*, edited by Caitrin Lynch and Jason Danely, 1–20. New York: Berghahn Books.

Davey, Judith, G. Nana, V. de Joux, and M. Arcus. 2004. *Accommodation Options for Older People in Aotearoa/New Zealand*. Wellington: New Zealand Institute for Research on Ageing/ Business and Economic Research.

Demuth, Andreas. 2000. "Some Conceptual Thoughts on Migration Research." In *Theoretical and Methodological Issues in Migration Research*, edited by Biko Agozino, 21–57. Hants: Ashgate.

Diversity and Contact (DivCon). 2015. "Diversity and Contact (DivCon)." Max Planck Institute for the Study of Religious and Ethnic Diversity. Accessed 10 March. https://www.mmg.mpg.de/349368/diversity-and-contact.

Dixon, Guy. 2016. "Retirees Roll up Their Sleeves to Help Refugees." *Globe and Mail*, 14 October 2016.

Donnella, Leah. 2017. "Will Racism End When Old Bigots Die?" *Code Switch*, 24 January 2017. https://www.npr.org/sections/codeswitch/2017/01/14/505266448/will-racism-end-when-old-bigots-die.

Donovan, Samantha. 2018. "Refugees Welcomed by Retirees in Eltham." ABC Radio News and Current Affairs, 4 August 2018. https://www.abc.net.au/radio/programs/am/refugees-welcomed-by-retirees-in-eltham/10073418.

Dore, Louis. 2016. "How Old People Have Screwed over the Younger Generation: In Three Charts." indy100, 29 March 2017. https://www.indy100.com/article/how-old-people-have-screwed-over-the-younger-generationin-three-charts—W1AA_n4nEb.

Dorling, Danny. 2016. "Brexit: The Decision of a Divided Country." the bmj (354), 6 July 2016.

Douglas, Mary. 1966. *Purity and Danger: An Analysis of Concepts of Pollution and Taboo*. London: Routledge.

Drozdzewski, Danielle, and Daniel Robinson. 2015. "Care-Work on Fieldwork: Taking Your Own Children into the Field." *Children's Geographies* 13 (3): 372–378.

Dunn, Kevin, James Forrest, Ian Burnley, and Amy McDonald. 2004. "Constructing Racism in Australia." *Australian Journal of Social Issues* 39 (4): 409–430.

Durie, Mason. 2010. "Heke Atu Heke Mai: Aotearoa, Global Transitions, and the Search for Common Ground." *Pathways, Circuits and Crossroads*, City Gallery, Civic Square, Wellington.

Eastwood, Clint. 2009. *Gran Torino*. Warner Bros.

Edens, John. 2017. "On the Ball: Migration 'Impacting Sport' as Auckland Youth Kick Rugby into Touch." *Stuff*, 20 Jan 2017. https://www.stuff.co.nz/sport/football/84747169/on-the-ball-migration-impacting-sport-as-auckland-youth-kick-rugby-into-touch.

Egoz, Shelley. 2000. "Clean and Green but Messy: The Contested Landscape of New Zealand's Organic Farms." *Oral History* (Spring 2000): 63–73.

Elder, Glen H., Monika Kirkpatrick Johnson, and Robert Crosnoe. 2003. "The Emergence and Development of Life Course Theory." In *Handbook of the Life Course*, 3–19. New York: Kluwer Academic.

Emerson, Robert M., Rachel I. Fretz, and Linda L. Shaw. 1995. *Writing Ethnographic Fieldnotes.* Chicago: University of Chicago Press.

Enguix, Begonya. 2014. "Negotiating the Field: Rethinking Ethnographic Authority, Experience and the Frontiers of Research." *Qualitative Research* 14 (1): 79–94.

Erel, Umet. 2011. "Complex Belongings: Racialization and Migration in a Small English City." *Ethnic and Racial Studies* 34 (12): 2048–2068.

Erickson, Jennifer. 2012. "Volunteering with Refugees: Neoliberalism, Hegemony, and (Senior) Citizenship." *Human Organization* 7 (2): 167–175.

Falzon, Mark-Anthony. 2009a. "Ethnic Groups Unbound: A Case Study of the Social Organization of Cosmopolitanism." In *Cosmopolitanism in Practice*, edited by Magdalena Nowicka and Maria Rovisco, 37–50. Farnham: Ashgate.

———. 2009b. "Introduction." In *Multi-sited Ethnography: Theory, Praxis and Locality in Contemporary Research*, edited by Mark-Anthony Falzon, 1–23. Ashgate: Farnham.

Fanslow, J., and E. Robinson. 2011. "Sticks, Stones or Words? Counting the Prevalence of Different Types of Intimate Partner Violence Reported by New Zealand Women." *Journal of Aggression, Maltreatment and Trauma* 20 (7): 741–759.

Fitzgerald, Ruth, and Linda Robertson. 2006. "Inhabiting the Places and Non-places of a Residential Home: A Case Study from New Zealand." SITES 3 (1): 48–71.

Flores-Herrera, Nancy Liliana Ivanova. 2015. "Narratives of the Self: The Impact of Migration on the Health of Latinos Living in Wellington, New Zealand." Master's thesis, Massey University.

Foster, George, and Robert Kemper. 2010. "Anthropological Fieldwork in Cities." In *Urban Life: Readings in the Anthropology of the City*, edited by George Gmelch, Robert Kemper, and Walter Zenner, 5–19. Long Grove, IL: Waveland Press.

Frey, William. 2014. "Five Charts That Show Why a Post-White America Is Already Here." *New Republic*, 21 November 2014. ———. 2015. *Diversity Explosion: How New Racial Demographics are Remaking America*. Washington, DC: Brookings Institutional Press.

Friesen, Wardlow. 2009. "The Demographic Transformation of Inner City Auckland." *New Zealand Population Review* 35: 55–74.

Frohlick, Susan. 2002. "You Brought Your Baby to Basecamp?" *Great Lakes Geographer* 9 (1): 49–58.

Gardner, Katy. 2002. *Age, Narrative and Migration: The Life Course and Life Histories of Bangali Elders in London.* Oxford, UK: Berg.

———. 2009. "Lives in Motion: The Life-Course, Movement and Migration in Bangladesh." *Journal of South Asian Development* 4 (2): 229–251.

Garro, Linda, and Cheryl Mattingly. 2000. "Narrative as Construct and Construction." In *Narrative and the Cultural Construction of Illness and Healing*, edited by Cheryl Mattingly and Linda Garro, 1–50. Berkeley: University of California Press.

Gendall, Philip, Paul Spoonley, and Andrew Trlin. 2007. "The Attitudes of New Zealanders to Immigrants and Immigration: 2003 and 2006 Compared." New Settlers Programme, Occasional Publication No. 17, Massey University, Palmerston North.

George, Molly. 2016. "Cosmopolitan Methods and Recruiting the Urban Stranger in Aotearoa New Zealand." *Sites: A Journal of Social Anthropology and Cultural Studies* 13 (1): 62–87.

George, Molly, and Ruth Fitzgerald. 2012. "Forty Years in Aotearoa New Zealand: White Identity, Home and Later Life in an Adopted Country." *Ageing & Society* 32 (2): 239–260. doi: 10.1017/S0144686X11000328.

Giles, Janice, and Carole Adamson. 2005. "The Social Sanctioning of Partner Abuse: Perpetuating the Message That Partner Abuse Is Acceptable in New Zealand." *Social Policy Journal of New Zealand* 26 (November 2005): 97–116.

Glass, Ira, and Mikki Meek. 2017. "Our Town—Part One." *This American Life*, Edited by Ira Glass. https://www.thisamericanlife.org/632/our-town-part-one.

Glick-Shiller, Nina, Linda Basch, and Cristina Blanc-Szanton. 1992. "Towards a Definition of Transnationalism: Introductory Remarks and Research Questions." In *Towards a Transnational Perspective on Migration: Race, Class, Ethnicity and Nationalism Reconsidered*, edited by Nina Glick-Shiller, Linda Basch, and Cristina Blanc-Szanton, i–xiii. New York: New York Academy of Sciences.

Glick-Shiller, Nina, and Georges Fouron. 1990. "'Everywhere We Go, We Are in Danger': Ti Manno and the Emergence of a Haitian Transnational Identity." *American Ethnologist* 17 (2): 329–347.

Glick-Shiller, Nina, and Andrew Irving. 2015. "Introduction: What's in a Word? What's in a Question?" In *Whose Cosmopolitanism? Critical Perspectives, Relationalities and Discontents*, edited by Nina Glick-Shiller and Andrew Irving, 1–22. New York: Berghahn Books.

Gmelch, George, and Sharon Bohn Gmelch. 2009. "Notes from the Field: Rural-Urban Difference and Student Fieldwork." *City and Society* 21 (2): 293–306.

Goodall, Heather, Stephen Wearing, Denis Byrne, and Allison Cadzow. 2009. "Fishing the Georges River: Cultural Diversity and Urban Environments." In *Everyday Multiculturalism*, edited by Amanda Wise and Selvaraj Velayhtahm, 177–196. Basingstoke: Palgrave Macmillan.

Gottlieb, Alma. 2012. "Two Visions of Africa: Reflections on Fieldwork in an 'Animist Bush' and in an Urban Diaspora." In *The Restless Anthropologist*, edited by Alma Gottlieb, 81–99. Chicago: University of Chicago Press.

Graham, Janice, and Peter Stephenson. 2010a. "The Experience of Loss and the Range of Contestation." In *Contesting Ageing and Loss*, edited by Janice Graham and Peter Stephenson, ix–xvii. Toronto: University of Toronto Press.

———. 2010b. "Introduction." In *Contesting Aging and Loss*, edited by Janice Graham and Peter Stephenson, ix–xvii. Toronto: University of Toronto Press.

Grainger, Andrew. 2009. "Rugby, Pacific Peoples, and the Cultural Politics of National Identity in New Zealand." *International Journal of the History of Sport* 26 (16): 2335–2357.

Granga, D. 2006. "From Potential Returnees into Settlers: Nottingham's Older Italians." *Journal of Ethnic and Migration Studies* 32 (8): 1395–1413.

Grillo, Ralph. 2010. "An Excess of Alterity? Debating Difference in a Multicultural Society." In *Anthropology of Migration and Multiculturalism*, edited by Steven Vertovec, 19–38. London: Routledge.

Grimshaw, Anna, and Amanda Ravertz. 2005. *Visualizing Anthropology*. Bristol, U.K.: Intellect Books.

Gupta, Akhil, and James Ferguson. 1992. "Beyond 'Culture': Space, Identity and the Politics of Difference." *Cultural Anthropology* 7 (1): 6–23.

Hall, Stuart. 1993. "Culture, Community, Nation." *Cultural Studies* 7 (3): 349–363.

Haltiwanger, John. 2017. "Data Suggests Younger People Are Increasingly Less Racist." Bustle Digital Group. Accessed 22 June 2018. https://www.elitedaily.com/news/politics/generation-apparently-way-less-racist-older-people-theres-hope/1958518.

Hannam, Kevin, Mimi Sheller, and John Urry. 2006. "Editorial: Mobilities, Immobilities and Moorings." *Mobilities* 1 (1): 1–22.

Hannerz, Ulf. 1990. "Cosmopolitans and Locals in World Culture." *Theory, Culture & Society* 7 (2–3): 237–251.

———. 2006. "Studying Down, Up, Sideways, Through, Backward, Forwards, Away and at Home: Reflections on the Field Worries of an Expansive Discipline." In *Locating the Field: Space, Place and Context in Anthropology*, edited by S. Coleman and P. Collins, 23–42. Oxford: Berg.

Hargreaves, Dougal. S., Felix. Greaves, Chorlotta Levay, Imogen Mitchell, Ursula Koch, Tobias Esch, Simon Denny, Jan C. Frich, Jeroen Struijis, and Aziz Sheikh. 2015. "Comparison of Health Care Experience and Access between Young and Older Adults in 11 High-Income Countries." *Journal of Adolescent Health* 57 (4): 413–420.

Havighurst, Robert. 1961. "Successful Aging." *Gerontologist* 1 (1): 8–13.

Hazan, Haim. 1984. "Continuity and Transformation among the Aged: A Study in the Anthropology of Time." *Current Anthropology* 25 (5): 567–578.

———. 2000. "The Cultural Trap: The Language of Images." In *Aging and Everyday Life*, edited by Jaber Gubrium and James Holstein, 15–18. Malden: Blackwell.

Heath, Anthony, and Lindsay Richards. 2016. "Attitudes Towards Immigration and Their Antecedents." In *Topline Results from Round 7 of the European Social Survey*. London: European Social Survey.

———. 2018. "How Do Europeans Differ in Their Attitudes to Immigration? Findings from the European Social Survey 2002/3-2016/17." Organisation for Economic Co-operation and Development, Social, Employment and Migration Working Papers.

Hendrickson, V. L. 2019. "New Zealand Locks Its Doors from the Inside." *New York Times*, 24 February 2019. https://www.nytimes.com/2019/02/22/realestate/new-zealand-locks-the-doors-from-the-inside.html.

Hiebert, Daniel. 2002. "Cosmopolitanism at the Local Level: The Development of Transnational Neighborhoods." In *Conceiving Cosmopolitanism: Theory, Context, Practice*, edited by Steven Vertovec and Robin Cohen, 209–223. Oxford: Oxford University Press.

Hill, Richard S. 2010. "Fitting Multiculturalism into Biculturalism: Maori-Pasifika Relations in New Zealand from the 1960's." *Ethnohistory* 57 (2): 291–319.

Ho, Elsie, Sybil Au, Charlotte Bedford, and Janine Cooper. 2003. *Mental Health Issues for Asians in New Zealand: A Literature Review*, edited by Mental Health Commission. Hamilton: University of Waikato.

Hochschild, Arlie Russell. 2000. "Global Care Chains and Emotional Surplus Value." In *Global Capitalism*, edited by Will Hutton and Anthony Giddens. New York: New Press.

Hockney, Jenny, and Allison James. 2003. *Social Identities across the Life-Course*. Houndmills: Palgrave MacMillan.

Holmes, Janet, Meredith Marra, and Bernadette Vine. 2012. "Politeness and Impoliteness in Ethnic Varieties of New Zealand English." *Journal of Pragmatics* 44 (9): 1063–1076.

Hudson, Maria, Joan Phillips, and Kathryn Ray. 2009. "'Rubbing Along with the Neighbours': Everyday Interactions in a Diverse Neighbourhood in the North of England." In *Everyday Multiculturalism*, edited by Amanda Wise and Selvaraj Velayhtahm, 199–215. Basingstoke: Palgrave Macmillan.

Hueber, Andre. 2011. "Claims Auckland Immigration Flawed." *The Aucklander*, 17 November 2011.

Hutching, Megan. 1999. *Long Journey for Sevenpence: Assisted Immigration to New Zealand from the United Kingdom, 1947–1975*. Wellington: Victoria University Press.

Huyssen, A., ed. 2008. *Other Cities, Other Worlds: Urban Imaginaries in a Globalizing Age*. Durham, NC: Duke University Press.

Ip, Manying. 2003a. "Maori-Chinese Encounters: Indigine-Immigrant Interaction in New Zealand." *Asian Studies Review* 27 (2): 227–252.

———, ed. 2003b. *Unfolding History, Evolving Identity: The Chinese in New Zealand.* Auckland: Auckland University Press.

Jordan, Miriam. 2019. "Reporting on the Retirees Making Migrants' Journeys a Little Easier." *New York Times*, 29 May 2019.

Kahn, Joel. 2003. "Anthropology as Cosmopolitan Practice?" *Anthropological Theory* 3 (4): 403–415.

Kant, Immanuel. 1974. *Anthropology from a Pragmatic Point of View.* Translated by Mary J. Gregor. The Hague: Martinus Nijhoff.

Kaufman, Sharon. 1986. *The Ageless Self: Sources of Meaning in Later Life.* Madison: University of Wisconsin Press.

———. 1993. "Reflections on 'The Ageless Self.'" *Generations* 17 (2): 13.

Keeling, Sally. 1999. "Ageing in (a New Zealand) Place: Ethnography, Policy and Practice." *Social Policy Journal of New Zealand*, no. 13. https://www.msd.govt.nz/about-msd-and-our -work/publications-resources/journals-and-magazines/social-policy-journal/spj13 /ageing-in-place-ethnography-policy-practice.html.

Kennedy, Paul. 2009. "The Middle-Class Cosmopolitan Journey: The Life Trajectories and Transnational Affiliations of Skilled EU Migrants in Manchester." In *Cosmopolitanism in Practice*, edited by Magdalena Nowicka and Maria Rovisco, 19–36. Farnham: Ashgate.

Kenny, Charles. 2017. "The Data Are In: Young People Are Increasingly Less Racist Than Old People." *Quartz*, 24 May 2017. https://qz.com/983016/the-data-are-in-young-people-are -definitely-less-racist-than-old-people/.

Khoo, Gaik Cheng. 2009. "Kopitiam: Discursive Cosmopolitan Spaces and National Identity in Malaysian Culture and Media." In *Everyday Multiculturalism*, edited by Amanda Wise and Selvaraj Velayhtahm, 87–104. Basingstoke: Palgrave Macmillan.

Kiata, Liz, and Ngaire Kerse. 2004. "Intercultural Residential Care in New Zealand." *Qualitative Health Research* 14 (3): 313–327.

King, Michael. 2003. *The Penguin History of New Zealand.* North Shore, Auckland: Penguin.

Kirkpatrick, Heather. 2013. *Mary Meets Mohammad.* Australia: Waratah Films.

Koopman-Boyden, Peggy. 2011a. s.v. "Older People." *Te Ara: The Encyclopedia of New Zealand.* Accessed 17 March 2020. http://www.TeAra.govt.nz/en/older-people.

———. 2011b. s.v. "Older People: Politics and Advocacy." *Te Ara: The Encyclopedia of New Zealand.* Accessed 17 March 2020. http://www.TeAra.govt.nz/en/cartoon/26712/winston -peters-2005.

Kottasova, Ivana. 2016. "British Millennials: You've Stolen Our Future." *CNN Money*, WarnerMedia.

Kukutai, Tahu H. 2008. "The Structure of Maori-Asian Relations: An Ambivalent Future?" *New Zealand Population Review* 33/34: 129–151.

Kukutai, Tahu H., and Robert Didham. 2009. "In Search of Ethnic New Zealanders: National Naming in the 2006 Census." *Social Policy Journal of New Zealand* 36, 46–62.

Kunovich, Robert M. 2004. "Social Structural Position and Prejudice: An Exploration of Cross-National Differences in Regression Slopes." *Social Science Research* 33 (1): 20–44.

Kymlicka, Will. 2012. "Multiculturalism: Success, Failure and the Future." In *TransAtlantic Council on Migration.* Washington, DC: Migration Policy Institute.

La Grow, Steven, Stephen Neville, Fiona Alpass, and Vivien Rodgers. 2012. "Loneliness and Self-Reported Health among Older Persons in New Zealand." *Australasia Journal of Ageing* 31 (2): 121–123.

Lamb, Sarah. 2009. *Aging and the Indian Diaspora: Cosmopolitan Families in India and Abroad.* Bloomington: Indiana University Press.

———. 2014. "Permanent Personhood or Meaningful Decline? Toward a Critical Anthropology of Successful Aging." *Journal of Aging Studies* 29 (2014): 41–52.

Lamphere, Louise, ed. 1992. *Structuring Diversity: Ethnographic Perspectives on the New Immigration.* Chicago: University of Chicago Press.

Laurier, Eric, and Chris Philo. 2006. "Cold Shoulders and Napkins Handed: Gestures of Responsibility." *Transactions of the Institute of British Geographers* 31 (2): 193–207. doi: 10.1111/j.1475-5661.2006.00205.x.

Lawton, M. P. 1990. "Knowledge Resources and Gaps in Housing the Aged." In *Aging in Place,* edited by D. Tilson, 287–309. Glenview: Scott Foresman.

Leavey, Gerard, Sati Sembhi, and Gill Livingston. 2004. "Older Irish Migrants Living in London: Identity, Loss and Return." *Journal of Ethnic and Migration Studies* 30 (4): 763–769.

Lochore, Revel Anson. 1951. *From Europe to New Zealand: An Account of Our Continental European Settlers.* Wellington: A.H. & A.W. Reed, New Zealand Institute of International Affairs.

Longhurst, Robyn, Lynda Johnston, and Elsie Ho. 2009. "A Visceral Approach: Cooking 'at Home' with Migrant Women in Hamilton, New Zealand." *Transactions of the Institute of British Geographers* 34 (3): 333–345.

Macaraeg, Sarah. 2018. "Retirees and Refugees: How 93-year-old Julia Allen Builds Community through ESL." *Memphis Commercial Appeal,* 20 November 2018. https://www.commercial appeal.com/story/news/2018/11/21/refugees-retirees-memphis-resettlement-esl-volunteering -world-relief/1895125002/.

MacPherson, Cluny. 2005. "Reinventing the Nation: Building a Bicultural Future from a Monocultural Past in Aotearoa/New Zealand." In *Race and Nation: Ethnic Systems in the Modern World,* edited by Paul Spickard, 215–238. New York: Routledge.

Marotta, Vince. 2000. "The Ambivalence of Borders: The Bicultural and the Multicultural." In *Race, Colour and Identity in Australia and New Zealand,* edited by John Docker and Gerhard Fischer, 178–189. Sydney: University of New South Wales Press.

Massey, Doreen. 2005. *For Space.* London: Sage.

Massey University. 2011. "World Cup Shows Rugby Is Our 'Surrogate Religion.'" Massey University. Last Modified 27 October 2011. Accessed 27 April http://www.massey.ac.nz /massey/about-massey/news/article.cfm?mnarticle_uuid=F7A79FDB-E0AC-2F3F-5E16 -17D74A87E6EE.

Maydell-Stevens, Elena, Anne-Marie Masggoret, and Tony Ward. 2007. "Problems of Psychological and Sociocultural Adaptation among Russian Speaking Immigrants in New Zealand." *Social Policy Journal of New Zealand* 30 (30): 178–198.

Mayhew, Pat, and James Reilly. 2009. "The New Zealand Crime and Safety Survey." *Family Violence Statistics Report.* Wellington: Families Commission.

McCarthy, Tom. 2008. *The Visitor.* Anchor Bay Entertainment.

McMillan, Kate. 2004. "Developing Citizens: Subjects, Aliens and Citizens in New Zealand since 1840." In *Tangata, tangata: The Changing Ethnic Contours of New Zealand,* edited by Paul Spoonley, Cluny MacPherson, and David Pearson, 265–290. Southbank, Victoria: Thomson Dunmore Press.

Monaghan, John, and Peter Just. 2000. *Social and Cultural Anthropology: A Very Short Introduction.* Oxford: Oxford University Press.

Moody, Harry. 2009. "From Successful Aging to Conscious Aging." In *The Cultural Context of Aging: Worldwide Perspectives,* edited by Jay Sokolovsky, 67–76. Westport: Praeger.

Moore, Peter. 2016. "How Britain Voted at the EU Referendum." YouGov UK, 28 June 2016. https://yougov.co.uk/topics/politics/articles-reports/2016/06/27/how-britain-voted.

Munn, Nancy. 1992. "The Cultural Anthropology of Time: A Critical Essay." *Annual Review of Anthropology* 21: 93–123.

Myerhoff, Barbara. (1979). *Number Our Days: Culture and Community among Elderly Jews in an American Ghetto.* New York: Meridian.

Myers, Dowell. 2007. *Immigrants and Boomers: Forging a New Social Contract for the Future of America.* New York: Russell Sage Foundation.

Nava, Mica. 2006. "Domestic Cosmopolitanism and Structures of Feeling: The Specificity of London." In *The Situated Politics of Belonging.* Edited by Nira Yuval-Davis, Kalpana Kannabiran, and Ulrike Vieten. London: Sage.

New Zealand First. 2005. "Securing Our Borders and Protecting Our Identity." *Scoop,* 27 May 2005. https://www.scoop.co.nz/stories/PA0505/S00702.htm.

New Zealand Government. 2008. "SuperGold Benefits for Travel, Hearing Aids." New Zealand Government, 23 May 2008. https://www.beehive.govt.nz/release/supergold-benefits-travel-hearing-aids.

New Zealand Herald Staff. 2010. "Paul Henry Suspended." *New Zealand Herald,* 5 October 2010. http://www.nzherald.co.nz/nz/news/article.cfm?c_id=1&objectid=10678313.

New Zealand Immigration. 2016a. "Investor Visas". *Immigration New Zealand.* Accessed 2 May 2021. https://www.newzealandnow.govt.nz/investing-in-nz/visas/investor-visa.

New Zealand Immigration. 2016b. "Summary of Terms: Health Requirements for Residence in New Zealand." *Immigration New Zealand.* Accessed 15 May 2020. http://glossary.immigration.govt.nz/healthrequirementsresidence.htm.

New Zealand, Ministry of Social Development. 2010. "People." Accessed 1 April 2016. http://socialreport.msd.govt.nz/people/ethnic-composition-population.html.

Newton, Kate. 2015. "Sikh Leader to Meet after Turban Ban." Radio New Zealand. Last Modified 18 June 2015. Accessed 29 February 2016. http://www.radionz.co.nz/news/national/276581/sikh-leaders-to-meet-after-turban-ban.

Ni Bhroin, Riona. 2012. "Half the World Away: A Qualitative Study Exploring Migration and Motherhood in New Zealand." Master's thesis, Massey University.

Nippert, Matt. 2015. "The Big Read: Crafar Farms Saga Over." *New Zealand Herald,* 21 December 2015. http://www.nzherald.co.nz/business/news/article.cfm?c_id=3&objectid=11564446.

Noble, Greg. 2009. "Everyday Cosmopolitanism and the Labour of Intercultural Community." In *Everyday Multiculturalism,* edited by Amanda Wise and Selvaraj Velayhtahm, 46–65. Basingstoke: Palgrave Macmillan.

Novek, Sheila, Toni Morris-Oswald, and Verena Menec. 2011. "Using Photovoice with Older Adults: Some Methodological Strengths and Issues." *Ageing & Society* 32 (3): 451–470.

Nowicka, Magdalena, and Maria Rovisco, eds. 2009a. *Cosmopolitanism in Practice.* Aldershot: Ashgate.

———. 2009b. "Introduction: Making Sense of Cosmopolitanism." In *Cosmopolitanism in Practice,* edited by Magdalena Nowicka and Maria Rovisco, 1–16. Farnham: Ashgate.

NZPA (New Zealand Press Association). 2009. "Peters Back with Anti-immigration Speech." Fairfax Media Digital. Last Modified 9 October 2009. Accessed 29 February 2016. http://www.stuff.co.nz/national/politics/2948589/Peters-back-with-anti-immigration-speech.

———. 2011. "Dominion Road Identified as Auckland's Chinatown." *New Zealand Herald,* 20 June 2011. http://www.nzherald.co.nz/nz/news/article.cfm?c_id=1&objectid=10733420.

Oakley, Robin. 2010. "Empowering Knowledge and Practices of Namaqualand Elders." In *Contesting Aging and Loss*, edited by Janice Graham and Peter Stephenson, 47–62. Toronto: University of Toronto Press.

Okely, Judith. 1992. "Anthropology and Autobiography: Participatory Experience and Embodied Knowledge." In *Anthropology and Autobiography*, edited by Judith Okely and Edith Callaway, 1–28. London: Routledge.

Olwig, Karen Fog, and Kirsten Hastrup. 1997. "Introduction." In *Siting Culture: The Shifting Anthropological Object*, edited by Karen Fog Olwig and Kirsten Hastrup, 1–14. London: Routledge.

Ong, Aihwa. 2002. "Flexible Citizenship among Chinese Cosmopolitans." In *The Anthropology of Politics*, edited by Joan Vincent. Oxford: Wiley-Blackwell.

Pardo, Italo, and Giuliana Prato. 2012. "Introduction: The Contemporary Significance of Anthropology in the City." In *Anthropology in the City*, edited by Italo Pardo and Giuliana Prato, 1–28. Surrey, England: Ashgate.

Parker, David. 2018. "Foreign Buyers Ban Passes Third Reading." New Zealand Government. 15 August 2018. https://www.beehive.govt.nz/release/foreign-buyers-ban-passes-third-reading

Pettigrew, Thomas F. 2006. "A Two-Level Approach to Anti-immigration Prejudice and Discrimination." In *Cultural Psychology of Immigrants*, edited by R. Mahalingam, 95–112. Mahwah, NJ: Erlbaum.

Pew Research Centre. 2011. *The Generation Gap and the 2012 Election*. Washington, DC: Pew Research Centre.

Phillips, Jock. 2013. "History of Immigration: Assisted Immigration Revives: 1946–1975." Last Modified 21 August 2013. Accessed 7 March 2016. http://www.TeAra.govt.nz/en/history-of-immigration/page-14.

Phillips, Time and Phillip Smith. 2003. "Everyday Incivility: Towards a Benchmark". *The Sociological Review*. 51 (1): 85–108.

Phillipson, Chris, and Thomas Scharf. 2005. "Rural and Urban Perspectives on Growing Old: Developing a New Research Agenda." *European Journal of Ageing* 2 (2): 67–75.

Pink, Sarah. 2006. *The Future of Visual Anthropology*. London: Routledge.

Pollock, Karen. 2012. "Health and Society: Socio-economic Status, Ethnicity and Health Inequality." Last Modified 13 July 2012. http://www.TeAra.govt.nz/en/health-and-society/page-2.

Pool, Ian. 2015. "Death Rates and Life Expectancy: Māori Epidemiological Transition." Last Modified 15 January 2015. Accessed 18 February 2016. http://www.TeAra.govt.nz/en/graph/26605/life-expectancy-at-birth-maori-and-non-maori.

Prakash, Gyan. 2015. "Whose Cosmopolitanism? Multiple, Globally Enmeshed and Subaltern." In *Whose Cosmopolitanism? Critical Perspectives, Relationalities and Discontents*, edited by Nina Glick-Shiller and Andrew Irving, 27–28. New York: Berghahn Books.

Prato, Giuliana. 2012. "Anthropological Research in Brindisi and Durres: Methodological Reflections." In *Anthropology in the City: Methodology and Theory*, edited by Italo Pardo and Giuliana Prato, 79–100. Farnham, Surrey: Ashgate.

Radice, Martha. 2000. *Feeling Comfortable: The Urban Experience of Anglo-Montrealers*. Saint Nicolas, Quebec: Presses Universite Laval.

———. 2011. "Ethnography of the Street." *Anthropology News* 52 (3): 13.

Radio New Zealand. 2011. "Grey Power Wants Review of Asian Immigration in Auckland." Radio Broadcast, Auckland.

Radvansky, Gabriel, David Copeland, and William Von Hippel. 2010. "Stereotype Activation, Inhibition and Aging." *Journal of Experimental Social Psychology* 46 (1): 51–60.

Ramadan, Tariq. 2015. "Cosmopolitan Theory and the Daily Pluralism of Life." In *Whose Cosmopolitanism? Critical Perspectives, Relationalities and Discontents*, edited by Nina Glick-Shiller and Andrew Irving, 57–64. New York: Berghahn Books.

Rapport, Nigel. 2005. "The Narrative as Fieldwork Technique: Processual Ethnography for a World in Motion." In *Constructing the Field: Fieldwork in the Contemporary World*, edited by Vered Amit, 71–95. London: Routledge.

———. 2012. *Anyone: The Cosmopolitan Subject of Anthropology*. New York: Berghahn Books.

Rapport, Nigel, and Ronald Stade. 2007. "A Cosmopolitan Turn: Or Return?" *Social Anthropology* 15 (2): 223–235.

Robbins, Bruce. 1998. "Actually Existing Cosmopolitanism." In *Cosmopolitics: Thinking and Feeling Beyond the Nation*, edited by Pheng Cheah and Bruce Robbins, 1–19. Minneapolis: University of Minnesota Press.

Rodriguez-Galan, Marta. 2013. "Grandmothering in Life-Course Perspective: A Study of Puerto Rican Grandmothers Raising Grandchildren in the United States." In *Transitions and Transformations: Cultural Perspectives on Aging and the Life Course*, edited by Caitrin Lynch and Jason Danely, 137–150. New York: Berghahn Books.

Roggeveen, Edward. 1996. "Dutch Immigrants in New Zealand, 1945–1964." Master's thesis, University of Auckland.

Rowles, Graham. 1983. "Place and Personal Identity in Old Age: Observations from Appalachia." *Journal of Environmental Psychology* 11: 103–120.

Rowles, Graham, and Hege Ravdal. 2001. "Aging, Place and Meaning in the Face of Changing Circumstances." In *Challenges of the Third Age: Meaning and Purpose in Later Life*, edited by Robert S. Weiss and Scott A. Bass. Oxford: Oxford University Press.

Roy, Eleanor Ainge. 2016. "Prestigious Academic to Quit New Zealand after Autistic Son Refused Residency." *Guardian*. Accessed 16 February 2016. https://www.theguardian.com/world/2016/feb/16/prestigious-academic-to-quit-new-zealand-after-autistic-son-refused-residency.

Russell, Cherry. 2010. "Drunks, Bums, and Deadbeats? A Biographical Perspective on Gender, Aging and the Inequalities of Men." In *Contesting Aging and Loss*, edited by Janice Graham and Peter Stephenson, 87–102. Toronto: University of Toronto Press.

Saville-Smith, Kay. 1993. "The State and the Social Construction of Ageing." In *New Zealand's Ageing Society: The Implications*, edited by Peggy Koopman-Boyden, 76–94. Wellington: Daphne Brassell Associates Press.

Schofield, Verna, Judith Davey, Sally Keeling, and Matthew Parsons. 2006. "Ageing in Place." In *Implications of Population Ageing: Opportunities and Risks*, edited by Jonathon Boston and Judith Davey, 275–306. Wellington: Institute of Policy Studies, Victoria University of Wellington.

Schonwalder, Karen, Soren Peterman, Jorg Huttermann, Steven Vertovec, Miles Hewstone, Dietlind Stolle, Katharina Schmid, and Thomas Schmitt. 2016. *Diversity and Contact: Immigration and Social Interaction in German Cities, Global Diversities*. London: Palgrave Macmillan.

Sharlach, Andrew, and Keith Diaz Moore. 2016. "Aging in Place." In *Handbook of Theories of Aging*, edited by Vern Bengtson and Richard Settersten, 407–425. London: Springer.

Sheller, Mimi, and John Urry. 2006. "The New Mobilities Paradigm." *Environment and Planning A* 38 (2): 207–226.

Sherman, Jamie. 2009. "The Colour of Muscle: Multiculturalism at a Brooklyn Bodybuilding Gym." In *Everyday Multiculturalism*, edited by Amanda Wise and Selvaraj Velayhtahm, 161–176. Basingstoke: Palgrave Macmillan.

Skrbis, Zlatko, and Ian Woodward. 2013. *Cosmopolitanism: Uses of the Idea*. Los Angeles: Sage.

Smith, Ian. 2008. "Maori, Pakeha, Kiwi: Peoples, Cultures and Sequence in New Zealand Archaeology." In *Islands of Inquiry: Colonisation, Seafaring and the Archaeology of Maritime Landscapes,* edited by Geoffrey Clark, Foss Leach, and Sue O'Connor, 367–380. Canberra: ANU E Press.

Smith, Linda Tuhiwai. 1999. *Decolonizing Methodologies: Research and Indigenous Peoples.* London: Zed Books.

Sokolovsky, Jay, and Joan Sokolovsky. 1982. "Familial and Public Contexts for Aging: Growing Old in a Rapidly Changing Mexican Village." In *Aging and the Aged in the Third World,* part 2, 111–144. Williamsburg: Faculty Books, Department of Anthropology, College of William and Mary.

Spoonley, Paul. 2011. "Remaking National Identity and Citizenship in Contemporary Aotearoa/New Zealand." Paper presented at Interrogating Multiculturalism in Aortearoa New Zealand: an Asian Perspective, Dunedin, New Zealand, 19–20 February.

———. 2014. "Will Rugby Remain New Zealand's National Game?" *Bulletin.* Accessed 27 April 2016. http://www.asianz.org.nz/bulletin/will-rugby-remain-new-zealands-national -game.

Spoonley, Paul, and Richard Bedford. 2012. *Welcome to Our World? Immigration and the Reshaping of New Zealand.* Auckland: Dunmore.

Spoonley, Paul, and Philip Gendall. 2010. "Welcome to Our World: Attitudes to Immigrants and Immigration." In *New Zealand and International Migration: A Digest and Bibliography,* no. 5, edited by Andrew Trlin, Paul Spoonley, and Richard Bedford. Palmerston North: Integration of Immigrants Programme, Massey University.

Stacey, Jackie. 2015. "Whose Cosmopolitanism? The Violence of Idealizations and the Ambivalence of Self." In *Whose Cosmopolitanism? Critical Perspectives, Relationalities and Discontents,* edited by Nina Glick-Shiller and Andrew Irving, 34–36. New York: Berghahn Books.

Staples, Brent. 2016. "Voters Who Long for 'Leave It to Beaver.'" *New York Times.* Accessed 22 September 2018. https://www.nytimes.com/interactive/projects/cp/opinion/election-night -2016/where-nostalgia-fits-in.

Statistics New Zealand. 2004. *Report of the Review of the Measurement of Ethnicity.* Wellington.

———. 2010. "Loneliness in New Zealand: Findings from the 2010 New Zealand General Social Survey." Accessed 8 April 2016. http://www.stats.govt.nz/browse_for_stats/people _and_communities/older_people/loneliness-in-nz-2010-NZGSS/loneliness-in-nz.aspx.

———. 2014. 2013 "Census QuickStats about Culture and Identity." Wellington.

———. 2015. "National Ethnic Population Projections: 2013 (base) to 2038." Press release. Wellington: Statistics New Zealand.

———. 2016. "Recorded Crime Offenders Statistics: Unique Offenders." Statistics New Zealand. Accessed 25 March 2016. http://nzdotstat.stats.govt.nz/wbos/Index.aspx?DataSetCode =TABLECODE7412#.

Statistics, Office for National (UK). 2018. "Ethnicity Facts and Figures." *Ethnicity in the UK,* 22 August 2018. https://www.ethnicity-facts-figures.service.gov.uk/uk-population-by-ethnicity /demographics/age-groups/latest.

Stephenson, Peter. 2010. "Age and Time: Contesting the Paradigm of Loss in the Age of Novelty." In *Contesting Aging and Loss,* edited by Janice Graham and Peter Stephenson, 3–26. Toronto: University of Toronto Press.

stevieco411. 2016. "Votes for Brexit . . . Will Die before Being a Victim of That Decision!" Accessed 2 May 2021. https://imgflip.com/i/16d9m2.

Stoller, Paul. 2012. "Afterword." In *The Restless Anthropologist,* edited by Alma Gottlieb, 159–163. Chicago: University of Chicago Press.

Strauss, Anselm, and Juliet Corbin. 1998. *Basics of Qualitative Research*. Thousand Oaks, CA: Sage.

Tan, Lincoln. 2016. "The Big Read: Why Are Migrants Snubbing NZ's Regions?" *New Zealand Herald*, 4 January 2016. Accessed 25 March 2016. http://www.nzherald.co.nz/nz/news/article.cfm?c_id=1&objectid=11569008.

Tolich, Martin. 2002. "'Pakeha "Paralysis': Cultural Safety for Those Researching the General Population of Aotearoa New Zealand." *Social Policy Journal of New Zealand* 19 (December): 164–178.

Tomkiw, Lydia. 2016. "Europe Refugee Crisis: How Retirees in Germany Are Helping Syrians." *International Business Times*, 5 February 2016. https://www.ibtimes.com/europe-refugee-crisis-how-retirees-germany-are-helping-syrians-2292304.

Torres-Gil, Fernando, and Karra Bikson Moga. 2002. "Multiculturalism, Social Policy and the New Aging." *Journal of Gerontological Social Work* 36 (3–4): 13–32.

Tourism New Zealand. 2011. "100% Pure History." *Tourism New Zealand*. Accessed 26 October 2011. http://www.tourismnewzealand.com/about-us/100percent-pure-history/.

Tremewan, Christopher. 2005. "Ideological Conformity: A Fundamental Challenge to the Social Sciences in New Zealand." *Sites: New Series* 2 (1): 1–44.

Trundle, Catherine. 2010. "Against the Gated Community: Contesting the 'Ugly American Dream' through Rural New Zealand Dreams." In *Local Lives: Migration and the Politics of Place*, edited by Brigitte Bonisch-Brednich and Catherine Trundle, 31–48. Farnham: Ashgate.

Tsing, A. 2005. "Introduction." In *Friction: An Ethnography of Global Connection*, 1–19. Princeton, NJ: Princeton University Press.

TVNZ (Television New Zealand). 2011. *Close Up*. "Chinatown," 21 June 2011.

Valentine, Gill. 2008. "Living with Difference: Reflections on Geographies of Encounter." *Progress in Human Geography* 32 (2): 323–337.

Vanleerberghe, Patricia, Nico De Witte, Claudia Claes, Robert Schalock, and Dominique Verte. 2017. "The Quality of Life of Older People Aging in Place: A Literature Review." *Quality of Life Research* 26 (11): 2899–2907.

Van Maanen, John. 1988. *Tales of the Field: On Writing Ethnography*. Chicago: University of Chicago Press.

Vertovec, Steven. 2009. "Cosmopolitanism in Attitude, Practice and Competence." Max Planck Institute Working Paper 09-08. Accessed 17 May 2016. http://pubman.mpdl.mpg.de/pubman/item/escidoc:1126666/component/escidoc:2056850/WP_09-08_Vertovec_Cosmopolitanism.pdf.

———. 2010a. "Introduction: New Directions in the Anthropology of Migration and Multiculturalism." In *Anthropology of Migration and Multiculturalism*, edited by Steven Vertovec, 1–19. London: Routledge.

———. 2010b. "Super-Diversity and Its Implications." In *Anthropology of Migration and Multiculturalism*, edited by Steven Vertovec, 65–95. London: Routledge.

———. 2015a. "Introduction: Formulating Diversity." In *Routledge International Handbook of Diversity Studies*, edited by Steven Vertovec, 1–20. London: Routledge.

———. 2015b. "Introduction: Migration, Cities, Diversities 'Old' and 'New.'" In *Diversities Old and New*, edited by Steven Vertovec, 1–22. Basingstoke: Palgrave Macmillan.

Victor, Christina. 2005. *The Social Context of Ageing: A Textbook of Gerontology*. London: Routledge.

Volunteering New Zealand Incorporated. 2015. "Statistics on Volunteering." Volunteering New Zealand Incorporated. Accessed 4 April 2016. http://www.volunteeringnz.org.nz/policy/statistics/.

von Faber, Margeret, and Sjaak van der Geest. 2010. "Losing and Gaining: About Growing Old 'Successfully' in the Netherlands." In *Contesting Aging and Loss*, edited by Janice Graham and Peter Stephenson, 27–46. Toronto: University of Toronto Press.

von Hippel, William, Lisa Silver, and Molly Lynch. 2000. "Stereotyping against Your Will: The Role of Inhibitory Ability in Stereotyping and Prejudice among the Elderly." *Personality and Social Psychology Bulletin* 26 (5): 523–532.

Wahl, H., and F. Lang. 2003. "Environmental Gerontology at the Beginning of the New Millennium: Reflections on Its Historical, Empirical and Theoretical Development." *Gerontologist* 43 (5): 616–627.

Walker, Ranginui. 2004. *Ka Whawhai Tonu Matou: Struggle without End.* Auckland: Penguin Press.

Walrond, Carl. 2016. "Dalmations: Farming, Fishing, Winemaking." *Te Ara: The Encyclopedia of New Zealand.* Last Modified 13 July 2012. Accessed 7 March 2016. http://www.TeAra .govt.nz/en/dalmatians/page-4.

Ward, Colleen, and En-Yi Lin. 2005. "Immigration, Acculturation and National Identity in New Zealand." In *New Zealand Identities: Departures and Destinations*, edited by James Liu, Tim McCreanor, Tracey McIntosh, and Teresia Teaiwa, 155–173. Wellington: Victoria University Press.

Ward, Colleen, and Anne-Marie Masgoret. 2008. "Attitudes toward Immigrants, Immigration and Multiculturalism in New Zealand: A Social Psychological Analysis." *International Migration Review* 42 (1): 227–248.

Wardle, Huon. 2000. *An Ethnography of Cosmopolitanism in Kingston, Jamaica.* Lampeter: Mellen.

Warnes, Anthony, Klaus Friedrich, Leonie Kellaher, and Sandra Torres. 2004. "The Diversity and Welfare of Older Migrants in Europe." *Ageing & Society* 24 (3): 307–326.

Watson, Sophie. 2009. "Brief Encounters of an Unpredictable Kind: Everyday Multiculturalism in Two London Street Markets." In *Everyday Multiculturalism*, edited by Amanda Wise and Selvaraj Velayhtahm, 125–139. Basingstoke: Palgrave Macmillan.

Welcome to Eltham. 2016. "Eltham Seniors Welcome Refugees." Facebook, 26 October 2016. https://www.facebook.com/WelcomeToEltham/videos/?ref=page_internal

Wendt, Claus, Monika Mischke, Michaela Pfeifer, and Nadine Reibling. 2012. "Confidence in Receiving Medical Care When Seriously Ill: A Seven-Country Comparison of the Impact of Cost Barriers." *Health Expectations* 15 (2): 212–224.

Werbner, Pnina. 1999. "Global Pathways: Working Class Cosmopolitans and the Creation of Transnational Ethnic Worlds." *Social Anthropology* 7 (1): 17–35.

———. 2006. "Vernacular Cosmopolitanism." *Theory, Culture & Society* 23 (2–3): 496–498.

Wessendorf, Susanne. 2013. "Commonplace Diversity and the 'Ethos of Mixing': Perceptions of Difference in a London Neighbourhood." *Identities: Global Studies in Culture and Power* 20 (4): 407–422.

———. 2014a. "'Being Open, but Sometimes Closed.' Conviviality in a Super-Diverse London Neighborhood." *European Journal of Cultural Studies* 17 (4): 392–405.

———. 2014b. *Commonplace Diversity: Social Relations in a Super-Diverse Context, Global Diversities.* London: Palgrave Macmillan UK.

Westerhof, Gerben. 2010. "'During My Life So Much Has Changed That It Looks Like a New World to Me': A Narrative Perspective on Migrating in Time." *Journal of Aging Studies* 24 (1): 12–19.

Whitlock, Scott. 2016. "Journalist on MSNBC: GOP Convention Full of 'Angry,' 'Old' 'White People.'" mrcNewsBusters, 21 June 2016. https://www.newsbusters.org/blogs/nb/scott -whitlock/2016/07/18/journalist-msnbc-rnc-convention-full-angry-old-white-people.

Wiles, Janine, Ruth Allen, Anthea Palmer, Karen Hayman, Sally Keeling, and Ngaire Kerse. 2009. "Older People and Their Social Spaces: A Study of Well-being and Attachment to Place in Aotearoa New Zealand." *Social Science & Medicine* 68 (4): 664–671.

Wiles, Janine, Annette Leibing, Nancy Guberman, Jeanne Reeve, and Ruth E. S. Allen. 2012. "The Meaning of 'Ageing in Place' to Older People." *Gerontologist* 52 (3): 357–366.

Wilkinson, Abi. 2016. "Stubborn Old People Who Want to Leave the EU." *Telegraph*, 29 March 2016. https://www.telegraph.co.uk/opinion/2016/03/29/stubborn-old-people -who-want-to-leave-the-eu-are-condemning-the/.

Williamson, Rebecca. 2016. "Vernacular Cosmopolitanisms in Suburban Peripheries: A Case Study in Multicultural Sydney." *Sites: A Journal of Social Anthropology and Cultural Studies* 13 (1): 111–133.

Wilmshurst, Janet, Atholl Anderson, Thomas Higham, and Trevor Worthy. 2008. "Dating the Late Prehistoric Dispersal of Polynesians to New Zealand Using the Commensal Pacific Rat." *Proceedings of the National Academy of Sciences* 105 (22): 7676–7680.

Wilson, Graham K. 2017. "Brexit, Trump and the Special Relationship." *British Journal of Politics and International Relations* 19 (3): 543–557. doi: 10.1177/1369148117713719.

Winkler, Hernan. 2015a. "In Aging Societies, Will Young Liberals Become Old Conservatives?" *Eurasian Perspectives,* 12 June 2015b. https://blogs.worldbank.org/europeandcentralasia /aging-societies-will-young-liberals-become-old-conservatives.

———. 2015b. "Why Do Elderly People Oppose Immigration When They're the Most Likely to Benefit from It?" *Future Development,* 7 March 2015. https://www.brookings.edu/blog /future-development/2015/07/22/why-do-elderly-people-oppose-immigration-when -theyre-most-likely-to-benefit/.

Wise, Amanda. 2009. "Everyday Multiculturalism: Transversal Crossings and Working Class Cosmopolitans." In *Everyday Multiculturalism,* edited by Amanda Wise and Selvaraj Velayhtahm. Basingstoke: Palgrave Macmillan.

Wood, Phil, and Charles Landry. 2007. *The Intercultural City: Planning for Diversity Advantage.* London: Earthscan.

Wright, Oliver, and Jerome Taylor. 2011. "Cameron: My War on Multiculturalism." *Independent,* 5 February 2011. http://www.independent.co.uk/news/uk/politics/cameron-my-war-on -multiculturalism-2205074.html.

Young, Iris Marion. 1990. *Justice and the Politics of Difference.* Princeton, NJ: Princeton University Press.

Zodgekar, Arvind. 2005. "The Changing Face of New Zealand's Population and National Identity." In *New Zealand Identities: Departures and Destinations,* edited by James Liu, Tim McCreanor, Tracey McIntosh, and Teresia Teaiwa, 140–154. Wellington: Victoria University Press.

INDEX

Note: Page numbers in *italic* type refer to illustrative matter.

abuse of resources, 70–71, 75, 130
abusive relationships, 151n5
academic population, 63
Adam, Barbara, 137, 138
African New Zealanders, *10,* 54, 68, 89–90, 92, 104, 110, 113. See also *names of specific nationalities*
Age, Narrative and Migration (Gardner), 29
Age Concern New Zealand, 102–103, 104, 139
aging: contesting polarized views of, 142–144; as liability or asset, 146–148; migration and, 29–32; older people, as category, 14–15, 28; in place, 144–146; studies on, 26–27, 28; successful aging paradigm, 27–28, 143. *See also* older New Zealanders
Ahmed, Anya, 29, 51
Alan (research participant), 20, 51–52, 107–108, 120, 124
All Blacks (rugby team), 114
Allport, Gordon, 125–126
American New Zealanders, 77, 97
Amin, Ash, 138, 139, 140
Andrews, Molly, 27–28, 143
Ann (research participant), 55, 82, 83–84, 112
anthropology. *See* ethnographic fieldwork; research methods; urban ethnography
Aotearoa New Zealand, overview, 7–9, *10,* 41
artistic design and property, 70
"Asian Angst" (*North and South*), 67–68
Asian New Zealanders: in Auckland, 34–36, 50, 52; crimes by, 66–68; population statistics of, 7, 8, *9, 10,* 21; racism towards, 90–91; social groups of, 20, 35–36. *See also* Helen (research participant); Li-Na (research participant); *names of specific nationalities;* Xui Li (research participant)
assimilation, expectations of, 7–8, 53, 60–62, 67, 78. *See also* immigrants; multiculturalism
asthma, 75

Auckland: about, 9, *10,* 33; Asian New Zealanders in, 34–36, 50, 52; China Town (proposed), 9, 50–51, 84, 88; population changes in, 22, 54–56, 84; Queen Street, 45; as research site, *11,* 38, 39; studies on aging in, 31; urban changes to, 45–46, 47, 49
The Aucklander (publication), 87
Australia, 2, 5, 88, 94, 127, 147
author's positionality, 18–20, 38–39. *See also* ethnographic fieldwork; urban ethnography

Barret, Patrick, 145
Baumann, Gerd, 26
Beaglehole, Ann, 60–61
Be A Tidy Kiwi campaign, 111. *See also* tidyness
Beausoliel, Emily, 42–43
Belich, James, 61, 72
Bell, Claudia, 111
Beth (research participant): before-and-after comparisons of, 45–46, 50; on food diversity, 66; on immigrant workers, 53, 63; on population diversity, 78; on resourcefulness, 47
biculturalism, 8, 22, 81–83, 85, 132. *See also* indigeneity; Māori; multiculturalism; national identity; Pākehā; Treaty of Waitangi (1840)
biosecurity, 66. *See also* crime and safety
Bönisch-Brednich, Brigitte, 61, 115
Brexit, 2–3, 29, 127, 141. *See also* United Kingdom
British New Zealanders, 7–8, 53, 56, 60. *See also* Jane (research participant)
British Society for Gerontology (BSG), 3

Cable, Vince, 3
cadence. *See* pace of life
Cambodian New Zealanders, 8, 54, 56. *See also* Asian New Zealanders

ABOUT THE AUTHOR

MOLLY GEORGE is a social anthropologist and a research fellow at the University of Otago. Her main areas of interest are migration and aging, but her research includes a wide variety of topics from children's playground behavior, to family sleep practices in Māori and Pacific families, to refugee health care. She is originally from the United States and resides in a little house on a hill in Dunedin, New Zealand. She is also a mum, a wife, a sister, and a daughter, and has become even more grateful for the stunning view out her kitchen window during the COVID-19 lockdown.